SIMPLY DEVINE

Memoirs of a Hall of Fame Coach

BY
DAN DEVINE
WITH MICHAEL R. STEELE

SPORTS PUBLISHING INC.
WWW.SPORTSPUBLISHINGINC.COM

Editor: Rob Rains
Director of Production: Susan M. McKinney
Dustjacket and photo insert design:Terry Neutz Hayden

ISBN: (Notre Dame version: 1-58261-007-x)
(Missouri version: 1-58261-204-8)
Leatherbound edition ISBNS:
(Notre Dame: 1-58261-231-5)
(Missouri: 1-58261-232-3)

SPORTS PUBLISHING INC.
804 N. Neil
Champaign, IL 61820
www.sportspublishinginc.com

Printed in the United States.

To all of my players and coaches

———————————

Contents

Acknowledgments

Coach Devine's lovely family was always generous with hospitality, warmth and memories. They made it much easier to understand the man and his work. Our wives, Jo Devine and Gerianne Steele, have always been supportive, and this project was no different. Thank you, Jo and Geri.

Diane Bratman, Coach Devine's secretary, helped as the project went forward in very distant places. John Heisler, after two decades of assistance for both of us from the Sports Information Office at Notre Dame, never failed to produce pertinent results when called upon—which was often.

Fathers Theodore Hesburgh and Edmund P. Joyce were extremely generous with their time and insights. They offered their considerable support in the formative stages of the project. We are both deeply indebted to them for their examples, guidance and love.

Lyn Leone has been a generous, helpful resource.

Emil T. Hoffman, former Dean of the Freshman Year at Notre Dame, and University of Missouri Chancellor Richard Wallace have provided key glimpses into Coach Devine's career and professional responsibilities and practices at their respective universities.

The Athletic Directors at Arizona State, Missouri and Notre Dame, along with the CEO of the Green Bay Packers, graciously agreed to offer retrospective views, the pooling of which shows remarkable consistency across five decades in the life of Dan Devine. Special thanks thus go to Kevin White of ASU and Notre Dame, Mike Alden of Missouri, Bob Harlan of the Packers, and Mike Wadsworth of Notre Dame. Journalist Bob Broeg has made a great contribution based on 40 years of friendship with Coach Devine.

Thanks to having coached with and against hundreds of coaching peers and thousands of players, Dan Devine has touched virtually all corners of the modern collegiate and professional game. We wish to offer our gratitude to Joe Paterno, Joe Garagiola, Don Shula, Dr. Fred Brossart, Johnny Roland, Hank Kuhlmann, Ted Hendricks, Woody Widenhofer, Vagas Ferguson, Jerome Heavens, Terry Murphy, Ed Bauer, Bill Walsh, John Ralston, Joe Montana, Steve Orsini, Joe Yonto, Brian Boulac and George Kelly. All of them have been deeply significant figures in the life and career of Dan Devine, and all have been thoughtful and helpful in the various phases of this project.

Cheryl Norman, Joe Paterno's assistant at Penn State, and Chad Moller of the Sports Information Office at Missouri both provided timely and helpful information.

Dave Diles, formerly of ABC sports, and a longtime friend of Coach Devine, very kindly shared his insights from a crucial time in Coach Devine's career. Few know the football scene better than Dave Diles, and his views have been very helpful.

We have been working on this project for nearly two years. We would be remiss if we did not note the sad passing of many people who would have been integral parts of the finished product, people near and dear to Coach Devine. They include Harry Caray, Ray Nitschke, Curtis Jones, Willie Fry and David Huffman. All of these people would have been contacted or actually were contacted for their significant thoughts. We miss them, one and all, very much and ask for God's blessing upon them and their families.

—*Mike Steele*

Athletic Director Don Faurot and President Elmer Ellis gave me my first five-year contract at Missouri. I want to thank them for hiring me and showing their confidence in me. I also want to thank Ole Olejniczak and the board at Green Bay for hiring me and giving me a five-year contract. At Notre Dame, I'd like to thank Athletic Director Moose Krause and Father Ed Joyce and Father Ted Hesburgh for offering me a five-year contract.

I've written this book simply because I wanted to tell the story of two young people, married in 1947, and their trip down the path of life together.

As always, I thank Jo for her support.

—*Coach Dan Devine*

Prologue

by

JOE GARAGIOLA

Introduce Dan Devine to one of your friends and you end up trying to explain him . . . and that you will never be able to do because he takes you down so many roads.

His coaching record is all over this book, and yet when you meet him you have to think, how could he coach at such a high-profile school like Notre Dame? Coach in the National Football League, are you kidding? You have to be tough to coach there. Yet he coached the Green Bay Packers. Dan Devine is nice and he's tough. I believe that somewhere on his body he has a Good House-keeping Seal of Approval, but he has been able to hide it when he has to get the job done.

I expect the unexpected to happen when I'm around him. While he was being honored at Arizona State University and he was in the middle of his thank-you speech, the ASU marching band came into the gym playing at full volume and led us all out to the stadium. Was it preplanned? I don't think so. At a banquet honoring the Fiesta Bowl teams, we were visiting and talking about championships, when he wanted to show me his championship ring. He lifted his hand, turned the ring towards me, but forgot he was holding a Coke. His tie took the brunt of the spill. Preplanned? I don't think so. We are both Catholic, and one day I got a call from Dan, asking me to emcee a banquet. It didn't surprise me when I learned it was for the Lutheran Convention. I am always treated to his Will Rogers side—he never met anyone he didn't like.

He is my friend, and friends never disappoint you. Even in the toughest situations, he remains Dan Devine. Let me explain that to you.

Our second son, Steve, always wanted to go to Notre Dame. That is all he talked about while in grade school. When he did go there, our telephone calls were more pep-ups for us than for him. He would always say, "I can't believe I'm here. This is great. I can see the Golden Dome from here . . .," and so on.

When Steve was in high school, we took a trip to St. Louis. It was perfect. Missouri was playing Notre Dame in Columbia. Steve couldn't wait to see that game and neither could I.

Dan heard that we were coming to the game, so he invited us to watch the game from the Missouri sideline. We had never seen a game that close up, so we accepted his invitation. Dan knew, and I knew, that although Steve was on the Missouri sideline, he would be rooting for Notre Dame.

The game was a beauty, and it looked like Missouri might upset the great Notre Dame team. Two things happened in the game that told us what Dan Devine was all about.

Technically, I can't explain it, but I know that a Joe Theismann pass could have been intercepted. It was a wobbly pass that could have been caught by a defender, but it dropped to the ground and Notre Dame still had the ball. When the Missouri player who could have had the chance to intercept the ball came out of the game, we watched to see the coach's reaction. Dan put his arm around the youngster and, although we don't know what he said, the youngster walked away with his head held high.

The other play was an all-out blitz that had Joe Theismann surrounded to the point that he must have known how General Custer felt. Missouri players were all over him and, after getting away from two of them, he flipped the ball behind his back (à la Harlem Globetrotters style) and completed the short gain and made the first down.

There was a TV time-out, and Dan walked to the far end of the bench, where Steve and I were almost hiding. He winked at Steve and said something like, "We've got a real barnburner going here." Steve didn't know what to say or do. I joined him. Eventually, Notre Dame won that game. Later, we talked about the tough loss and how Dan still had enough control of himself to talk to the player who had missed an opportunity, and how, in the face of disappointment and the impossible Joe Theismann pass, he wasn't ranting and raving and going ballistic. He was setting an example for his players and a very impressionable youngster named Steve Garagiola. In that moment when he winked to Steve, he sent a powerful message. Coach Dan Devine showed us how to win, but more important, he showed us how to lose.

In baseball, there is an expression that any fielder can handle the good hops, but it takes a great one to handle the bad hops. Dan Devine is a great infielder. There are no bad hops he can't handle. I just want to borrow his outlook on life for one day and, maybe as a bonus, he might show me where that Good Housekeeping seal is.

Foreword

_____

by
JOE PATERNO
Head Coach, Penn State

Danny Devine and I became friends when we were young assistant coaches. He was at Michigan State and I was at Penn State. We would both attend coaching conventions and got to know each other there quite well. We had many friends and associates in common, such as Earle Edwards and Frank Kush, both of whom had connections with the State of Pennsylvania. Our friendship has lasted for nearly 50 years.

In my opinion, Danny has never been fully appreciated for the outstanding teams he produced on a consistent basis throughout his career. He is not one who promotes himself; he is always laid back, but still conducts himself as a very professional person. His teams were characterized by precision, great organization, and a lack of mistakes. You had to beat his teams; he seldom beat himself. He stressed quickness and team cohesion.

On the personal level, he knew who he was, what he wanted to do and how to get it done. He always had a pleasant manner, but he had a steely character when necessary. His beliefs were strong, and he wouldn't let the clamor of the fans talk him out of his position. He is courageous and has a very strong character.

Danny Devine's contributions to football must include the way he could organize a staff to reach a common goal. In the clinics he worked in, you could see that he had an important impact on other coaches. I'd also have to say that the 1969 Dan Devine Missouri team we beat in the Orange Bowl was the first really modern offensive college football team—a Power I with two great wideouts, a big tailback and a big offensive line. Others used option football, but Danny didn't rely on this very much. His teams always knew how to call plays at the line of scrimmage; he knew how to incorporate good ideas; and he was a master at evaluating his personnel.

Before we played that Orange Bowl game, the two of us met for a private walk on the beach. We shared many good friends we could talk about, and we were deeply committed to producing quality football teams and quality young men. I count Danny Devine as one of my best friends in football and respect very much what he has added to this game and our lives.

It's about time that his full story has come out so he can finally gain the respect that he deserves.

Introduction

This book began with a phone call from Peter Bannon and, later, Mike Pearson, both from Sports Publishing. We discussed my writing a series of books on famous Notre Dame football coaches. After a full exchange of ideas, we settled on Dan Devine.

In August of 1998, along with my research assistant, Zack Barnett, and my son, Sean, I drove from Oregon to Phoenix to spend some quality time with Coach Devine. I felt blessed and honored.

In 1980, it had been my privilege to know and work with legends of Irish football history. I was aware of Dan Devine—certainly the great 1977 team's national championship was a key here—but I didn't really have a full sense of the man or all his accomplishments. Truth to tell, being in the orbit of Notre Dame football tends to give one a singular view of the football world. . . it starts and stops with the Golden Dome.

So, here I was in the presence of a man who is idolized in the State of Missouri, a man who had the second-most wins in college football at the time of his retirement. At that point, only Bear Bryant had more wins in major college football than Dan Devine—and Devine's teams were unbeaten in three games against Bear Bryant's Alabama squads. Devine met and defeated the following football coaching peers and luminaries, among others:

Sammy Baugh
Bear Bryant
Joe Paterno
Paul Brown
Joe Schmidt
Bobby Dodd

Abe Gibron
Tom Landry
George Welsh
Weeb Eubank
Bo Schembechler
Bud Grant
Bud Wilkinson
Bump Elliott
Pete Elliott
Eddie Crowder
Jack Mitchell
Chuck Fairbanks
Pepper Rodgers
Dallas Ward
Frank Broyles
Bill Parcells
Murray Warmath
Bob Devaney
Rip Engle
Wayne Hardin
Ben Martin
Bill Peterson
Fred Akers
Ray Graves

It's a safe bet that there are not many people walking the earth who can make a claim as strong as this one. Dan Devine, elected to the College Football Hall of Fame the first year he was eligible, after a fine start in coaching at East Jordan, Michigan, where his teams were undefeated for two years, has been one of the most significant figures in the coaching histories of three excellent college football programs—Arizona State, Missouri and Notre Dame. He coached teams that were either top ranked or threatened to be top ranked—six different teams at three schools in four different decades: ASU in 1957; Missouri in 1960, 1965 and 1969; and Notre Dame in

1977 and 1980. In the sixties, his Missouri team was the only major college team to avoid having more than three losses in a season.

Though it has been 20 years since Dan Devine last prowled the sidelines, his amazing success as a coach is underlined when one evaluates his win-loss record against the traditional powers. The Nebraskas, Michigans, Alabamas and others have retained a consistent level of success throughout the years, appearing season after season in the Top 25 poll. And the final 1999 rankings included those same familiar names. Here's Coach Devine's career record versus the "big boys."

Nebraska	8-5
Michigan	4-1
Kansas State	12-1
Michigan State	5-1
Alabama	3-0
Florida	1-0
Miami	6-0
Arkansas	1-0
Minnesota	3-0-1
Oregon	1-0
Texas	1-0
Illinois	3-0
Purdue	5-1

Devine's teams were undefeated against eight of these 13 teams, compiling a 53-9-1 record, a winning percentage of .849 that spells consistency!

And while coaching at the college level, 94 percent of those players who played four years for him obtained at least an undergraduate degree. Hundreds of them also completed their graduate studies.

After his years in the NFL, where he was NFC Coach of the Year in 1972, he quickly recognized the skills, leadership and potential of a skinny kid buried far down in the Notre Dame depth chart—Joe Montana. He has coached teams to impressive victories in five different bowl games and is a leader in bowl-game achievements for Missouri and Notre Dame. His winning percentage is the highest of any coach of these two schools in bowl games. As Missouri's Athletic Director, he hired the man, Norm Stewart, who led the Tigers to more than 600 basketball wins before retiring in 1999.

Earlier in his career at Missouri, Devine was a campus leader in the effort to bring love, respect, decency and full citizenship to African-American players and students. He served his country with distinction in World War II and, later, as a member of the White House Conference for a Drug Free America, a cause for which he toured the country for several years. He has a multimillion-dollar building named in his honor at the University of Missouri and has been awarded two honorary doctorates. And he has helped raise a family of seven children, ending his football career to devote himself to helping his life's partner, Jo, in her battle with multiple sclerosis. In that regard, he has received a Lifetime Achievement Award from the Multiple Sclerosis Institute.

In addition to his achievements in collegiate football, he has also been recognized as an NFL Man of the Year. In 1972, his Green Bay Packers won the Central Division title, and he received the Professional Football Writers of America Coach of the Year award. The Green Bay Packers Hall of Fame Association presented him with both the NFC Coach of the Year and NFL Man of the Year awards.

We live in an age in which those few with similar attainments in life seem to have egos that require massive care and feeding. This is hardly the case with Dan Devine. He is low-key, quiet, thoughtful, almost self-effacing. I am sure that there are competitive fires burning within his rather slight frame—he was an accomplished athlete in any sport he tried, he has risen to the challenge of building programs wherever he coached and his career saw him follow in the wake of giants. It takes a certain measure of ego and competitive ire to have done these things with the standard of success reached by Dan Devine.

My guess is that many of those who lost against him did so partially because they underestimated the man. Or they thought they had him figured out, knew his tendencies—then learned too late that they should have done more homework. If you're Dan Devine, this can be seen as a tremendous hidden advantage.

After giving all of this much thought, it still strikes me that I have not fully come to an understanding of the motivational factors at work within Dan Devine. I am willing to chalk it up to the sheer mystery and complexity of the human personality. There is also the possibility that someone as gifted as Dan Devine cannot successfully articulate precisely those factors that drive him, much as the great hitters in baseball find it difficult to express the niceties of their craft. Finally, there is the tendency for the greats to let their deeds serve as their words. All of these factors, and others, have been at work in this case. And reaching a complete understanding could serve to dull the appreciation of the man.

Let me offer you the reader some insights that will help as you follow Dan Devine's story. There are two patterns in his story that are highly meaningful: One, mark those times when something very significant is happening when Dan is in an automobile, on a journey somewhere. These are often very inspirational moments, and they are good analogues to the notion of one's life as a journey. The other pattern that strikes me is the one of returning home. Coach Devine seems to have made every effort to create a "family" atmosphere to surround the players and coaches on his teams. These teams would often have to leave their home environs, face a daunting foe, overcome adversity, achieve triumph—and then return home to the cheers and intense emotion that attend victory.

Dan Devine's life can be tracked through these emotions. . . and many of them are powerful, positive highs. There are also some lows, but there is *always* a return to home, to love and to unity. In a very important way, this is a key measure of the man.

And now is the time for Dan Devine to tell his story, in his own words.

Chapter One

LUCKY ME

People who are lucky enough to be blessed with a great family during their lifetimes should be eternally grateful. I really believe I've been blessed with two families in my lifetime, and for that I am thankful beyond words.

My "real" family—my wife Jo, our seven children, 16 grandchildren and two great-grandchildren—has made my life a complete joy. My "extended" family—all the players I coached over the years and the other coaches and administrators with whom I worked —made my job fun and enjoyable every single day.

I was lucky enough to work at a job and in a profession that I truly enjoyed. From the days when Jo and I left our home in Minnesota to begin a coaching odyssey that took us to East Jordan, Michigan, Michigan State, Arizona State, Missouri, the Green Bay Packers and Notre Dame, our life was rich and rewarding.

In college, I was the quarterback of my football team and Jo was the homecoming queen, and we've been sweethearts ever since. Jo and I were married in March 1947. We had seven children—six girls and a boy. Our twins are the oldest, Jennifer and Mary Jo. A student manager interrupted a practice one day at Michigan State to tell me Jo was having labor pains, and that night our daughter Dede was born. The night before our annual spring game in East Lansing in 1954, son Daniel J. Devine II was born—Tiger would become his nickname. Sarah was born three years later, and was baptized in a small Catholic church on the Arizona State campus.

Lisa was born just as the family was settling into life in Columbia, and Jill was born the weekend of Missouri's big game against the Air Force Academy.

Starting at birth, our family's life has revolved around football. My kids were at practices, attended games, and enjoyed many private moments with players who were very kind to them.

Jo and I have always appreciated the loyalty and support of my brothers and sisters and her brothers. I have a great love for them, and they in turn love me and my family very much. All of our family members have been great cheerleaders and fans for all of my teams, especially Jo's mother, who lived with us in Missouri for 13 years, following the early and sudden death of Jo's father.

I was lucky enough to coach some of the greatest players in college football, and players who might not have been true stars on the field but were stars off of it, graduating to become successful doctors, lawyers, engineers, businessmen and educators. For everyone who knows the likes of Joe Montana, Johnny Roland and Roger Wehrli, I can name three more players who might not be as well known but who were just as enjoyable to coach and watch develop as outstanding young men.

I was blessed to coach for four years in Title Town, USA, the home of the best franchise in pro football, the Green Bay Packers. Our teams weren't as successful as I would have liked, but I wouldn't have traded the experience for anything.

I was honored to add my name to the list of those who have coached football at the University of Notre Dame, the job many consider the best college coaching job in the country. It truly was a blessing to be associated with that special group of people.

In addition to coaching at the University of Missouri, I was privileged to serve two stints there as athletic director and was recently presented with an honorary doctorate. A building on the Columbia campus bears my name. ASU was a special growing experience.

Of all of the relationships I have enjoyed over the years, no story better illustrates the combination of my love for football and my love for my wife Jo than an incident that happened in the mid-1960s, when I was coaching at Missouri.

Jo always kept a chart of a game, and I would consult those charts from time to time when I did not have access to a game film. On this particular day, I needed more help from Jo than just her chart.

I was watching the film of a game between Oklahoma and Oklahoma State, and I kept having a problem with part of the film. There was something I just wasn't getting. It was about 3 a.m., and Jo was sleeping soundly, but I just couldn't take it anymore. I woke her up and asked her to come down and look at the film with me, to see if together we could figure it out.

She did—the play I couldn't understand occurred when Oklahoma was called for being offsides. But Oklahoma State actually had 12 men on the field and the officials had missed that. OSU played 12 men, but Oklahoma received the penalty. That was just one example of many when Jo's observations were important to my coaching success.

Jo now suffers from multiple sclerosis, but she is a battler and has never let the disease get the best of her. I am as proud of her today as I was the day I married her, 53 years ago.

Back then, nobody knew what I would amount to. I was just a small-town boy from Proctor, Minnesota, the "Proctor Flash," as I was later called by Lute Olsen, the basketball coach at the University of Arizona. He was the basketball coach at Two Harbors, Minnesota, after I graduated from Proctor, our school's biggest rival, and home of my good friend Jim Hastings.

I used to get ribbed by my friends about being a member of the Duluth Area Hall of Fame, until they noticed other honorees included Bronko Nagurski, Ernie Nevers and Bud Grant. The ribbing suddenly came to a halt.

It's impossible for me to discuss all the super players, coaches and teams with whom I was associated. I'm going to try to name a few but I know there will be omissions, and for that I apologize in advance.

I was the offensive backfield coach when Earl Morrall played quarterback for Michigan State in 1954. Earl is now a community leader in Miami and a good friend. His greatness and leadership on the football field is remembered by many.

Leon Burton played at Arizona State as a freshman, sophomore and junior in 1955-57. Arizona State had many exceptional runners before and after Leon's arrival in 1955. But I believe he was the best true runner I ever saw. He had tremendous speed and agility. For the three years that he was on my team, he was the game breaker.

Dr. Fred Brossart was the first Phi Beta Kappa that I coached. He was a key performer in the Orange Bowl in 1959. He went on to become a star the next year, 1960. He paced the defense to Missouri's upset over Navy and Heisman Trophy winner Joe Bellino in the Orange Bowl. Fred made the trip from his home in Oregon to New York when I was inducted into the Hall of Fame.

The 1960 team's two starting guards, Paul Henley and Paul Garvis, were both on chemical engineering scholarships. One of the tackles, Dr. Ed Blaine, became an outstanding physiologist, and the other tackle, Rockne Calhoun, became a judge. These players were exceptional people as well as exceptional athletes. To be able to carry a full load of difficult college courses, and still accept the discipline and time commitment to play football, is truly remarkable.

Glancing up at the wall in my den, I see a picture of Bill Tobin. He was a star performer in 1961 and 1962. Bill was from the small town of Burlington Junction. I can only imagine how he must have felt playing in the Orange Bowl for his home state university, and kicking three extra points with President Kennedy watching and cheering. In 1962, he ran 77 yards for the winning touchdown against Georgia Tech in the Bluebonnet Bowl. Georgia Tech was ranked in the top 10 going into the game, so it was a big game for Missouri. There were several players on that team who went on to have successful careers in the NFL, including Andy Russell, a 10-year captain of the Pittsburgh Steelers, George Seals, Gus Otto and Jim Johnson. Jim is the defensive coordinator of the Philadelphia Eagles.

The 1963 Missouri team had many outstanding players. A young junior, Vince Tobin, was a standout—the same Vince Tobin who now is the successful coach of the Arizona Cardinals and younger brother of Bill Tobin.

Roger Wehrli, who played for Missouri and the St. Louis Cardinals, is the best football player to have not yet been picked for the Hall of Fame.

Each team has such special memories. It's hard not to mention them all. Rick Slager, the Notre Dame quarterback for the 1976 season, took us to the Gator Bowl and defeated Joe Paterno's Penn State team. The score was 20-9. He also quarterbacked the team to victories over Purdue, Michigan State, Alabama, Miami and more.

Coaching is certainly a difficult profession. Perhaps a better name for an assistant coach should be co-coach because he has to work so closely with the head coach. Some assistants are delegated more responsibility than others. Some are eventually appointed assistant head coach. Many have that stature on the staff even though they don't have that title. The other staff and players understand that the assistant head coach is second in command. My players understood that, if an assistant gave them instructions, they should accept those instructions as if they came from me. Loyalty on your coaching staff is the most important asset the staff can have; it is the only way the team and staff work and excel as a cohesive unit. This loyalty must be 100 percent and must work both ways. Decisions must be made under great pressure and emotion. It would be impossible to be correct every time. The assistant coaches have to know that the head coach will back them up in order to have the confidence to make those decisions.

Ninety-seven percent of the coaches on my staff understood me as a person and as a coach. I can be difficult to understand at times. Once the effort is made to make that connection, the process of understanding becomes simpler. The three percent who didn't understand me should not have applied to work on my staff. I was an assistant coach for five years. I never publicly questioned my boss; I felt that was the loyalty I owed him. I have encouraged my staff to question me privately if they disagreed with my decisions. I have changed my mind on the spot when their explanations sounded better than mine. I'm sure I may have questioned Biggie's or Duffy's philosophy at times. I probably said to myself, "If I ever get a head coaching job, I'll do it my way." I would like to tell young assistant coaches today: please consider the short amount of time in which decisions must be made, particularly on the field. There are many ways to do things, but one voice has to stand out, one voice has to make the decision.

One example comes quickly to mind—the Notre Dame/ Michigan game in 1980 between Sugar Bowl- and Rose Bowl-bound teams. That was the game where Blair Kiel made the great pass to Tony Hunter. Tony took the ball out of bounds with two seconds remaining in the game. In order to win the game, we had to kick a 51-yard field goal, into the wind, with an inexperienced kicker. Our only other choice was to go for a long pass. I made the decision immediately. I wanted to avoid a penalty and also I wanted to get the team out on the field with a decisive attitude. Harry Oliver kicked that field goal 51 yards into a strong wind to win the game for Notre Dame as the clock ran out. I often thought about how I made that decision so fast. I could have been wrong. It seemed right at the time. The best thing was to try and do it error free. Even my best friend thought it wasn't a good call. But he wasn't on the sideline to make the decision.

Starting at ASU in 1955 was really like on-the-job training. I was very fortunate to assemble a small, hardworking, intelligent staff, even though we had a very low budget. We had one thing in mind— to win, and we did.

We had two great line coaches on the same staff. Frank Kush was a highly successful college coach and later became a head coach in the NFL and head coach in the USFL.

After spending 16 years with me at ASU and Missouri, Al Onofrio became the upset king of college football as Mizzou's head coach. I was not an easy man to work for, so I know that those 16 years may not have been all pleasant. He hung in with me. I will always be indebted to him for his loyalty and skill. Frank was still in the army in Georgia and Al was the golf coach at ASU when my first spring practice meetings started. I was very fortunate to get both of those talented people.

Cecil Coleman was also a fine coach. He later became the Athletic Director at Illinois. Tom Fletcher was on the staff when I arrived. He went on to coach the Pittsburgh Steelers.

Bob Carey was the first coach I hired at ASU. He was Frank's teammate at Michigan State. He was captain of the 1951 team

Michigan State and voted first-team All-American. He was also a starter for the Los Angeles Rams. I was fortunate to get him at ASU even for just one year before he went back to pro ball. Bob was from Charlevoix and played in that great East Jordan/Charlevoix series.

After the 1957 season, we moved on to Missouri. It was mainly for financial reasons. Al Onofrio, Tom Fletcher and our 1956 Captain, Charley Mackey, went with us. Frank Kush became the head coach at ASU. Frank hired Dick Tamburo, who later was athletic director at Missouri and ASU. He also hired pro and college coach Chuck Fairbanks. Both Dick and Chuck were Michigan State graduates. Chuck was also from Charlevoix.

Doug Weaver joined our coaching staff at Missouri. He was a teammate of Frank Kush's at Michigan State. He was an intellectual and very good football coach. Doug left my staff to become head coach at Kansas State. He went on to become Athletic Director at Georgia Tech and Michigan State. Doug also received a law degree along the way. I retained Clay Cooper and Harry Smith. They both had coached for Don Faurot. Harry Smith made the 50-year All-America team as a guard from Southern California.

Merv Johnson joined the staff for the 1960 and 1961 Orange Bowl teams. He was later the offensive coordinator and assistant head coach when Notre Dame won the 1977 National Championship. Merv was also the top assistant for Frank Broyles at Arkansas and Barry Switzer at Oklahoma. Bill McCartney and Woody Widenhofer were both on the staff. They both went on to become successful head coaches. Bill and Woody were roommates on those Orange Bowl teams.

Curtis Jones coached and played for me. He was a gifted coach and a good friend. He died suddenly during the 1998 season. His son Corby was a tremendous quarterback for Missouri.

Charlie Rash, from Shelbina, Missouri, was one of my first captains. He coached at Missouri and the Air Force Academy for Ben Martin and at Tennessee for Doug Dickey. Charlie and several other brilliant young coaches were killed in a tragic train-car collision while coaching at Tennessee. I'm sure that he would have had a great career as a head coach had he been granted the time. We lost so many good men along the path of life.

Rollie Dotsch coached for me at both Missouri and Green Bay. He won the "Coach of the Year" award in the USFL. Rollie died much too soon when he was an assistant for the Minnesota Vikings. Rollie died the night before he was to leave with his family on vacation to Arizona and the desert that he loved.

Bart Starr was the quarterback I was planning to start when I went to Green Bay. Injuries in 1970 and 1971 prevented him from playing. He was a big help to the staff during 1971, and in 1972 he became a full-time coach.

Two of Missouri's greatest players coached at Green Bay for me. Hank Kuhlmann is still actively coaching in the NFL, while Johnny Roland holds many of the St. Louis Cardinals' rushing records. He is still successfully coaching for the Arizona Cardinals.

Johnny Polonchek played for Michigan State when I was an assistant coach. He coached for me at Green Bay and went on to become assistant head coach at New England. Elijah Pitts was a great running back for Vince Lombardi. He joined my Packer staff in 1971 and was a great asset. Francis Peay played for me at Missouri and Green Bay, joined us at Notre Dame, and went on to be a very successful coach at Northwestern. Gary Barnett, who played for me at Missouri, succeeded Peay. Both are outstanding people.

All of the accomplishments in my life have been shared by Jo and our kids, and, now, by our grandchildren. I am just as proud of what they have accomplished in their lives, and have even more hope for what they will accomplish in the future.

Our grandchildren include Kelly, Kristy and Kasey Carver; Keary and Darius Husain; Danielle, J.J. and Crystal Yazzie; Kathleen and Daniel J. Devine III; Kelsey and Kyle Avery; Jacob and Arlo Horvath; Sam Spencer and Jesse Devine. Our great grandsons, "Alexander the Great" and Joseph Daniel Haggerty, have begun the hope of the next generation.

All of those kids are growing up in a much different world than I knew as a boy. It is my prayer that their lives will become as complete and rewarding as mine has been. It's been a wonderful journey; no one could ask for anything more.

Chapter Two

PROCTOR, MINNESOTA

My earliest memory is waking up as a cold and confused four-year-old, riding in a Model T Ford in the middle of a blizzard. I was crying as Aunt Mamie tried to comfort me; my Uncle Joe was driving. It was 1928, and my aunt and uncle had picked me up at the train station in Duluth, Minnesota, and were taking me back to their home in nearby Proctor, Minnesota.

I'm certain I had no idea at the time what was happening, but my parents had sent me to live with my aunt and uncle because of financial desperation. My father ran a general store in Eau Claire, Wisconsin, but he was ill, which limited his ability to feed and clothe our family. I was the second oldest boy out of nine children.

As the days turned into weeks and months, I realized I was not going to be returning home. Many nights I cried myself to sleep. Uncle Joe and Aunt Mamie tried to be the best parents they could be, and their son, Rich, was a real friend. Uncle Joe worked on the docks in Duluth, transporting ore from the iron range to the waiting ships. In the winters, when the ore was too frozen to move, he would sometimes go to Gary, Indiana, to work in the steel mills. It had to be as tough on them to have me living with them as it was for me.

I never tried to find out more about why my parents had sent me away. It was a decision that I'm sure affected their lives as well.

One aching feeling that never left me was how desperately I missed my family.

Growing up during the Depression was hard for everybody, and I tried to do what I could to help out my aunt and uncle. In high school, I had a paper route. We did not have running water in the house, so it was my job to wake up every day at 5 a.m., prime the family's well and put water on the kerosene stove. Then I had to pick up the newspapers and deliver them, which, in the winter months, usually was either on skis or snow shoes. I had to be back home by 6 a.m. to get cleaned up and ready for school. If I was late and missed the bus, I had to walk to school carrying either my horn or baseball glove.

Returning home in the afternoon was more challenging, because it was uphill most of the way. For some reason, that hill today doesn't look nearly as steep as it did back then.

It was also my job to gather and chop the firewood. It was mostly tamarack, left over from burned-out timber stands. We had a wood-burning stove in the middle of our small living room, and we heated water and cooked our food on a kerosene stove. We raised hogs and always had a big garden. Aunt Mamie was great at canning and preserving as much food as possible, and we always had plenty of jams and preserves. One memory I have never forgotten is how we kept carrots fresh in the cellar by storing them in sand.

It was during high school that I first showed interest in sports. I wasn't certain at that time what I wanted to do with my life, and our school didn't have career counselors or anybody like that to give you ideas. Most of the adults in Proctor worked for the railroad. The two people who I paid the most attention to, however, were Mr. Nelson and Mr. Johnson, the coaches at the high school. They gave me my start in football, basketball, baseball, track and hockey.

I always enjoyed playing sports. Our basketball and football teams practiced at the elementary school, which was about two miles from our home. When practice was over, my friends and I usually walked home. As was the case when walking home from school, the last part of the trip was uphill, and it always seemed the wind was blowing directly in my face. Nobody knew anything about wind-chill factors back then, but in those winter months it had to be 40 degrees below zero or worse.

I became more interested in sports than my schoolwork, often becoming so tired that after dinner, when I was supposed to be studying, I would fall asleep. Even though I know I could have done better, I look back and realize I received a good education both in high school and college.

One of the best things about the high school in Proctor was the athletic facilities. We even had a glass-enclosed, Olympic-sized swimming pool. Proctor's residents took pride in the success of the school's athletic program, in part because we were a town of less than 2,000 people and were the smallest school in the conference. Three of the town's residents went on to either coach or play for the Green Bay Packers.

Because we didn't have a lot of money, I had to make a lot of the equipment for whatever sport I was playing. I played hockey without skates. Once I made a basketball hoop out of a used Arco coffee can. It was too small for a regular basketball, so I played using a softball. My uncle got me a backboard and basket.

It was hard to find time to do everything that had to be done in a day. In addition to going to school, playing sports and studying, I had a lot of part-time jobs while in high school. I worked in a grocery store and on the ore docks, and later, while in college in Duluth, I worked for Tri State Sports, a sporting goods store.

As anybody who grew up in that era could tell you, it was a simpler time and we didn't have many of the problems that kids today face. Proctor was a small, all-white town, and most of the residents were Lutheran and of Scandinavian descent. I was a minority because I was Catholic.

I remember playing against one black player in high school. I don't remember ever playing against any Hispanics or Native Americans. The three owners of the sporting goods store where I worked in college were the first Jewish people I ever met. The one I remember best was Morris Claskey. One Christmas, he gave me a set of lights for our family to use for decorations. He was always sending me home with gifts and things we never could have afforded.

Uncle Joe was Lutheran and Aunt Mamie was Catholic. We didn't have a Catholic high school in Proctor, so I went to the public school. Catholicism to me was not a Sister rapping me on my knuckles in school; it was the long prayers I said before each and every game I played. I suppose I was praying to win; but I tried to camouflage those thoughts by promising God that if He'd let me get this one victory, I would never do anything wrong again.

My religion always was important to me, and I became more outspoken and public about my beliefs later in life, especially when I went to Notre Dame.

My friends and I played basketball at the YMCA in Proctor, because it had a gym. Once, during a shirts-and-skins game, I threw the ball on the floor in a burst of anger. I immediately knew I shouldn't have done it, but Mr. Nelson, the coach, sat me on the bench and forced me to watch my friends play. That taught me the lesson to never let my anger get the best of me, which I tried to remember even during my coaching career. The other important lesson I learned was not to overcoach.

Of course, on December 7, 1941, tensions around the world escalated. While I was too young to serve in the Armed Forces at that time, I did realize that we were helping in the military buildup for our country by steaming ore in Proctor. When the commander of the Japanese fleet that attacked Pearl Harbor, Admiral Yamamoto, was told that it was a sneak attack, he said, "All we have done is arouse a sleeping giant and filled him with a terrible resolve." From that time, the United States performed a miracle of converting a peacetime economy to a wartime economy . . . and probably the closest to perfect unity was achieved in our country. That is why I tell my children and grandchildren, when they ask questions, that they had to live in that time to understand all that transpired and culminated in the dropping of the atomic bomb on Hiroshima.

When I was a junior in high school, on a Sunday night in early December, I went to a movie at the Northshore Theater in Duluth. The manager came out and announced that Japan had bombed Pearl Harbor. Like thousands of Americans, I didn't know where Pearl Harbor was. I later found out that there were two boys from Proctor at Pearl Harbor—one killed on December 7, 1941—and that brought it into a lot sharper focus.

The following Monday morning at Proctor High School, there was an assembly for the entire student body. The assembly was so crowded that some of the boys had to sit on the floor. Usually that would have meant a chance to horse around. However, on *this* morning, there was an almost eerie silence. From a big radio in front of the crowd came the voice of President Roosevelt. He gave his now famous speech about December 7, 1941, being "a day that will live in infamy." He read off a list of other places that Japan had bombed that same day, but the key was that they had bombed Pearl Harbor.

I knew this was a big thing and that we would all ultimately be in the service. We all started thinking about that in the back of our minds. I'd had a brief experience flying in an open-cockpit two-seater bi-plane and was fascinated by flight. My aim and ambition was to become a pilot. After graduation from high school, I was classified I-A by my draft board, but there were so many people volunteering, they weren't drafting men as young as I was.

I worked for the railroad for a quarter instead of going directly to college. I went to Fort Snelling in Minneapolis to enlist in the Army Air Corps, but I failed a depth perception test. I still have some problems with depth perception— as many football fans have told me during my career. Then I came back and entered Duluth State for the winter quarter.

As time went on, little things gave me greater confidence. I never lacked a particular type of confidence—after all, at 14 I was a regular in football and basketball in a good conference. The Duluth State team was good. It hadn't been hit hard by the draft; it was an experienced team. I was a freshman and walked in late after the basketball season had started. I still made the starting five by the time the season was halfway over. Making that starting unit was good for my morale. My good friend Jim Hastings, from Two Harbors, also made the team. At the end of the season we said goodbye.

I still wasn't drafted and wouldn't be for some time, so I went back to Fort Snelling and tried to enlist for the second time. Again, I failed the depth perception test, but the doctors were very encouraging to me and gave me some hope. The decision wasn't permanent. If I could pass the depth perception test, I could join the Army Air Corps as a cadet. The Army Air Corps liked to brag that they could give you the same education in two years that West Point and Annapolis gave in four years. I believe that's true. So I rested my eyes and went back to take the depth perception test for the third time. I guess that third time was the charm . . . finally I passed!

I never went back to Proctor. I took the clothes I had with me and got on a troop train bound for Florida. I started basic training in early 1943. That was probably the most intense training I've ever experienced. For example, I never dreamed that I could learn to send and receive wireless code. You had to be able to send and receive so many words a minute of wireless code, or you washed out. There were so many academic and physical reasons to fail, but I made it. These achievements really helped to build my confidence.

After basic training, I was sent to Springfield College in Massachusetts. Dr. Naismith invented basketball at Springfield College. The original gym and baskets are still there. I took math and science courses taught by Ed Hickock, who was also the basketball coach at Springfield. He later became a member of the National Basketball Hall of Fame and was the president of the National Coaches Association.

The Army Air Corps did not allow its cadets to play football. The Navy Air Corps was allowed to play, and Iowa Pre-Flight had a great team. The other service academies also had very good teams. The Army Air Corps at Springfield was a very competitive group of young men, and we were not allowed to compete athletically. Hickock decided to start a basketball team by taking two men from each of the five classes. This very competent group of players was known as "Hickock's Mathematicians." I started, and we practiced and played in our free time. Making the first team gave my confidence another big lift.

Then I had to make it with the big boys in gunnery school. I got my B-17 gunner's wings and also fired and qualified from a B-24 bomber. I then hit a series of frustrations . . . too many people, waiting too long between each step. After gunnery school, I went to advanced bombardier school and received my wings at Carlsbad, New Mexico. I had all this education, but I never got assigned to a crew. On my discharge papers, it stated that I also held all of the navigator ratings except celestial, and that I was a B-29 oxygen, first aid, and personal equipment officer. I had complete authority over this area. All of this was first-class training, but I was extremely anxious to move on. I was disappointed that I never got assigned to a B-17 or B-24 crew.

I was given other assignments that my commanding officer said were very important. While stationed at Carlsbad, I often flew with pilots who had served their tours of duty but who still needed to fly four hours a month to stay polished. They liked to fly with me because of my accuracy as a bombardier. We would go on training missions and drop bombs on a target on the bombing range. This got old pretty fast, and I was anxious to do what I had been trained to do—be a combat bombardier.

My commanding officer finally recognized my frustration when I told him that I had to get out of there and do the things that I was trained to do. He thanked me for my service to him and the Army Air Corps. My gunnery wings were in a B-17, which is a non-pressurized, open airplane. You shot the machine gun like you were shooting at ducks. You led the target, figuring the altitude and wind in your head. After talking with my Colonel, I was surprised to receive orders to report to B-29 gunnery, which was totally different from what I had been doing. The B-29 was a new aircraft, bigger than anything I'd ever seen, and it also had other differences, including a pressurized cabin. In B-29 gunnery, the gunsight figured in the wind and the altitude, and you just put the gunsight directly on the target. I was sent to Henderson Field to learn the gunnery of the B-29, because when the bombardier wasn't in the bombing run, he was basically the nose gunner.

Toward the end of my training for B-29 gunnery, I was approached by four enlisted men. Two were quite a bit older, and two were my age. They asked me if I would join the crew that they were putting together. I was on cloud nine! By then I was a flight officer with my gunner's wings twice and my bombardier's wings. I was so flattered and pleased. As we were discussing the final agreement, we learned that the atomic bomb had been dropped, and the war ended before we ever got into action. I always felt that my contributions to the war effort had not been significant, although my commanding officer told me several times they were.

Of course, I was very happy that we had saved so many American lives. I think you had to have gone through all of this to understand the necessity for dropping the bomb. I understand that many people felt there were other means to end the war, but I see the many American lives that were saved.

When the war ended, I was extremely well qualified for my job as a bombardier. The war ended so abruptly that I had my choice of staying in the peacetime Army Air Corps or taking a discharge. I took a discharge because I really had no interest in the peacetime Army Air Corps. I had enlisted because of the war, and now it was over. My purpose for remaining in the service was gone.

Minorities in the United States contributed to the war effort in a most significant way. It was the first exposure for many people to others who were different from themselves, people who were not white and Christian.

The Japanese-Americans comprised the 442nd infantry. It was the most highly decorated battle unit in the history of the United States Army. The Native Americans comprised the Navaho Code Talkers. There were 350 Marine Navaho Code Talkers. They developed and used a secret code based on the Navaho language for relaying orders and information. Thousands of lives were saved by having secure communications. African-Americans are most famous for the Tuskegee airmen. They flew escort missions over Germany in P-51 fighter planes. They were considered one of the top fighter squadrons. The Hispanics developed into excellent servicemen who made great sacrifices for their country. All of these and other minorities gave their service courageously.

When stationed in New Mexico, I was on official duty to El Paso when I saw a big football stadium. . . the Sun Bowl. At that time there were six bowl games, the Rose, Cotton, Sugar, Orange, Gator and the Sun Bowl. I had the driver drop me off to see the Sun Bowl. Since I was from northern Minnesota, I had been a fairly frequent visitor to Memorial Stadium, where the Golden Gophers played in their heyday, the thirties and early forties. In those days, they were always fighting for the national championship. They did win it in 1936, 1940 and 1941. I went into the Sun Bowl, looked at the empty stadium and wondered what it would be like to play there. In a little more than 10 years after that visit, I would be coaching Arizona State against Texas Western on this field, their home field. Texas Western had Don Maynard and Jesse Whittenton. I told my squad that winning this game would earn them the conference championship. It did.

While coaching at Michigan State, I was very close to being called back to service in Korea. I would have gone without hesitation, but Jo and I had too many babies by then for me to be eligible.

As quickly as the United States had mobilized at the start of the war, we demobilized just as quickly, as tens of thousands of men and women were discharged almost overnight. I arrived home, in Proctor, in late November. It was ore-steaming time, and I took a job steaming ore. I got a sort of glorified supervisory job. Still, it was dirty and sweaty work, and I coughed constantly. I was teaching the job to the young guys, so I was still exposed to the steaming. At this point, I still didn't know what I wanted to do with my life. There was a program for veterans to get a small amount of money until they found jobs. I was steaming ore, so I passed it up.

I had several contacts from my time in the service. The contacts were in basketball, football and baseball. I started to receive phone calls at home from Frank Puglesi, the head basketball coach at Duluth State. Duluth State later became the University of Minnesota at Duluth. There were so many people going back to school that there were many good athletes, so I was pleased to get the call. Frank invited me to come to the school and said he would help me all he could. I qualified for the GI bill, so I really didn't need much financial aid until I got married. I didn't answer Frank right away, and he finally called and said I should get down there before the season was over. He said that I should check in at Washburn Hall and report for practice the next night. So I did!

We had a good team playing against some really great players. I was team captain, and playing for Coach was a great experience. I wouldn't trade it for anything. I was *happy*! I met a beautiful, intelligent, perfect girl—Joanne Brookhart. I enjoyed classwork too. I had some great teachers in anatomy, physiology, psychology and history. Math and the sciences were more difficult for me, but history was a piece of cake. I was also interested in the new concept of physical education.

In the spring of 1946, Jo and I were starting to talk about our future together. We weren't married until the spring of 1947, so we put a lot of thought into it. One thing was clear, I wanted to get through school as quickly as I could, even if it meant giving up eligibility in football and basketball. In the summer of 1946, I got the chance to be a playground director at a large playground. In my second summer of working at this playground, I would have lunch at a small restaurant that made good hamburgers. Money was pretty tight. On Mondays, Wednesdays and Fridays, I would have a small hamburger. On Tuesdays, Thursdays and Saturdays, I would have their small hamburger and a small glass of milk—but I couldn't afford that milk on the other days.

My hours working at the playground were from noon to 9 p.m. This allowed me to take two courses in each of the two summer sessions at UMD. The university granted me credit for the math and science that I took in bombardier training. With the previous credits I had earned and the summer school credits, it gave me a head start for the rest of my life. Up until that time, I thought that tomorrow would always take care of itself. When Jo entered the picture, my focus changed.

I hadn't played football for Coach Lloyd Peterson, and there were three veteran classes coming out at one time. There were 140 men on our football squad. For the opening game, I was the number-two quarterback. In that game, I moved the team at the end to score and we won. We ran the single wing and the Split-T. The quarterback was an active person. I wasn't so small then that I couldn't play blocking back in the single wing. I was born with the instinct to be a pulling guard; it was easy for me to pull to the right and trap out on the end in our off-tackle play. Going into the second game, I was the starting quarterback. The original starter was moved to the halfback position. In the 1946 season, we won games, and I learned a lot of football.

The following summer, I went back to summer school and changed to another playground. Jo and I decided that I would skip basketball in the '46-'47 season. This was difficult for me to do, but I had trouble the year before playing basketball and keeping up my grades. So there really wasn't much choice. In the 1947 football season, I was elected captain of the football team. In retrospect, I realize what an important role the captain plays on the team.

Some of my current arthritis problems probably originated from blocking those 230-pound defensive ends on the off-tackle play. Since I played 60 minutes, I probably also got clipped by an overeager wide receiver or tight end. That finished my playing career at Minnesota-Duluth, because I skipped basketball again. In the spring I was awarded the Outstanding Athlete Award by the university alumni. Years later, they gave me an award as a distinguished alumnus. Minnesota-Duluth had been a good choice for me. I received a good education. The athletic program was challenging, and I learned a great deal about being a coach. There was a good balance between academics and sports.

My cousin Rich, who was five years older than me, was the most intelligent person I've ever known. He showed me a great deal of love and consideration at this time. I'm deeply indebted to him for his understanding of my need for an anchor in my life. Jo became that anchor.

Chapter Three

EAST JORDAN AND MICHIGAN STATE

Even though I loved sports and considered myself pretty knowledgeable, I don't think I really ever planned to become a coach. Back in the 1930s and 1940s, that just didn't seem to be the type of career to which a young man aspired. We didn't have guidance counselors at our high school to advise about college and careers. It seemed most high school kids finished their education, and then had to try to make up their minds what they were going to do with their lives.

Proctor was a railroad town. Almost everybody got out of school and went to work for the railroad. It was an era where people never really moved in pursuit of a job. Kids were born in a town, grew up there, married, lived and worked there, retired there and died there. The jobs on the railroad paid well, and most people were very content to live their lives that way.

My education had been well-rounded, especially adding the training I had received in the military, but I really didn't think I wanted to stay in Proctor and work for the railroad.

Because I was married, of course, the decision about where I was going to work and what I was going to do wasn't mine alone. Jo had a big voice in deciding our future together, and she knew how much I liked sports. When I heard there was an opening for a football coach at a high school in Michigan, in a town called East Jordan, Jo and I decided to pursue it.

After graduating in the spring of 1948 from Minnesota-Duluth, I worked at the college placement office. A lot of schools were looking for football coaches, but most wanted someone with experience. The Superintendent of the East Jordan school district was an older gentleman named Ernie Wade. He told the placement office he would consider a qualified candidate even if he had no coaching experience. I applied.

For my interview, I took a Greyhound bus from Duluth to Charlevoix, praying the rosary the entire way. I hitchhiked the rest of the way to East Jordan.

Mr. Wade had a reputation as someone who didn't support athletics; but I think he really did care. If I was going to get the job, I needed to know if he would support me, and if I would get the cooperation I would need to be successful. The more I talked with him, the more I was determined to get the job.

We talked about the kids, and how they were treated. I was concerned the school didn't have a trainer; but that was considered a luxury then that many small schools simply couldn't afford. The longer we talked, the more we seemed to develop a mutual respect. Before I was due to return to Duluth, Mr. Wade offered me the job and I accepted.

It so happened that a fair was being held at the high school that night, so I went out there and introduced myself to several of the boys on the football team. Their attitudes impressed me and made me even more excited to get to work. The challenge of trying to guide these kids and mold them into good young men, in addition to being good football players, seemed to be just the thing I was looking for.

I really was just glad to have made a decision, to have a job and some direction for my life. Jo and I had become parents of twin daughters Jennifer and Mary Jo six months earlier, and, because we had no hospitalization insurance, we were still paying those bills. Even though I knew this job wasn't going to make me rich, some money would be coming in, and that was better than none.

Jo and the twins were still in Minnesota, so I took the bus back to collect our belongings and prepare for the move. We decided that I would go to East Jordan for the start of practice and the school year in August, find a place to live, then come back over the Labor Day weekend and pick them up.

I left Duluth driving a 17-year-old 1931 Plymouth. The trip was made more difficult by the fact that a bridge had yet to be built across the Straits of Mackinac. It was a long, hot trip.

Being apart from my family was tough. I was happy when the Labor Day weekend arrived, and I drove back to Duluth to pick them up. We packed everything we owned into that old Plymouth.

Everything in that car was valuable to us, because it was everything we owned. After getting the car loaded, we took off and drove straight through to East Jordan, but not without a couple of incidents. The generator died, and the formula for the babies spoiled as we waited for the ferry. We made up our minds that, no matter what went wrong, we knew we were going where God wanted us to go.

We made it to East Jordan and began to settle in. We had an apartment in a home on the lake. The home owners, Bud and Mary Strehl, were waiting for us with big smiles, and even better, with hot food they had been preparing for a Labor Day barbeque. We went to bed tired, but happy, and with full stomachs.

The Strehls were wonderful people. We became close friends with them and also with Bud's cousin, Frank, and his wife, Betty Jo, who lived across the street. They now live in Tucson. Frank lost both legs in France during World War II, but he never let that slow him down. Being around him and Betty Jo is inspiring. They are godparents to our son, Tiger.

East Jordan is a very pretty town on the shore of Lake Charlevoix. In the fall, the leaves would turn colors, and, in the winter, we would skate on the lake. Once we saw fishermen on the lake moving their shacks after cutting big holes in the lake to go ice fishing, we stopped skating at night.

It was a good place to live; and Jo and I and the twins were very happy. The town's biggest industry was the foundry, and its principal product was manhole covers. I've seen manhole covers made in East Jordan all across the country, even in New York. East Jordan also had a cherry processing plant.

Most of the residents were avid fishermen and boaters because of the lake. Being a new and young coach, I took my job seriously and didn't give myself as much time to enjoy those activities and the town. I wish I had done more of those things.

It didn't take long to educate myself as to why East Jordan had been looking for a new football coach. The Red Devils had not won a game in two years. Despite that lack of success, I was impressed with the character of the young men on our team, especially a sophomore quarterback named Brian Boring. He was the type of kid who typified everything that was good about East Jordan. No matter where else I went during my coaching career, I was always fortunate to have at least one player on my team who was like Brian, just a class individual who stood out above everybody else.

As we prepared to open the season, I was so nervous and excited that I couldn't eat for two days. Our opponent was Grayling High School, and I tried my best to act confident and relaxed so the kids wouldn't get too nervous and worked up. I'll never forget the first play I called. It was "47-X," a counter play where the quarterback faked a handoff to the fullback, then handed it to the halfback, who was supposed to run off tackle. We snapped the ball, and Brian faked the handoff to Joe Hammond, then actually gave the ball to Max Summerville. The hole opened as the Grayling defenders all went after Hammond, who had carried out the fake perfectly. Little Max, who would go on to become a successful coach, rambled through the opening in the line and kept going. He ran right up the middle of the field and didn't stop until he had crossed the goal line, after a run of 67 yards. Remember, this team had not won a game in two years and really had not even scored much. We had just scored a touchdown on our first play of the season.

The hardest thing for me and the players was to remember that the game wasn't over just because we had scored. It had only begun. We did manage one more touchdown later in the game, and our defense played well. We were able to break that long losing streak with a 14-7 win.

East Jordan's biggest game each year was against Charlevoix, which had produced Bob Carey, the captain of Michigan State's 1951 football team and probably the school's greatest player at that point in its history. Carey later would become a coach with me.

We had continued our good play after the opening game and came into the battle against Charlevoix undefeated. Charlevoix also was undefeated—and enjoying a 57-game winning streak. In the 1947 matchup of the two teams, Charlevoix had won 66-0.

The whole town of East Jordan was excited about the game, which was played at home that year; and our team didn't let the town down. We didn't win, but we didn't lose either. We played to a 0-0 tie, earning a tie for the league championship. Nobody in the stands wanted to leave when the game was over. The team had come a long way in a year, and I was very proud of all of the players.

It also was the first time I realized that a coach can feel just as good as a player about winning. I was extremely happy and proud of everything we had accomplished in a short amount of time.

My salary for that year was $2,900. To earn that money, in addition to coaching football, basketball and baseball, I taught classes in history, political science and citizenship. One of my students, Puddy Thomson, later married Chuck Fairbanks, who went on to coach at the University of Oklahoma and in the pros. He was one of the players on that Charlevoix team, and was a very good one.

Because my salary didn't really bring in enough money to cover all of our expenses, I tried to pick up extra money wherever I could. I played basketball in a semi-pro league on Saturday nights for a team called the Charlevoix Knight Owls, earning $50 per game. The owner was Johnny Knight, who also owned a softball team that I played for in the summer. I also worked in the East Jordan recreation department during the summer, and even sold encyclopedias for a short period.

I don't think kids today understand how hard it was back then to make money, and how hard people had to work in order to have a decent lifestyle and pay all the bills. It never bothered me to work; I enjoyed it, and I enjoyed every job I've ever had. It probably didn't hurt that the success of the football team had opened some doors for me to other businesses and job opportunities in the town.

The football team's success was a hot topic all winter, and, when it came time for the school's annual spring awards banquet, the leaders of the town wanted to invite a speaker from a major college. We put in a call to Michigan State, where Biggie Munn was the head coach, and were pleased they agreed to send their offensive line coach, Duffy Daugherty, to speak at our banquet.

Duffy did a great job. When the banquet was over, he decided to spend the evening at our home on the lake. It was the first time we had ever met, and we hit if off immediately. There was a difference in our ages, but luckily I've always been able to communicate with people who are both older and younger than me. I think that's a skill any successful coach needs or he isn't going to last long.

Duffy always related well to people. Because he liked almost everyone he ever met, he also was willing to do anything for them. That, in turn, gave people a good, warm feeling about Duffy.

I don't think there ever was a person who did more for other people, at least in athletics, than Duffy Daugherty. We stayed up late that night talking. Duffy spent the night sleeping on the couch in the living room because we only had one bedroom. When Jo and I awoke in the morning and walked into the living room, he had one twin under each arm. That's how our long and great relationship began.

The success of the 1948 team raised the expectations of the people in East Jordan for the 1949 football season, and the kids were more than up to the challenge. We, again, were undefeated going into the game against Charlevoix. For the second year in a row, we tied, this time 13-13.

The success of the team in both seasons gave us celebrity status across the state. We were noticed because we still were the smallest school in our conference, with only a few more than 200 students, and for years had had trouble even convincing enough of the boys to come out so we could field a team.

The fans were as excited about the team as the players. They became fiercely loyal and followed us all over northern Michigan. People who saw our games and high school games in Detroit thought we were comparable; and Charlevoix did send many players on to Michigan State. We had an all-state player in Tuck Thomson, who later became the brother-in-law of Chuck Fairbanks.

It was a big year for me, because out of the friendship with Duffy, he invited Jo and me to attend many of the Michigan State games that year. The schedule worked out great, because we played on Friday night, then were able to drive to East Lansing for the Spartans' games on Saturday. One of the games we watched was the battle against Notre Dame, who was headed to the national championship behind the play of Leon Hart and Emil Sitko.

Against Michigan State, Sitko scored the winning touchdown on a dive that looked like he had been shot out of a cannon. The crowd and school officials didn't seem too upset by the loss because they respected the fact that Notre Dame was willing to schedule Michigan State and helped the Spartans get into the Big Ten Conference.

Through my developing friendship with Duffy, I got to know several members of the Michigan State coaching staff. Jo and I were invited to attend postgame parties at the home of Biggie Munn, the head coach, and his wife, Vera. Even though I was making only $3,100 a year—I got a big $200 raise after our success in 1948—the way Jo and I were treated by everyone associated with Michigan State made us feel like royalty.

During the winter of 1949, Duffy and I talked often; and he kept encouraging me to move to East Lansing and go to graduate school at Michigan State. He didn't promise anything for the future, but he said I could work with the football team as a graduate assistant. Even though Duffy was technically an assistant coach, he had a lot of friends in high places and was usually able to get what he wanted.

Jo and I talked about it, and we decided, unless we were content to remain in East Jordan for the rest of our lives, this was probably an opportunity that we shouldn't pass up. I thanked everybody in East Jordan who had been so kind and supportive of us. We rented a van, loaded it with our furniture and other belongings and our family took off for the next chapter in our lives.

As had been the case when I was hired in East Jordan, I really had no idea what I was getting myself into at Michigan State. I knew I was going to be going back to school and would be doing some kind of assistant coaching with the football team, but I had no idea what my exact duties would be.

Looking back on it, I guess we were a little naive to have given up a secure job for a real unknown. We didn't even have any idea where we were going to live. Thankfully, Duffy came through and helped us line up a place in a wartime surplus barracks where many other students lived. It wasn't the most attractive place around, but it was clean and safe and had the advantages of being close to campus and the football offices.

One of the first people I met after arriving at Michigan State was Chuck Davey, a great boxer on the Spartans' excellent boxing team. We just happened to meet my first day of class and developed a good friendship. He went on to fight for the welterweight championship of the world against Kid Gavilan in Chicago. He's gone on to become a successful businessman in Detroit.

The instructors at Michigan State were very good, particularly in the classes I took in sports physiology. This was in an era when physical education still wasn't treated seriously by a lot of people and at a lot of schools. I was fortunate to get a very good education in the field. The teachers had all earned doctorate degrees and could have just as easily been teaching in a lot of other departments on campus.

One thing that didn't change about my life was that I still tried to pick up extra money any way I could. I was lucky enough to hook up with a basketball team made up of seniors from the football team. We played in a league and were paid $75 a game. One of my teammates was Sonny Grandelius, who later became head football coach at Colorado. It also was my job to set up the games and make all of the arrangements, including drawing up the contracts. This helped me get to know the players well and many of us remain good friends today, although we don't get to see each other as often as we'd like.

I also picked up some extra money by refereeing high school basketball games, and Duffy helped out by sending some requests for a banquet speaker my way. I know he made more money for the assignments he accepted, but I was grateful to have the extra money.

I got involved with the football team right away, and one game I'll never forget was the battle against the University of Michigan. This was in 1950, and the rivalry then was just as intense as it is today. We were playing at Michigan, and I remember walking onto the field and looking up at nearly 100,000 people in the stands. I had never seen a crowd like that in my life. On the field, the Michigan band was playing, and it looked like they stretched from one end zone to the other. I was so nervous I felt like crawling in a hole and disappearing for the entire game.

The rules about where coaches could be for games was different back then. In addition to having a coach scout from the press box, you were allowed to have a scout in each end zone. I was assigned the north end zone, and, as I walked up the steps to the top of the stands, waiting for the game to start, I remember telling myself, "Devine, you can go in a hole now, just panic, not do anything, or choose to try to do something constructive for the Spartans."

For the first half I sat up there and took copious notes. At halftime, I climbed down the steps and went to the locker room to make my report, and the first person I ran into was Duffy. He was waiting for the team to get a drink and settle down, so I took the opportunity to tell him what I thought after watching the first half.

"Duffy," I said, "it looks to me like the 4-trap and the dive at 7 are plays that we should be using."

If looks could kill, I would have been dead on the floor of the locker room. Duffy was in no mood for advice from anyone, much less someone like me, who still wasn't certain exactly what I was doing or what I was talking about. I remember thinking, "Well, that was pretty brash," but I still trusted my opinion and what I thought were plays that could work for our offense.

I went outside for a couple of minutes, hoping I hadn't made a big mistake, then walked back in the locker room. On the blackboard, I saw that Duffy had diagrammed the two plays I had suggested. My heart jumped for joy—the team was going to take my advice. I was now more nervous than I had been before the game began. Michigan State had not won at Michigan in 13 years, and the two plays that I suggested, and were now drawn up on the blackboard, might be the difference between the team winning and losing.

I went back to the end zone for the second half and was ecstatic when team captain and fullback LeRoy Crane ran a fullback spinner on the 4-trap for a touchdown that put us ahead. We won by the score of 14-7.

It was a much different scene in the locker room after the game. It was the first and only time I ever saw a university president in tears after a game. That was how badly Michigan State President John Hannah wanted to win the game, and how much he thought it was going to mean in the state for his school. I didn't know then that I was going to be back in the same locker room in the future, first as the head coach of the University of Missouri, and, later, as the coach at Notre Dame. Both times we would be celebrating highly emotional wins, when the Tigers won by scoring on the final play of the game, and when the Irish blocked an attempted field goal on the final play of the game to win. I was lucky enough to be the head coach of teams that played three games at Ann Arbor and three games at East Lansing; and I'm proud to say my teams won all six of those games.

Earning my graduate degree qualified me to become a full-time assistant coach with the Spartans, earning $7,500 a year. That was a lot of money in the early 1950s, and Jo and I felt comfortable enough to buy our first house. Still, we needed financial help, and we got it from Duffy. He co-signed the note at the bank. He was always the type of person who would do anything he could to help his friends.

I quickly learned that both Biggie and Duffy were very organized. I didn't realize at the time how influential both of them would be in my life. Looking back, I can see how much of my strategies and philosophies about coaching and administering a staff came from both of them. Biggie and Duffy were completely different individuals. Duffy was a brilliant man and a great football coach who could jump from one wavelength to the next in a blink of an eye. He wasn't able to focus and concentrate as long as Biggie could, however.

Biggie gave me the job of coaching the junior varsity, a team made up mostly of freshmen, who, at the time, were normally not eligible to play on the varsity squad. Colleges have done away with junior varsity teams now because freshmen are eligible to play right away. Colleges don't want to "waste" that year if a player is good enough to play immediately. Players who are not quite that advanced are able to redshirt for a season, meaning they are eligible to practice but can't play in the games. That, in effect, gives them a fifth year of eligibility.

In 1951, freshmen normally were not allowed to play, but the outbreak of the war in Korea changed the NCAA rules. With so smany young men going into the service, the colleges didn't want to not have enough players on their teams. So they amended the rule to allow freshmen to play.

This didn't really change my job, because we still had a junior varsity team; but I lost some players I might have otherwise had on my team. I was lucky, however, because what I almost lost was my job.

Soon after the war began, all officers who were on flying status at the end of World War II received a letter informing us we would be recalled for duty in Korea, unless we had four or more dependents. We already had the twins and, then, in two weeks, our daughter Dede was born. That gave me the four dependents, which exempted me from going to Korea.

Jo and I had talked about it, and we were prepared if I had been sent to Korea. She would have taken the kids back to Duluth to stay with her parents. I never will know what would have happened to my coaching career if that had happened.

Instead, the year I spent as the junior varsity coach probably was the most beneficial year I had in all of my preparations to become a head coach on the collegiate and professional levels.

Biggie turned over all of the responsibilities for running the team to me. I had to make all of the travel arrangements, including the buses, hotels, meals, practice facilities, dressing rooms, etc. I learned that I really was in charge as I was working on the plans for our trip to Columbus to play Ohio State, a game that I thought would interest Biggie.

I had my plans all made, but I wanted to make certain they were OK with Biggie. I had everything typed up, and I took it into his office one day and handed it to him. Biggie glanced up from what he was doing, barely looked at what it was and tossed it back to me. He said, "We hired you as head junior varsity coach—this is your job."

Biggie looked as if he was mad that I had bothered him about such a thing, but he was the kind of guy who was hard to read. You couldn't always tell if he was displeased or not, or whether he was secretly pleased, but wanted to act like he was mad to try to teach you a lesson. He wanted to make you believe it was your job. He wanted you to feel comfortable and confident about the decisions you made and not worry that he would be standing over your shoulder second-guessing or correcting you all the time.

This experience, combined with the in-game decisions that had to be made while coaching on the sideline, gave me experience that any young coach would have died for. I was still in my early 20s, coaching kids only a few years younger than me; and I learned what I needed to do to be successful.

We had a good year on both the junior varsity and varsity levels, and that made for a good work environment. The coaches were happy, the players were in a good mood and everybody was united, working toward one goal. We beat Michigan and Ohio State, and I quickly learned those were the two most important games on the schedule.

Later that season, the varsity started receiving national attention. We beat Frank Leahy's Notre Dame team 35-0 on national television, and that was unheard of. The program was being noticed by other coaches and by schools in need of new coaches, and we started to lose assistants to other programs. Forest Evashevski left after the 1951 season, and that left an opening for Biggie to fill on his staff. He had a lot of qualified people who had coached under him, and I didn't know who was going to get the job.

I wasn't really expecting it. After all, I was only a year out of graduate school and had spent one season as the junior varsity coach. If Biggie had called me into his office and said he was picking someone else, and that he wanted me to keep doing what I was doing, I would have understood and been perfectly content and happy. Instead, he called and told me he was making me one of his four full-time assistants.

My particular job in 1952 was working as the freshman coach, but all of us did a little bit of everything, whatever Biggie asked us to do. The other three assistants were Duffy, Steve Sebo and Earle Edwards. We had about 15 graduate assistants and part-time coaches available as well, all of whom had played at Michigan State, but I felt like one of the big boys. It's incredible when you look back now and realize that we won a national championship that year, with a full-time staff of five coaches. Major Division I programs today have three times the number of coaches and other people working on all of the administrative jobs that have to be done. It was a different era back then, that's for sure.

It was a great time in my life. I was making a salary that we could live on, we had a nice home, and I was building good relationships with the other coaches and players. I even was included in the group that could eat at the training table, a nice perk around any football team.

Being the freshman coach was similar to being the junior varsity coach, although, as one of the four full-time assistants, I also had responsibilities for the varsity practices and games. I had about eight graduate assistants working under me. They might not have realized it, but I learned a lot from every one of them. It was hard work, because the freshmen usually played on Friday afternoon and then I had to help prepare for the varsity game on Saturday.

I kept the same job in 1953. The varsity had another big season, losing only one game en route to a share of the Big Ten championship. We were ranked third in the country as we prepared for the Rose Bowl on January 1 against UCLA.

For the bowl game, Biggie gave me the assignment of working with Mel Allen, who was going to be doing the play-by-play broadcast of the game on national television. The Rose Bowl is billed as the granddaddy of the bowl games, and that definitely was true in the 1950s. It was the one game that everybody in the country watched; and Biggie wanted Allen to know as much as possible about our program, and about our preparations and plans for the game.

Mel and I spent a lot of time together leading up to the game, and, in the process, we became good friends. We went over all of our game films from the season; and Mel definitely knew as much as anyone about our team and what we were going to try to do against UCLA.

Biggie was a great coach, but one of the reasons the teams at Michigan State were so successful in those years was because of the work of the assistant coaches. It's just as true today in both the college and pro ranks. A head coach probably gets too much of the credit when a team wins and too much of the blame when a team losses. The assistants do an awful lot of work and are really responsible for much of the game plan and decisions that are made.

We had a wonderful staff and received a nice addition in 1953 when Biggie added Bob Devaney, another high school coach. Bob, of course, went on to great success at Nebraska, where he became a rival as well as a good friend.

We won the Rose Bowl, 28-20, scoring the final touchdown on a 92-yard punt return by Billy Wells. That capped a great week for Wells, who looked as if he was about 14 years old.

He had a crush on Debbie Reynolds, the actress, and really wanted to meet her. Two nights before the game, we had a big party for both teams, and Bob Hope was the master of ceremonies. It had been arranged for Reynolds to be there, and she was hiding behind a curtain. Hope brought Wells up to the stage, and was kidding him, when Debbie snuck out from behind the curtain and came up and tapped Billy on the shoulder. When he turned around and saw her, he about went crazy.

Hope really got into it, and set it up so that, if Michigan State won, Reynolds would agree to go on a date with Billy. I wonder how long it took Wells to remember that after he scored the winning touchdown.

Wells and Reynolds did go on the date, and stayed out all night. That was the end of the relationship, although I do know they saw each other occasionally over the years. Wells ended up acting in some movies after his college days were over.

After the game, the staff went through a major change. Biggie gave up coaching to become the athletic director, and Duffy was named head coach. It was a good move for me, because Duffy and I were close. I moved up to become the offensive backfield coach and earned the nonexistent, at least on paper, title as Duffy's number-one assistant.

Even though they were extremely close, much like a father and son, Biggie and Duffy had moments when their relationship was scarred. Watching these two guys who I admired at odds with each other was the only unpleasant experience I had while at Michigan State.

I learned so much from both of them, and one of the things I learned was how fragile relationshps on a coaching staff can be, and also how important it is for a team to be successful. Duffy had played for Biggie, but that didn't mean they agreed on every issue and every decision.

Major college football is a stressful profession. Coaches have to be able to deal with the pressure that comes with the job or they are going to fail. You have a high profile, and emotions run very high. It's not unusual for there to be disagreements that boil over and get ugly. Some coaches are able to deal with the pressures of winning and losing better, but for some it really is an emotional roller coaster every week.

In the years I was an assistant, and, even later, as a head coach, I don't think I ever reached the point where I considered losing a football game worse than death. Some coaches did. I was as competitive as anybody who ever coached the game, and I wanted to win. No one, I guarantee, ever took losing harder than I did.

Biggie and Duffy both were so kind and understanding and helpful to me. They were also tough with me, and gave me a good kick in the pants whenever I needed it. I owed a great debt to both men, both personally and professionally.

Several years after Biggie took over as athletic director, he suffered a stroke. Everyone was stunned and saddened, and I think that made the fallout between Biggie and Duffy even harder for everyone involved.

My role on the staff changed under Duffy. One of the things he thought I could bring to the team was help in recruiting. I guess he liked my personality, or he thought I could get along well with the recruits, their families and their high school coaches. Recruiting good players is, of course, the first requirement for building a successful program in any sport. It doesn't matter how great a coach is; if he doesn't have decent players on his team, he is not going to win.

I enjoyed the recruiting part of the game, as any good coach should; but I also enjoyed the in-game strategy involved in coaching and making split-second decisions on the field. I saw how Biggie and Duffy approached their work, including the before-game preparations, the halftime adjustments that had to be made, and the differences when it came time to prepare for a bowl game. As with all of my experiences at Michigan State, every facet of the game was helping nurture and prepare me for the day when I was to become a head coach.

The players at Michigan State taught me a lot as well. Some who stood out, for a multitude of reasons, were LeRoy Crane, Sonny Grandelius, Dorne Dibble, Bob Carey, Al Dorow, Billy Wells, Johnny Wilson, Doug Weaver, Tom Yewcic, Evan Slonac, LeRoy Bolden, Ellis Duckett, Walt Kowalczyk and Earl Morrall. Carey was also a three-year starter in basketball and competed in the shot put for the track team. As far as I know, he is the last person to win nine varsity letters during his athletic career at a Big Ten school.

Wilson was a Rhodes Scholar and in a class by himself as just an outstanding person. Weaver went on to become a good coach and later served as athletic director at Georgia Tech and Michigan State.

We played against some outstanding players as well, including Leon Hart (one of only two linemen to win the Heisman Trophy), Emil Sitko, Bill Wightkin, Bob Williams, Johnny Lattner (another Heisman winner), Don Kramer and, of course, Hopalong Cassidy at Ohio State. Watching all of them, and scores of other greats, added to my knowledge and love of the game.

The biggest thing I learned at Michigan State was the importance of loyalty, hard work and intelligence. You can't expect to be successful as a coach at any level, in any sport, without a combination of those three things.

Biggie and Duffy were very loyal to me, and I felt I was loyal to them. They expected and deserved loyalty from the assistant coaches and the players. Both men worked extremely hard, and they worked their players hard. When the players came into that program, they knew the commitment they were making. If they weren't willing to live up to it, Biggie and Duffy made it easy for them to leave. There's no doubt that a large portion of the success of those teams was because of the amount of work they put in to make certain they were successful.

Intelligence is a hard skill to measure, and it's definitely an oversimplification. You just knew, by your practice and experience, when was the right time to call for a fake field goal or a fake punt. Those decisions aren't just gambles or lucky guesses. A smart coach knows his players, knows the game, and knows the right time to call plays like that, or even a quarterback sneak or a 50-yard bomb. You can't take courses in intelligent coaching, you can't teach it. It comes from understanding and studying and appreciating the game and your players. It's an intangible, immeasurable skill, but it's one all good coaches have in common.

I was happy that Duffy had taken over as the head coach; and I was very comfortable with what I was doing at that stage in my life and career. I really was not contemplating making any major changes anytime soon, but then something totally unexpected happened. Arizona State was looking for a new head coach, and I turned out to be the guy they wanted.

Chapter Four

ARIZONA STATE

Maybe because I never really set out to become a coach, at any level, I never gave much thought to becoming a collegiate head coach. With some young assistant coaches that I see now, that is their entire goal, striving to get that first head coaching job. I don't know why, but it honestly wasn't ever a goal of mine.

It especially was not a goal when I was still in my mid-20s and had only been an assistant at the college level for four years and a coach at all for six. That was why I was so taken by surprise when I found out Arizona State officials wanted to talk to me about their head coaching position.

The officials there were looking at me, I think, because of the success of the Michigan State program and also because of my age. I think they wanted a young guy because the school had some difficulties in the past, and in the 1950s was not as successful and glamorous a program as it is today. They knew they didn't have the ability to attract a proven head coach, or even some of the more established, higher profile assistants, so they were willing to take a chance on a young guy that they thought might be able to grow into the job.

I found out later what helped lead Arizona State to me were some very strong recommendations from the people I had worked with, like Duffy and Biggie. One of the coaches on the staff there had coached against me when I was playing in college, and I found out later he had given me a strong recommendation as well. Because I had tried to be friendly to everybody I met in the game, everybody that ASU contacted was very supportive, and I really appreciated it.

When I found out the ASU people wanted to talk to me, I was flattered, but also a little scared. I went out there to interview for the job and tour the area, and I really received first-class treatment from the university president, Dr. Grady Gammage, Athletic Director Clyde Smith and all of the other people I met with.

I was very impressed with the area, with all of the resort hotels and developments, and I had no doubts that the predictions the area would turn into a gold mine would be correct. I only wish I had had more money then so I could have invested it wisely and been well off financially forever.

All of the school officials talked openly about their hopes for the future, for the school in general and also for the football program. They wanted to come clean with the NCAA and clear up the mistakes they had made in the past, which were the reason they were on probation. During my interview with Dr. Gammage, he only wanted to know two things—would I run a completely honest program, and would my student athletes make normal progress in their classes and graduate?

I knew the answer to the first question was yes. I could never imagine doing something illegal in my program, and I assured Dr. Gammage that my program would be clean and honest. As far as what my student athletes would do, I answered the question the only way I knew how, which was that I would make that one of my goals and would do my best. Having him ask those questions impressed me and told me what I needed to know about Dr. Gammage and his priorities, and I had no doubt he was going to turn that school into one of the leading universities in the country, which is exactly what he did.

I also came away impressed with Clyde Smith, who had been the head coach at Indiana. He was the coach when the Hoosiers beat Frank Leahy's undefeated Notre Dame team in a major upset in 1950.

Despite my immediate fondness for those people, and the fact I knew it would be a tremendous challenge to take over as the head coach, I didn't say yes to the job offer right away. I went back to Michigan and sat down with Jo, and we kicked around all of the advantages and the negatives about the job.

Was I ready for a head coaching position? Honestly, I didn't know. But if I turned this offer down, how long would it be before another school came along, and where would that school be? Would it be as good a situation as Arizona State? There was no way to tell.

I was confident in my abilities, and I knew I had been trained well. Could I have learned more staying and working on Duffy's staff for a few more years? Certainly. Could I also learn while running my own program at Arizona State? That answer was also yes.

There were risks involved in taking the job. The school was on probation, and that always hurts your recruiting and is used against you by other programs going after the same kids. The area was just beginning to come alive, and the program was not as established and successful as Michigan State. If I was not successful, how much would that hinder me in trying to get another coaching job?

The more Jo and I talked about the possibility, however, the more it grew on me. It was very similar to the situation when we went to East Jordan and also when we went to Michigan State. We were taking a risk then, too; we didn't know what the future would hold or how things would work out. In both cases, things had worked out well, and we had to have faith that they would work out again in Arizona.

Before I completely made up my mind, I sat down with Duffy and asked for his advice and opinion. He told me to do whatever I thought was the best decision for me, Jo and the family. I knew he honestly meant that.

I also talked to Biggie, and he said, "You're ready for a head coach job. I've watched you since you were head coach for the junior varsity team. I liked the way you handled everything. Most of all I like the way you handled the players. You don't run a popularity contest. You simply try to get the best out of the material that you have. You hope that they like you later on when they understand what you were trying to do."

The final decision then came down to Jo and me. She was a perfect coach's wife and always was willing to sacrifice for the betterment of my career. If she didn't want to go to Arizona, she hid her feelings well. We knew finances would be a major factor in the decision. Because it was a smaller school in a smaller conference, they didn't pay nearly as well as Michigan State. They were offering me $8,900 a year, which wasn't much more than I was making, but the fringe benefits were better. They were going to give me a car, which we didn't have at Michigan State, an expense account for recruiting trips and a membership in a country club.

One of the other major risks was a state law in Arizona that limited all contracts to one year, because I would be an employee of the state. There were no multi-year contracts, so the only guarantee I had that I would not be bounced in a year was the word of Dr. Gammage and Clyde Smith. I decided I believed them and would take them at their word. I called and took the job.

Clyde wanted to introduce me at a big banquet that was already scheduled in Phoenix, so I flew down and he picked me up at the airport, which had only one small terminal. The first thing I realized is that I wasn't dressed for Arizona. I was wearing a heavy suit perfect for winters in Michigan, but we were going directly from the airport to the banquet and I had no time to pick up another suit or go to the hotel. At the banquet of the Press Box Association, I sat in front of all these blazing lights, and I felt I was going to melt away. I was hot and tired, and the room was packed with media and boosters and celebrities there to play golf in the pro-am of the Phoenix Open. I wondered if I had made the right decision in accepting the job.

Looking into the bright lights I couldn't see anybody, but I knew the room was filled with people. It was my job to give the main speech because I was being introduced as Arizona State's new head coach, and the banquet was being televised. I have no idea what I said or how I looked, but somehow I got through the whole ordeal. The beat writers who covered ASU from the two newspapers in town, Ben Foote of the *Phoenix Gazette* and Dean Smith of the *Arizona Republic*, were both there, and I think they could tell how nervous I was. They both were very kind to me and treated me well, as they have throughout my life.

Clyde helped me find a house in Tempe where I could rent a room while I was getting organized, before Jo and the kids came out to join me. It was the spring of 1955 and Tempe was a small, sleepy little college town. I immediately fell in love with the place. It seemed more like heaven to me than any place I had ever been.

I quickly fell into a routine that I enjoyed tremendously. I began my day by walking eight blocks, which took about 15 minutes, to the 6 a.m. Mass at Mount Carmel Catholic Church. It was a very quiet and peaceful way to begin each day. Over the years I've fallen out of the habit of being a daily communicant, and if I had it to do over again, I would be there every morning.

The church, which has now been refurbished, was small but beautiful. The Pastor was Father Daniel McCready, a fantastic man. We became close friends and still see each other occasionally. The original church is still on the ASU campus. Today, Jo and I help support a huge project that will make the old church fully accessible to all who are physically disabled. We're pleased that Father Nathan Castle, the current director of All Saints Catholic Newman Center, is so dedicated to this noble cause.

After Mass, I walked across the street to The Varsity Inn, where the staff and I met for breakfast. They had the world's best doughnuts and sweet rolls. The owner was Nels Jensen, and he treated us very well. After breakfast, we moved on to the stadium, where we sat in a room with a blackboard and came up with our plans for everything we wanted to cover in spring practice. We had everything timed out to the minute so everybody knew what they would be doing every minute and there would be no confusion or anybody wondering where they should be or what they would be doing next. That organization helped us not only in practice but later in our game routine.

At Michigan State, the daily practice schedule was just handed to me every day. Biggie and Duffy were different in a lot of ways, but they both were extremely organized. One of the biggest changes in becoming a head coach was that the responsibility for organizing practices and what everybody should be doing fell on my shoulders, but I honestly thought they had trained me well enough that I was ready for that responsibility.

It helped that I was blessed with an excellent staff. Two of my assistants went on to successful head coaching careers themselves, Frank Kush and Al Onofrio. Frank turned out to be the winningest coach in Arizona State history, and Al was the upset king when he was coaching Missouri in the 1970s. His teams upset Notre Dame in South Bend, Alabama at Birmingham, Southern Cal in Los Angeles, Ohio State at Columbus, Nebraska at Lincoln and Oklahoma at home. Looking at that list now makes you shake your head. It seems unbelievable, but all you have to do is check the record book to see that it really did happen. Al's teams even beat Frank's ASU team twice, both with shutouts.

Al had more experience, but Frank was young, like me. Al had gotten out of football and actually was coaching golf at Arizona State when I talked him into coming on board our staff. That took a little while, and he didn't make up his mind until we had already started practice.

Frank almost missed the start of practice. He was going to coach both the offensive and defensive lines, but he was still in the Army at Fort Benning, Georgia. He drove nonstop to Tempe, arriving just in time for the first day.

Our other assistants were Bob Carey, Tom Fletcher and Bill Kajikawa. Gene Fetter was with us for a while as well, and later we added Cecil Coleman, who had played at ASU and was a good coach.

Carey had starred with the NFL Rams until an injury ended his career. Kajikawa's story was incredible. Even though he was born and raised in the United States, he had to overcome the negative attitudes of many Americans toward persons of Japanese heritage during World War II. After numerous attempts failed, he finally was allowed to enlist in the 442nd Infantry, which was made up of Japanese-Americans. It became the most highly decorated battle unit in the history of the United States Army.

Bill's daughter, Dr. Christine Wilkinson, later became interim Athletic Director at Arizona State and I think some day will be the president of a major university.

It was tough being away from Jo and the kids, but it made sense for them to stay in Michigan and complete the school year. I was so busy trying to get organized and make certain I did everything right that I probably wouldn't have had much time to be a good father or husband anyway. I tried to stay in touch as much as possible with letters and telephone calls, and I wanted them to be as excited as I was about our new home and the opportunities it presented for us. I kept describing how beautiful the area was, but also how different it was than anything we had ever known in Minnesota or Michigan. It was really my first extended stay in the southwest, and I had no idea how beautiful the area was, especially in the spring.

It was easy to take the 70-degree days when I knew there were freezing temperatures and snow on the ground back in Michigan. That made Jo and the kids want to get out there as quickly as possible.

There is a trade-off with the weather in Arizona, however, which I quickly found out. If you live there year round, you get great weather for several months, and then you have the summer. Jo and the kids were prepared for what I had described, but what greeted them in June was something completely different. I went back and picked them up, and we drove across the country—with no air conditioner. We were greeted in Arizona by monsoon dust storms and temperatures that climbed past the 100-degree mark every day. Jo thought I had been lying to her about the weather, and I had to tell her it really would be nice again in the fall.

I learned that the weather always is a factor in whatever you do in Arizona, especially in preparing for a football season. The team now begins its practices up in the mountains, where it is cooler. We didn't have access to a place like that in 1955, but even if we had, I think my decision would have been to stay in the Valley. I just thought it would help better prepare the team if we practiced in the same conditions in which we would be playing games. Before classes began, we actually had three practice sessions a day, one in the early morning, one in the evening and one, without pads, in the middle of the day to work on conditioning.

I thought that was going to be a factor in our performance, especially early in the season when we would be playing teams that weren't used to the heat. While I wanted to see that our players were in the best condition possible, I wanted to find out more than that about them. I studied each of their academic profiles, seeing what progress they were making in school, and I wanted to check their attitude and morale. What I found was that we had some good football players and guys with big hearts. We had inherited some good players from the previous coaches, but we really had to get to work to build that team from the ground up.

I've always believed that in order to play well in games, you have to practice well. Probably because of my lack of experience and the fact it was my first head coaching job, I may have been a little too intense with that first group of players. We spent hours as a staff planning every detail of practice, and we followed that schedule religiously. We might have been guilty of practicing too hard, but that wasn't the way I saw it back then. I convinced our players how important the extra conditioning was, and how that was going to make a difference in whether we won or lost, and they accepted it.

One thing I learned from Biggie that I began using in my practices was to run a lot of the offensive plays against big bags. They didn't move, but a lot of the defensive players in those days didn't move much anyway. It helped the offensive guys learn what they were supposed to do on particular plays, and it increased their confidence they could run the play effectively and that it would work. We used them for practicing assignments, takeoffs and even improving the guys' morale. I spent a lot of time working with the players on the field, but I also quickly learned the advantages of overseeing practice from a tower, where you can see everything that is going on. Players want to be appreciated and complimented when they do something well, and it's easier to do that if you're watching the entire field and not on the ground working with one particular group.

On one blackboard we listed all of the things we wanted to accomplish before the end of spring practice. On another we listed all of the things we needed to do before our first game, which was going to be against Wichita State. They had a good team and were coming off the championship of the Missouri Valley Conference, having defeated Sid Gilman's Cincinnati team. Jack Mitchell, the coach, had moved on to Arkansas, and one of his assistants, Pete Tillman, had taken over.

The scouting of opposing teams was a lot different than it is now, and I think that forced us to concentrate more on what we did well as a team and just hope it would work against whatever defense they decided to use. Now scouting opponents is one of the most sophisticated areas of the game, but we didn't have the resources available to find out everything we could about an opponent back then.

Maybe the lack of knowledge about an opponent forced us to get to know our own players and their abilities better. We set up the offense and defense basically the same as the teams had run at Michigan State, but with a few different wrinkles of things I had been successful using as a head coach at East Jordan.

I had made up my mind when I took the job that if I wasn't successful, it was not going to be because I didn't try and didn't work hard enough. I remember sitting in my office that spring, which overlooked the university's tennis courts, and saw my assistants out playing tennis. They needed that break, and it was good they were out there relaxing. I probably should have been out there with them, but I thought by spending the extra time in the office, I was going to learn something that I otherwise might have overlooked. I didn't want to have any question unanswered, and to have anything come up in a game that we weren't prepared for or didn't know how to handle. I wanted the team to have confidence in me and the other coaches that we knew what we were doing and would call the right play in the right situation during a game.

One thing I knew immediately as a head coach was that I was only going to be successful if I had good players. Recruiting players was something I had done well at Michigan State, and I knew that was going to be my biggest challenge at Arizona State. At Michigan State it was easy to show off the campus and the school. The campus was beautiful, with a nice student union, several cafeterias and a big stadium. We had two great natural rivals in Michigan and Notre Dame, which were always national powerhouses. We had the support of the alumni and the school's administration, so it was an easy job trying to get kids to want to come to school there and play football.

When I got to Arizona State, we didn't have all of those things working for us. It actually was still a college at that point, not even a university. The school was building to that, thanks to the work of Dr. Gammage and others, but they knew it would take time. Even though I think Dr. Gammage was a lot like my first boss at East Jordan, Ernie Wade, who didn't care much for sports, he recognized the importance of the athletic program and realized its value in helping build the school the way he wanted to build it. He also gave me a goal—he wanted to beat the rival University of Arizona once every three years. If I could do that, along with running a clean program, he told me I could stay at ASU for the rest of my life.

Naturally, there weren't as many people in Arizona as in Michigan back then, so I knew we couldn't rely on just getting all of the local kids if we were going to become successful. One of the kids I had been familiar with in Michigan was a running back named Leon Burton, who was from Flint.

Duffy was recruiting him for the Spartans, but when Leon was involved in a car accident and we didn't know if he was going to be able to play, Duffy backed off. I wanted Leon badly. He might have been the best running back I've ever seen. I still wonder how good he would have been had he been on a National Championship-caliber team, but he was extremely good for us.

In the first game of his freshman season, he rushed for 235 yards—on only five carries—against Hardin-Simmons, which was coached by the legendary Sammy Baugh. When Baugh took over as head coach of the New York Titans of the upstart American Football League a few years later, the first player he signed was Leon Burton.

Leon went on to lead the nation in yards per carry in 1957. One play I'll never forget occurred in our game against Idaho. We had a comfortable lead, but were faced with a fourth down and 1 on our own 21-yard line. We decided to go for the first down, but instead Leon took an option play wide around end and was off for a 79-yard touchdown.

In addition to going after Leon, I relied on my contacts and friendships that I had made around the country to spread the word that we were looking for some good football players. We got kids from Milwaukee, Chicago and a few from California, and luckily they all turned out to be good kids and good players.

The NCAA wasn't as powerful then as it is today, and there were not as many guidelines and restrictions as there are on coaches and schools today. If you made arrangements with the principal in advance, you could visit a player almost any time you wanted. There was no limit on how many times you could visit a kid, so it was an area where you could outwork your opponents in convincing a kid to sign with you.

One thing that surprised me in Arizona was the attitude of some of the people toward minorities. Later at Missouri I became known as the coach who integrated the program, but that was a different place at a different time. I had seen prejudice before, and I didn't like it then.

Back in high school in Proctor, the band was on a trip and my best friend, Danny Cullen, was sitting behind me on the bus. He knocked my band hat down over my eyes. It was just a prank, somebody acting up, and it didn't bother me. I just responded by saying, "Danny, you're a darned dago." I didn't think anything more about it until the trip was over, and another of my friends came up to me.

The friend told me that when I said that, it made a girl who was sitting by her, Kathleen Marino, start to cry. I was completely astounded. "I made her cry?" I asked. She repeated that I had made her cry. It turned out that her father had a nickname around Proctor which she didn't like—Dago Mike—and my comment toward Danny had hurt her very much. Of course I had no intention of hurting her feelings or those of anybody else. I didn't have the tact to go up and apologize to her then, but I'm doing so now. I honestly don't believe anybody in Proctor meant any harm with comments like those, it was just a product of the times. But I never forgot that and how my comment had made Kathleen cry, and I was determined never to let something like that happen again.

We didn't really run into any racial problems during our first season, but in 1956 we played at Hardin-Simmons, which is located in Abilene, Texas. At that time, it was our routine to segregate black and white players for housing and eating. It seemed like I was always the last person to find out about problems like that, but when I heard that was our plan, I went to our Athletic Director and told him I didn't think we should play the game under those conditions. He agreed, and we said that if our entire team could not stay in the same hotel and eat in the same restaurant, we were not going to play the game.

Our entire team walked into a nice hotel in Abilene, and only one person, an older gentleman dressed like a cowboy, raised his eyebrows as we walked through the lobby before he went back to reading his newspaper. My hard stance forced the school to change its policy, and I'm proud of that.

Luckily we didn't have distractions like that as we prepared for our first game of the 1955 season, against Wichita State. As we got closer to the game, I was nervous and excited, but I really believed we had practiced well and were prepared. Our athletic director, Clyde Smith, told me I had the team too worked up.

We tied the game 20-20. It would have been nicer to win, of course, but I couldn't really complain. It was the closest thing to a win I ever experienced.

That turned out to be the springboard we needed for a good season. One of the teams we beat was Hardin-Simmons, in a game at Tempe, a team ASU had never beaten. Sammy Baugh was the coach, and that probably intimidated me more than it did any of our players. We had one of those games where everything just seemed to fall into place. Even our third-string quarterback, playing defense, intercepted a pass and returned it 65 yards for a touchdown. We won the game 69-14.

After the game, I hesitated to start walking across the field because I didn't know what to say to Baugh. I was afraid he would be critical of me and our team, thinking we had piled on the points. I was hoping he would spend the time talking with his staff and we could skip the traditional coaches shaking hands at midfield. As I looked up, however, I couldn't miss him coming to me, wearing his traditional big hat and cowboy boots. He came right up to me and stuck out his hand and drawled, "Danny, don't feel bad, these things just happen."

Sammy Baugh already had been one of my heroes, but I gained even more respect for him that day. I got to know him very well, and he is a tremendous person.

We enjoyed a great season, losing only to San Jose State in San Jose, as the year came down to the annual matchup against Arizona. I had been conditioned about the importance of beating your in-state rival during my years at Michigan State and our annual games against Michigan, and I quickly learned the battles against Arizona were just as important to the people at Arizona State. I should have realized that immediately when one of the first things Dr. Gammage told me was how he wanted to beat the Wildcats.

At Michigan State it was like we had two seasons, all of the other games and then the Michigan games. I found out it was the same thing at Arizona State. What you did in all of the other games was important, but even if you lost them all—but beat Arizona—it would be considered a good year. Arizona had won the games the two previous years by the lopsided scores of 35-0 and 54-14, but those games weren't as bad as the one in 1946, when Arizona won 67-0.

Those losses helped create an organization called the Sun Angel Foundation, which is still in existence today. The organization raises funds for the ASU athletic and academic programs, trying to avoid embarrassments like those losses to Arizona. Before the Foundation was formed, there was another group, known as the Thunderbirds, made up of people who were trying to promote the state and the area. They were involved in more activities than just ASU athletics, like starting the Phoenix Open golf tournament, but they cared about ASU and contributed money to the school as well.

Everybody in Tempe was looking forward to the Arizona game in 1955, thinking we had the best chance we had had in a while to win. An overflow crowd showed up, and a lot of people had to sit on the grass. It was a great defensive game, but we, unfortunately, were on the losing end, 7-6.

Our best all-around player was Bobby Mulgado, and he played a great game, except for missing an extra point that was the difference in the game. It was just one of those kicks that didn't go through the goalposts. Everybody in town was disappointed, and I began counting the days until the next Arizona game.

We still finished in first place in our conference, and after the season, there was a bowl game matching the all-stars from the Border Conference against the Skyline Conference, which is now the

WAC. Because we won the conference, I was named head coach of the team for the game, which was called the Salad Bowl. Sammy Baugh was my assistant, and I thought that would mean all of the reporters would flock to him. As it turned out, Sammy went to play golf and I got stuck with all of the interviews. I was really hoping I could spend more time with Sammy to pick his brain, but he spent so much time on the golf course that I never got that chance.

The one thing that game did do was give us a better way to end the season than the loss to Arizona. While fans started marking off the days until the next game, I didn't need a calendar. That loss haunted me for a year, even as we went through the summer and the rest of the 1956 season.

We had a good team again in 1956, and I was pleased with the progress the team was making. We again only had one loss going into the Arizona game, which that year was scheduled at Arizona, in Tucson.

A big crowd showed up again at what was at the time the biggest stadium in our conference, and this time we got the job done, winning 20-0. I really believe that victory was the springboard to our 1957 team becoming so successful, one of the best teams I ever had the pleasure of coaching.

It probably was a little more enjoyable to me because I considered leaving Arizona State after the 1956 season. The coaching job at the University of Houston was open, and they asked me to come in for an interview. I wasn't planning on going, even though I was flattered they had called. As an excuse, I used the statement that there weren't many Catholics in Houston. Shortly after I said that on the telephone to a member of the school's Board of Regents, the telephone rang again, and this time it was the Bishop of Houston calling.

"Mr. Devine," he said, "I agree, yes, there aren't many Catholics in Houston. But you can help change that, and there are many, many wonderful Christians."

Well, I didn't have any idea how to respond to that, so I went in for the interview, still not expressing much interest. Finally, the man who had been the most persistent, Mr. Cullen, handed me a yellow pad of paper and told me to write down what I wanted— salary, length of contract, moving expenses, assistant coaches, their salaries. He was a big-time oil tycoon and I know he was going to fund the whole thing, that his goal was to make Houston a big-time academic and athletic institution. He said, "Everything you want, everything you put on that yellow pad, we'll do."

I have to admit that was pretty tempting, since I had just received a $500 raise at ASU for the coming season. Still, I just didn't have the right feeling about the job and I thanked him and said I was going to stay at Arizona State.

Looking back, I know I made the right decision. We went undefeated in 1957, finishing the year off with a 47-7 romp over Arizona. We had the top-rated offense in the country and finished 11th in the national polls, something that was the farthest thing from anybody's minds just three years earlier, when I had taken over the job. I still don't believe that team received the attention that it was due for its accomplishments.

It was the team's success which prompted the state to make the commitment to build Sun Devil Stadium, where the team still plays. Governor Ernest McFarland came to our team banquet at the end of the season and looked down at me and said, "Young man, we are going to build you a stadium and we'll build it with state funds." It really was a remarkable thing for him to say, since most of the leaders and power brokers in the state were graduates of Arizona.

The governor had become a fan, however, and had spent much of the year traveling with our team. He taped interviews during halftime that couldn't have been more positive if they had been scripted by the public relations department.

During the season, we defeated a lot of good teams with many great players who went on to succeed as players or coaches. Future Super Bowl coach Tom Flores was at the College of the Pacific, and after we won that game, their coach, Jack "Moose" Meyers, voted us number one in the coaches' poll for the rest of the season. It looked a little silly when you saw the other schools that were getting first-place votes—Oklahoma, Notre Dame, Alabama, Penn State, Colorado—but he really thought we deserved the vote. It helped our program gain national attention.

We also played against future Super Bowl coach Dick Vermeil, who was the quarterback at San Jose State, and two players from Idaho who went on to All-Pro careers in the NFL, Jerry Kramer and

Wayne Walker. Every time I run into one of these guys, the subject of how good our 1957 team still comes up.

The success of the team brought me a lot of personal attention and invitations which should have focused on the squad and assistants. I was booked as a speaker at the annual meeting of the National Football Coaches Association, meeting that year in New York. The president of the association was Don Faurot, the coach at Missouri and someone I had long admired from afar. He had invented the Split-T formation and had taught it to Bud Wilkinson, Bear Bryant, Jim Tatum and others. He had a reputation as the most ethical coach around.

Usually when I came back from playing golf, Jo handed me a stack of phone messages, many of the calls coming from athletic directors. Some of the calls I returned, but a lot of them I didn't. When Don called and left a message, Jo told me, "Don't you think you owe him a return call? You've talked so highly of him."

I returned his call, and was surprised to learn that he wanted to talk to me about becoming the next coach at Missouri. He was a good recruiter and was persistent enough that I finally agreed to come up to Columbia for a visit.

It was a memorable trip, starting with the plane flight from Phoenix to Kansas City. We had to make an unscheduled stop to add fuel, and that made us late getting into Kansas City. On the trip, the person sitting next to me spilled a cup of hot chocolate all over the only suit I had brought with me. The Missouri alumni who were waiting for my plane to arrive, and then to drive me to Columbia, had to wait somewhere because we were late, so they waited in the airport bar. Nondrinker Faurot was with them, and after we finally arrived about 1 a.m., we headed down the highway to Columbia.

Halfway between Kansas City and Columbia, we ran out of gas. I was wearing a lightweight Arizona suit on a cold December night in Missouri, exactly the opposite of what happened when I left Michigan State for Arizona. I was sitting in the car, shivering, wondering why in the world I had agreed to make this trip. Nothing fazed Don, however. He said he was going to hitch a ride to the next exit to get us some gas.

"Young fella, you just sit tight right there and I'll be right back," Faurot told me.

I was in the car alone, freezing and praying and telling myself that I should never do this again. I looked through the window at Don, who was standing on the side of the road and with one wave of his hand, flagged down a passing truck. The driver stopped, rolled down his window and leaned out and asked, "What do you need Don?" I knew then how powerful a person Don Faurot was in this state. He helped us get some gas, and we again were on our way.

Part of the interview process included a trip to Rolla in southern Missouri to meet the members of the University Board of Curators. The meeting was set for early the following morning, so our night's sleep was more like a nap. I was staying at Don's home, and his wife Mary prepared a lovely breakfast before we were back on the road, headed for the meeting with the Curators. Don drove with one hand the entire way, using his other to diagram plays in the dust on the car's dashboard.

After that meeting, we came back to Columbia and met with Dr. Elmer Ellis, the President of the University. I could tell right away that he was very committed to building up the school's athletic program to be the best it could be, as well as the rest of the university. He said all of the things I was hoping he would say.

I spent Sunday touring the campus, paying close attention to the huge library and medical center. The tour also included the athletic facilities, and I couldn't believe how poor they were. The press box was the worst one I had ever seen. I found out it was ranked as the poorest one in the country by the Football Writers Association. It was barely one story tall, so if a tall man stood up too quickly, he would hit his head on the ceiling.

The stadium also was ranked as one of the worst in the country. Brewer Field House, where the basketball team played, had been a classic in its day but it was now old and dilapidated. The school's basketball program was almost in as bad shape.

I learned the school had been in pretty serious debt when Faurot had taken over as head coach and athletic director in 1935. The people in charge of the school and the alumni and boosters around the state were not big spenders. The school also was hampered by a state law that prohibited any tax money being spent on the athletic program.

Faurot had done a lot of great things during his tenure, including improving the school's financial picture. The big break came in 1948, when the Tigers beat SMU and Heisman Trophy winner Doak Walker. The game is still remembered as one of the best in school history. Ten years later things were better, but I could see there was a lot of room for improvement and much more that needed to be done.

As part of the interview process, I met with people from the academic side of the university, including one of the deans. We had lunch at the Student Union and I could tell he wasn't much of a sports fan. He was very kind, but we didn't have a lot in common to talk about. After lunch, Don, myself and Art Nebel, the faculty representative and also a dean, went to Dr. Ellis' office.

It was obvious that Dr. Ellis was a sincere educator, but also a sports fan. We went over every issue that I could think of, and as we all got up and were preparing to leave, Dr. Ellis spoke up.

"Don, what are we paying for this position?" Dr. Ellis said. Faurot responded that the salary was $13,000. Dr. Ellis then said, "Let's pay this young man $15,000."

Dr. Ellis told me that if I took the job, his door would always be open. He told me I never needed an appointment to come see him, whether it was for a professional or a personal problem. It was clear to all of us in the room, myself, Faurot and the faculty representative, that I would have a direct line to the president, an important avenue for any head coach at a major university. I'm certain Dr. Ellis told me that because he wanted to make it clear that he was the man in charge who would be making all of the important decisions. I took his offer only once.

While I had been sitting in the freezing car on the side of the road, I had said a little prayer. "God, if you get me out of this and back to Arizona, I'll never do this to you again." It was two days later now, and I didn't know what to do as there was a private plane from Texas A & M at the airport to fly me to College Station.

As I flew back to Arizona, I kept thinking about how impressed I had been with all of the people I had just met, and not about all of the things that had gone wrong on the trip. I liked the members of the team I had met, and I knew the school had an excellent academic reputation. The journalism school was one of the best in the country and attracted top students. The beat writer who covered the team for the school newspaper, *The Missourian*, in 1960 was Neil Amdur, who later spent a long time as the sports editor of *The New York Times*. I found out the other academic disciplines were just as outstanding. Dr. Hugh Stevenson was the dean of the medical school and a very impressive man, and we became lifelong friends.

I was thinking about all of this on the plane ride home, and how it was going to be a tough decision for Jo and me. The kids were getting older, and we had only been in Arizona for three years and I really wasn't prepared to uproot the family and move halfway across the country again. Jo and I had fallen in love with the area, and there's a reason we moved back there as soon as I retired from coaching.

We had a team banquet scheduled to honor our undefeated 1957 team, the first in school history, and I didn't want news of my visit to Missouri to get out and spoil the evening. I wanted the focus to be entirely on the team and what they had been able to accomplish. I called Don and told him I planned to issue a statement saying I had no comment about my trip to Missouri and if further developments warranted, I would have something to say at that time.

I knew that kind of left Don up in the air, so I asked him, "Are you going to offer this job to someone else, because you can't depend on me taking it?" Don said, "No, we'll just wait. You're our number-one choice. We'll just wait to see what's going to transpire."

I assured Don that I would call him with my decision immediately after the team banquet.

The banquet was a huge success. It was at this banquet that Governor McFarland made his statement about building the school a new stadium. I was so confused about what I wanted to do. I loved what I was doing and I loved the people and the area in Arizona, but the hangup about only being able to offer a one-year contract really bothered me. Missouri was offering a five-year deal. The money was good, the program was more established and in a bigger and more well-known conference. Trying to win there would be another challenge, and that idea has always appealed to me.

After the banquet, I went off by myself and walked around the campus, thinking about what I was going to do. Jo had gone home after the banquet, but I think she had sensed I had made up my mind about what I wanted to do. I called her, and she gave me the same support she has always given me. Next, I picked up the phone and called Faurot.

"If you offer me the job, I'll take it," I said. "I'm clear here."

I knew he was going to offer it, but I had wanted him to wait and make it official until we had completed the banquet.

A lot of people around Arizona State were disappointed that I was leaving. The school band and a lot of students marched over to our house, showing their support. The gesture was tremendous and meant a great deal to me. I was almost overcome by the way they made me feel so wanted.

It was clear to me the opportunity that I had before me, however. It was true I was making another move, but I never thought of myself as some kind of football vagabond, jumping from one job to the next. In my mind, each time I changed jobs I was improving myself, both in an economic position and also in terms of becoming the best coach I could be. Finances always were important to me, as I think they were to anybody who grew up in the Depression. I always worried about having enough money, and especially to ensure that I had enough to pay for my kids' education. That was something that was very important to me.

Jo knew how important it was to be able to pay our bills, educate our kids and live the kind of lifestyle we wanted, and that was why she was willing to make a lot of personal sacrifices and support me in whatever direction my career went.

One of the reasons it was easier to reach the decision to leave Arizona State was that I knew I was leaving the program in much better shape than it had been when I arrived. Frank Kush was ready to be the head coach, and he elevated the program to another level. The Governor had committed to building the new and improved stadium. The school was off NCAA probation and now had a more established program, which made it easier to recruit better players.

I was pleased all of those things had happened, and I had no doubts there would be better days ahead for everyone associated with Arizona State.

As I prepared myself for the next stage of my life, I had to wonder: What was ahead for me?

Chapter Five

THE UNIVERSITY OF MISSOURI

My success at Arizona State gave me an improved level of confidence as I prepared to take over the Missouri program, but I have found that no matter how hard you try, you can never be fully prepared for every challenge and obstacle that is going to come your way.

At Missouri, I was taking over for Frank Broyles, who decided to leave after coaching there only one year to become the head coach at Arkansas. He enjoyed tremendous success with the Razorbacks and is still at the school as Athletic Director. Frank was and is a very good friend. He was disappointed at Missouri, which had won a total of 14 games in the previous four seasons. Frank didn't think he could be successful and win at Mizzou. He was quoted after moving to Fayetteville as saying, "They have their heads in the clouds. If they want to go to the Ivy League, they should go to the Ivy League." He was just frustrated, and I'm glad he enjoyed the success he did at Arkansas.

I wasn't really worried about the reasons Frank had decided he couldn't win at Missouri. I knew from having taken over a program at Arizona State that wasn't in very good shape that hard work and recruiting good players could make any program better. I had too much to worry about concerning my own work and duties to waste my time thinking about the past.

I quickly learned that the best thing I could do in my new job was to listen to every piece of advice and suggestion I got from Don Faurot. I should have realized it on that frozen highway when the truck driver stopped when we ran out of gas and immediately called him by name—he was Mr. Missouri. He was a living legend throughout the entire state.

Don had become the coach at Missouri in 1935, and after leaving for military duty, returned after World War II. He had plenty of job opportunities and offers to coach elsewhere, at larger and more well-known programs, and he turned them all down. The offer which received the most publicity was from Ohio State. His famous quote after rejecting the offer was, "I'd work for the University of Missouri for nothing." The rest of us in the Athletic Department would then add, "And he expected the rest of us to do the same thing."

He is known most around the country for his innovations within the sport. He is the father of the Split-T, one of the most major changes in football in this century. The theory of running outside the end without blocking the end was not accepted until Don did it and showed the other coaches that it could be done. Many coaches today, both in the college and pro ranks, don't realize how important Don's innovations were to changing the way football teams design their offense.

No matter how many changes and innovations have occurred, however, one fact has remained the same—the teams that win are the teams that display the better fundamentals, knowing how to block, how to tackle and how to run and pass the ball.

What mattered most to me was the schedule for the upcoming season and the quality of the players on our team. Simply because of its conference affiliation, Missouri was playing a tougher schedule than we had played at Arizona State. Oklahoma, Nebraska and Colorado were annually among the best teams in the country, we had a rivalry with Kansas that was almost like an in-state battle, and we had a tough nonconference schedule as well. I could tell right away there was no way we had good enough players to beat Oklahoma.

We were really weak in overall team speed, and that surprised me. We had one player—Norris Stevenson—who I thought was fast enough to be effective. We had some other quality players, like guards Charlie Rash and Don Chadwick, and Dan LaRose was a good enough end to become my first All-America selection at Missouri. I just wasn't certain if we had enough quality players to run the offensive schemes that I wanted to run.

No matter what the sport, the best coaches are the ones who adapt their philosophies to take the best advantage of the strengths and skills of their players. I knew this, but I also knew which offenses I thought worked the best and were the ones that I wanted us to feature.

For the juniors and seniors on our team, the change in coaches meant they were going to be learning a third operating system in a three-year span, and that's tough, no matter how skilled or intelligent a player is. We were going to run a multiple offense, with one basic play being the sweep, and I was confident that our guys would be able to pick it up effectively during spring practice and in the fall before we began our specific individual game preparations.

During the spring drills, I couldn't help but continue to notice a little spark plug of a guy who was playing on the scout team. Maybe it was his red uniform shirt which stood out, but he seemed to be stopping every play that came his way. The more I stopped and watched him, the more I liked what I saw. He had excellent pursuit of the ball and was a fundamentally sound tackler. One day I stopped practice and called him off to the side. He stood 5-foot-6. I just had to find out more about this guy.

"What's your name, son?" I asked.

He answered, "Rockne Calhoun, sir," as he attempted to stand as tall as possible.

"Were you named after Knute Rockne?" I asked.

He grew a foot and his voice boomed. "YES SIR," he said.

"Well, I'll tell you what," I said. "Take off that red shirt and don't ever put it on again. Go put on a black shirt."

The color of the shirts was the way we differentiated between the teams. The black shirts were the regulars, the players who were most likely to be involved in the games. The red shirts were the younger players and the extra guys we needed for practice, but those who really didn't stand much chance of getting in the games.

I made the move because I really was impressed with the way Rockne was playing, but it proved to be a good morale boost for the entire team. They saw that I wasn't afraid to move people around and reward someone who I thought was worthy. I think the move made everybody work harder in practice and improved the quality of our team.

Rockne turned out to be a regular and one of our team leaders on both the 1959 and 1960 squads. He is now a judge and has been a good role model for kids to emulate.

One challenge about becoming the coach of the Tigers that I wasn't prepared for had to do with racial differences. I mentioned the problem we had in Abilene, Texas, during one game at Arizona State and how we got that matter resolved so the black and white players would be treated equally. I didn't think for a minute we were going to have problems similar to those at Missouri, but I quickly found out I was being naive again.

Missouri had been a swing state during the Civil War, supplying troops to both the Union and the Confederacy. Nearly 100 years later, people were still split in their allegiances. It was true throughout the university, not just for the football team.

I called attention to the problem by asking how many black students were enrolled at Missouri, and was told they preferred their own school elsewhere in the state. We had a few black players on our team, and I wanted them treated the same as the white players. I also wanted to ensure they had the same treatment and respect in all aspects of their college life, not just what happened on the football field. All of our players on the team seemed to get along well with no problems, and I didn't see why it couldn't be that way across the entire campus.

Two problems had to be addressed. A fraternity on campus frequently waved a big Confederate battle flag in the middle of the student body section in the stadium. Also, the school marching band was playing "Dixie" as the school song. I thought both of those activities were offensive to our black players and other black students on campus. I didn't want to sweep these problems under the rug. I took a public stance that was opposed by a few fans and some people in the administration, but it was something I felt very strongly about. Luckily, I had support from key people and these problems were worked out.

What I didn't know at the time was that we were going to be battling with issues of racial discrimination for several more years, showing the magnitude and depth of this problem. There were far more difficult issues than I had ever anticipated. In 1957, federal troops were sent to Little Rock, Arkansas, to enforce a Supreme Court ruling against segregation in schools. Confrontations continued for several years after that.

During my first season at Missouri, 1958, we had an away game at Texas A&M, coached by the great Paul "Bear" Bryant before he moved on to Alabama, in College Station, Texas. Texas A&M is a great football environment, and the cadets there are very vocal and supportive of their team. They stood throughout the entire game, stomping their feet, and I knew I never would be able to hear through the headphones, so I didn't even bring them out on the field.

We knew the crowd was going to be loud, so we practiced all week in our fieldhouse with the speakers blaring to try to prepare our players for the game conditions we were expecting. We could prepare for that, but not for other problems we hadn't expected.

After we arrived at our hotel in College Station, we sat down for our pre-game meal of prime rib. It was not cooked well; the meat was actually cold. That got our trip off to a bad start. We didn't play well either.

Sometimes following a night game we have an organized team meal, but this was one trip where we had decided the kids would get meal money—$2 or $3—and be allowed to spend the evening out on their own. The team bus had parked near some A&M campus hangouts and restaurants, and the players had gone off on their own. I was still on the bus, replaying the problems from the game in my mind.

Our two captains, Don Chadwick and Charlie Rash, interrupted me by charging back onto the bus. "Coach, they aren't serving the black players," one of them said. The news surprised me, and I said, "I beg your pardon?"

They repeated what was happening, and I asked what they thought we should do. Both Don and Charlie said, "The white players don't want to eat."

I said, "OK, go get everybody and let's get back on the bus." I was shocked that this kind of prejudice was still taking place. I broke down and cried, believing I had let my team down. I prided myself on preparation, every detail, and even though we had lost the game, having our players run into problems like this was far worse than losing a football game. I should have known this was a possibility and been prepared for it. I vowed to never again let something like this happen to my team.

Even though I made that vow sitting on that bus, it did happen again, two years later, after we went into Norman and upset Oklahoma. The star of the game was Norris Stevenson, the first black player to be awarded an athletic scholarship at Missouri. The whole city of Columbia erupted in celebration after our win.

We got back in town on Saturday. Because of Norris' popularity, he was approached by some people about picketing a small greasy spoon restaurant off campus that would not serve blacks. Norris didn't want to be involved in this problem, so he and the other members of the team didn't join the picketers, but it just showed how widespread discrimination continued to be.

Our success that season earned us a spot in the Orange Bowl, and on the airplane trip to Miami, I was informed the airline was going to throw a party for the team that night—for the white players only. I was told the black players would have their own party.

The news just ripped me apart, and there was no way I was going to stand for it or let that happen. I pulled Norris Stevenson and Mel West aside and told them they were going to be the guests of my family at our party that night. They came, and other than the sick feeling I had all night created by the whole mess, everybody had a good time.

We had other isolated incidents of discrimination over the years, and it really wasn't until Johnny Roland arrived on campus that we put an end to racial problems. We were heading to Lawrence by bus to play Kansas, when we stopped for gas and to allow everybody to use the restroom. One of our seniors came up to me and asked if everybody could get a drink and something to eat.

My first instinct was to say no, but I finally said OK. What happened? The place where we had just happened to stop in a small town in Missouri was refusing to serve the black players on the state university's football team.

I asked the team, "Do you want to leave?" and got a unanimous response. Nobody had eaten or drunk anything.

"You guys get on the bus," I told the players. "Walk right straight out of here—nobody's going to harm the players. This is the result of one or two people who just feel this way. Don't yell at anybody or take it out on anybody."

I then did something that I'm not proud of. I took a $100 bill out of my wallet and threw it on the floor. I took my foot and rubbed that $100 bill into the kind of cruddy floor, turned and left. It was beneath the dignity of my job to do that. I looked up, and two of our black kids were watching me. One took me by one arm and the other took me by the other arm. "Coach, we're going to get on the bus now." I could never forget what they said; it was the same thing I was thinking: "Don't blame everybody in this room for this incident."

Then they said, "We need you at the game tomorrow. If you stay in here, you may incite a riot." They kind of half picked me up and we got on the bus and took off. Just as we left the parking lot, a police car showed up.

Again, I vowed to myself to never be caught unprepared like that again. Today the University of Missouri is a national leader in positive race relations.

All of those problems were a long ways off as we prepared for our first game in that 1958 season, against Vanderbilt.

I wasn't naive to think that our team would be able to be as successful as the undefeated team at Arizona State the previous year, for a variety of reasons. Still, I was disappointed when we lost the opener 12-8. We had a chance to win the game late, but couldn't get the ball into the end zone.

That continued to be a problem for the rest of our nonconference schedule. We got our first win, 14-10 over Idaho, but that was a team my ASU squad had beaten 41-0 a year earlier. That gave me a good idea of how much work we had to do to make our team as good as I wanted it to be.

We had good leadership on those early teams, but we just weren't as talented as you really needed to be if you wanted to be competitive. Our first captains were Charlie Rash and Don Chadwick, and the 1959 captains were Dr. Tom Swaney and Mike Magac. They all became successful in business and were terrific young men. Charlie later was killed in a train accident in Tennessee, where he was a coach, and Tom became an engineer for Boeing before he died from cancer.

We lost our next two games, 12-0 to Bear Bryant's Texas A&M squad, and then to SMU, whose quarterback was Don Meredith. We had a 1-3 record as we began preparations for our conference opener, at Kansas State.

This was a big game for us, and we pulled out a lot of tricks to try to jazz up our offense. Everything clicked, and we won 32-8.

That helped improve the players' confidence, and we followed that win by getting past Iowa State in a close game, then went into Lincoln and beat Nebraska 31-0. Rash and Chadwick were great leaders.

Our next opponent was Colorado, and they were a good team. They already had come extremely close to beating No. 1 Oklahoma earlier in the year and had an outstanding quarterback, Boyd Dowler, who went on to become an All-Pro wide receiver in the NFL. I really thought this would be a good test for us to see how far we had come in a short matter of time.

We fell behind 9-0, and I was worried because our quarterback, Phil Snowden, was limited in what he could do because of a fiberglass vest which he was wearing to protect sore ribs. Still, we rallied in one of the wildest fourth quarters I've ever seen and won the game 33-9. Our defensive quarterback, Bobby Haas, who later distinguished himself on offense, played great.

That game, which was at home, really energized our fans. I found out Missouri's pattern in recent years had been to play good teams tough for a half or three quarters, then manage to lose the game in the last 15 minutes. This game kind of reversed that trend, and nobody was happier than me.

Some of the alumni were so revved up by that game, they wanted to make certain I didn't become upset like Broyles had the previous year and decide I wanted to leave after the season was over.

They discussed ways to make certain I stayed, and eventually came up with an insurance policy worth $250,000. They paid the premiums, and the IRS ruled the policy was a gift. The policy called for my family to get the money if I died, or I would receive it after 20 years if I stayed at Missouri. When I became tenured in 1963 it became even more attractive.

It was a great gesture on their part, and I really appreciated the faith and confidence the power brokers at the university had shown in me. It helped take away a lot of my worries about providing for my family and let me concentrate entirely on trying to improve our football team.

We were 4-0 in the conference, but I knew we weren't that good, needing to look back only to our 1-3 start to the season. Next up was Oklahoma, in Norman, and I knew Wilkinson and his players were just licking their chops to get at us and knock us back down a rung or two.

The first half was a defensive struggle, and they scored the only touchdown. We weren't able to keep up in the second half, however, and the Sooners rolled to a 39-0 win.

I had never encountered a game like that, and had no magic words to tell the players afterward. Missouri had not won in Norman since 1936, and I guess I got a little overzealous and jumped on top of a training table and promised our seniors that in two years, in our next game at Norman, we were going to dedicate the game to them and we were going to win.

Our traditional last game was against Kansas, and I knew we had to forget about the Oklahoma game or we would get beat again. We had a 13-7 lead late in the game, but I made a bad decision and had us try for a short field goal instead of running out the clock, and Charlie Rash missed. KU got the ball back and came down and scored and tied the game, 13-13. We had to block the extra point to preserve the tie.

Our overall record was 5-4-1, the same record Broyles' team had a year earlier. I think everybody except me and our team was happy with that, but I was concerned because there were so many up-and-down moments during the year. We just weren't consistent enough, and consistency is one of the characteristics of a good team.

All I had to do for incentive that off-season, anytime I didn't feel like working, was to look at our schedule for the 1959 season. We opened the year with games at home against Penn State and Michigan on the road.

We lost the opener to the Nittany Lions and then faced Michigan at Ann Arbor. We played well, but the Wolverines kicked a late field goal and went ahead 15-14. It was raining and the wind was blowing in our face and we had to go 81 yards in the final two minutes with no timeouts. We did it with two seconds to play, with Bobby Haas scoring on a quarterback sneak that gave us a 20-15 victory. Our number-one quarterback, Phil Snowden, had to sit out this last brilliant drive.

I heard later that a lot of people, alumni and other fans, had turned off their radios after Michigan's field goal, believing the game was over. Later, after hearing the score, they kept checking to make certain it actually was correct and that Missouri had indeed won. In a lot of ways that win really proved to be the program booster we needed.

After the game, everybody was excited and wanted to get back into the dressing room to celebrate. We went up the tunnel, but the door was locked and nobody was there to let us in. The Michigan dressing room was right across the hall, and they were already inside. We stood out there in the tunnel for something like 10 minutes, and finally I had enough. The players were wet and cold.

"Take it down," I yelled to the players. That wasn't the kind of thing I would normally say, but it was obvious nobody was going to come along and open the door for us. Rockne Calhoun and Mike Magac, a huge guy from East St. Louis, took the door off its hinges and laid it on the floor. The players poured into the dressing room and the celebration began.

Fritz Crisler was the Athletic Director at Michigan, and he was really ticked off about the door. I was so happy—both because we had won and still remembered the Michigan State-Michigan rivalry—that I couldn't care less. It was his fault nobody had been there to open it for us or we wouldn't have had to take it down.

Our Athletic Director, Don Faurot, didn't get down to the dressing room until well after this had happened, but he quickly found out. Crisler didn't make any apologies for keeping our cold, wet team waiting for so long, and he kept bugging Don about the door. Don just kept smiling and saying, "Send me a bill Fritz, send me a bill."

I don't know how much the door cost or if Crisler ever did send him that bill, but if he did, the price was worth it.

We got a lot of national media attention after the victory, and I tried never to allow myself to get caught up with anything the reporters said. This game was a little different, however. The *Chicago Tribune* ran a big story about "the team that won't be beat can't be beat." It was the first time I had ever heard that expression used to describe a particular victory. Other papers reported much the same thing, and for many years after that I would occasionally pull out those clippings and require all of our players to read them while eating our pre-game meal. They took this seriously.

Edgar Hayes, writing in the *Detroit Times*, said, "If Danny Devine never wins another game, he can tell his six children (that's how many we had then) and their children of the fantastic victory snatched from the jaws of bitter defeat." Other stories and accounts of the game were just as inspirational to me and our players.

We celebrated and enjoyed the victory, but then had to face reality and the fact that our season was only beginning, not ending. We had a lot of games to play and if we didn't regroup quickly, everything we had gained by winning against Michigan could be lost just as easily.

We again beat Nebraska, 9-0, and in our next game, we were leading Colorado when we heard on the public address system that Nebraska had upset Oklahoma, handing the Sooners their first conference loss in 73 games. The conference had a rule that the champion could not go to the Orange Bowl two years in a row, so we knew that if we could beat Colorado, we would get the invitation to the game in Miami, the first trip for Missouri to that game since before World War II.

Unfortunately, we couldn't hold the lead and lost 21-20. That game convinced me to make a change in coaching philosophy because I thought one of the reasons we lost was that we didn't put enough pressure on the quarterback. From that game on, the rest of my career, our defenses were designed to put as much heat on the quarterback as possible.

Russ Sloan was the most valuable player as we beat Air Force 13-0 at home in a game that was nationally televised. Next we beat Kansas State 26-0. Our final game was against Kansas, and the winner would earn the automatic trip to represent the conference in the Orange Bowl.

Our players did a great job, and we were ahead 13-7 late in the game. We took an intentional safety and won 13-9. That set up the trip to Miami to face Georgia, ranked fourth in the country, and the Bulldogs' explosive quarterback, Fran Tarkenton.

The game really was a defensive battle, but we lost 14-0. Still, I was extremely proud of all our players and how much they had accomplished in a very short two-year span. The money the school received from the bowl appearance, along with alumni contributions, was used to finance an addition to the stadium.

Our team success again made me attractive to organizations that were putting together coaching clinics, and one of those set up by the Air Force gave me a chance to go to Europe in the summer of 1960. We were in Paris and Berlin, and the U.S. government helped arrange a tour for me behind the Iron Curtain.

I had a driver, and he took me from Garmisch-Partenkirchen to Munich. He was a German soldier, a sergeant. He could speak English, but when we passed a sign that read "Dachau," he forgot what English he knew.

I leaned forward toward the front seat and said, "Sergeant, is that where the concentration camp was in World War II?" He acted like he didn't understand the question, so I said, more sternly, "Sergeant, I asked you a question." I repeated the question, and he finally said, "Yes, sir."

I said, "I want to go there." He certainly didn't intend to take me there, but he had been told to do as I asked, so we drove to Dachau. I can't express in words what I saw and the emotions I felt. It made me sick, but at the same time, I was glad I had gone there. If everyone could see a place like Dachau, it might solve some of the problems we have in this world today.

After the side trip to Dachau, we went to a U.S. air base that had been given to Germany that day and I really felt strange, like I had stepped into the middle of a German war movie or something. The high-ranking German officers were wearing their Luftwaffe uniforms, and it was quite a sight seeing all of the silver planes with the black Iron Cross on them. Finally, I saw an old American C-47 approaching, and I knew it was coming to get me. I always had been a history buff and it was very educational to see everything I had seen in Germany, but I also was very glad to be getting out of there.

We flew to Chatereaux, France, and then I was driven to Paris. By this time I was getting very homesick, and I went up to a young Corporal and motioned to the plane which was preparing to leave for Philadelphia. I told him, "I'll be back in 20 minutes. I'd like to be on that plane to Philadelphia."

The Corporal looked at my papers—I had been given a temporary rank of Colonel for the trip—and said, "Your orders read Berlin." I am not a good faker, but this time I pulled one of my all-time fakes. I told the Corporal, "I'll be back in 20 minutes. Cut me new orders."

When I came back in the aforementioned 20 minutes, my knees were shaking. I didn't know what was going to happen, but it was very uneventful. The Corporal handed me the new orders, and I was headed to Philadelphia.

Having experiences like that help to make a lot of your problems in day-to-day life seem very minor in comparison, and I was able to keep that perspective fresh in my mind as we began to prepare for the 1960 season.

Going into a new season, you know some of your best players returning, but there are always the men who come out of nowhere. We knew Donnie Smith, Mel West and Norris Stephenson were quality players, but Ron Taylor and Ed Mehrer blossomed and were very much leaders on the 1960 team. Amongst the many others were Skip Snyder and Gordon Smith.

Going to the Orange Bowl the previous year had raised everybody's expectations about our team as we began the year. We won our first two games, 20-0 over SMU and 28-7 against Oklahoma State, and prepared for our next game, the first game ever at Penn State's new Beaver Stadium. We won 21-8 and began to climb up in the national rankings.

Our success continued with a 34-8 win against the Air Force Academy, a day also important to me because of the birth of my daughter Jill, who was given a game ball after the win. A 45-0 win the following week over Kansas State vaulted us into the top five teams in the country.

Three more victories followed—34-8 over Iowa State, 28-0 over Nebraska in Lincoln and 16-6 against Colorado. We were 8-0 and headed for a showdown at Oklahoma.

Everybody in Columbia was getting excited, and I do mean everybody. It was not the kind of town where people got excited easily, but being so close to an undefeated season and perhaps a ranking as one of the best football teams in the country was something for the entire town to rally behind.

It was brought out that I had promised our seniors two years earlier that on our next trip to Norman, we would win. Many of those seniors, now out in the workforce, made plans to come in to Norman and be there for the game. Oklahoma was still a very good team, even if they weren't as good as some of Wilkinson's teams during that era. The pregame hype began, and it increased to a roar the closer we got to game time.

Our defense was playing incredibly well—we had not given up a rushing touchdown all season. So what happened? On the first play from scrimmage, the Sooners ran a counter option. We tackled the fullback, but the halfback was the one with the ball. You could tell after five yards that he was going all the way, and he did, an 80-yard scoring run. The band broke into "Boomer Sooner," and the stadium went berserk. We couldn't hear ourselves think, or use the phones to communicate with the coaches watching from the press box.

Our team could have folded right there, but they didn't. They kept their poise and composure, and when we scored late in the first half, it was 20-7 with Missouri leading. The second half began with just as much intensity, and late in the third quarter, Oklahoma faced a fourth-down-and-one play. They went for it, but Dan LaRose, defensive end, stuffed the runner and we took over.

On the first play of the fourth quarter, Norris Stevenson took a pitchout and swept around right end, and nobody could catch him. He sprinted 76 yards for the touchdown that broke the Sooners' backs. I don't think anybody has ever run like that against Oklahoma. He also had a 65-yard run. We went on to a 41-19 victory.

The scene after the game was incredible, but that was just the preliminary celebration before we got back to Columbia. For road games in those days we flew on two DC-3s, and as the planes approached the Columbia airport, we saw that we had a problem. We had nowhere to land—more than 20,000 people had come out to the airport to welcome the team home, and they had taken over all of the highways, the runways, everywhere. The planes had to circle for a long time before the police were able to clear the runways and give us a place to land.

Fire trucks were waiting for us, and the players piled onto those trucks and we paraded back to campus. Everybody in town was out on the streets, and the sirens and horns were blaring on the fire trucks. The small, sedate town of Columbia had gone absolutely nuts.

Nobody wanted the celebration to stop. We paraded around the campus, finally stopping at an area known as "the Columns" for an impromptu pep rally. Rockne Calhoun got up to speak and was able to quiet the crowd. He talked about how, when he was a young boy growing up in the small Mississippi River community of Louisiana, Missouri, he didn't have a radio, but he would go into town and listen to the Missouri games on the radio at the barber shop. He told that crowd he had decided as a small boy there were only two things he wanted to do—he wanted to play for Missouri, and he wanted to beat Oklahoma. He concluded his speech by yelling, "Today I did both, and now I can die!"

I really think Rockne meant that he could die figuratively, not literally. Nobody knew exactly what to do or say or how to act, because none of us had ever been in this position before.

For the first time in school history, Missouri was ranked as the number-one college football team in the country in both the Associated Press and United Press International polls. The students and the media descended on the players at our practices, and nobody knew how to handle the situation. I know I did a bad job of coaching that week and preparing for our game against Kansas because of all the distractions, etc.

Reporters from all across the state and the country were showing up in Columbia, and Bill Callahan, our sports information director and a great friend, convinced me that I needed to give them whatever time and access they wanted. We weren't accustomed to getting all of that free publicity, and he kept telling me how great it would be to improve the recognition and reputation of our program.

He convinced me to devote more time to the media during the week, and that time had to come out of what I should have spent preparing for the Jayhawks. KU had a great team, too, led by quarterback John Hadl, who went on to a great NFL career. In fact, the entire Kansas backfield might have been one of the best ever in college football. Hadl was joined by Curtis McClinton and Bert Coan. Kansas was ready to play the game and we weren't, and the result was predictable—we lost.

The KU victory was later reversed when the conference learned that Coan actually had been ineligible for the game, a fact that Kansas officials knew before the contest was even played. However, by that time it didn't matter to anybody except the record keepers. The shame of it was that it cost our kids the recognition they should have received for going undefeated and winning the conference championship as well as the national championship.

I learned a lot that week, lessons which I remembered and applied for years into the future. I realized it was the head coach's job to handle the distractions, and I didn't get it done.

Minnesota finished the year at 9-1, and in those days the final polls came out before the bowl games. The Gophers, the champions of the Big Ten, were named the national champions before they lost in the Rose Bowl. We went back to the Orange Bowl, where we played Navy and won. If the final polls had not been taken until after the bowl games, Missouri would have won the national championship. The timing of the vote was later changed until after the bowl games, but by then it was too late to help us.

Our opponent in the Orange Bowl was Navy, which featured the Heisman Trophy winner, running back Joe Bellino. President-elect Kennedy, a decorated former Navy officer, attended the game with the Secretary of the Navy, but we didn't give them much to cheer about. We held Bellino to minus-four yards rushing and won the game 21-14, dominating more than the score would indicate. We held Navy to a composite minus-eight yards rushing.

Despite what the polls said, there was no doubt about who was the best team in the country. All of the Eastern media were covering the Orange Bowl and came away impressed with our players. That team was a national championship team and deserved to be recognized as such, and to this day my honest opinion is that I let it slip away from them. I can't go back and change it. That team bears a scar instead of a pat on the back, and it remains one of the biggest regrets of my life.

One of the biggest ironies of our 1961 schedule was that we opened with Minnesota, the team which had won the mythical national championship the year before. They had an excellent team, led by two tremendous players—Carl Eller and Bobby Bell. We won the game 6-0, and I know our players and fans got a lot of satisfaction out of that win.

We finished the year with a 7-2-1 record, including our fourth consecutive shutout over Nebraska. We lost to Oklahoma, 7-0, but did win our grudge match against Kansas, 10-7, gaining a little revenge from the loss (later overturned) the previous year.

Something which probably wouldn't happen today occurred after the regular season, when we were invited to play in two bowl games. Our players were tired and burned out, so when we put it to a vote among the players about what they wanted to do, they voted to stay home and not go to either one of the games.

I actually was proud of them for taking that stance and realizing they were behind in their classwork and needed to get caught up. It was tough from a financial standpoint, because the move cost the university some money, but the administration supported the players' decision and we stayed home over the holidays.

Part of the fun in those years was that my kids were getting old enough to understand what I did for a living and to develop a knowledge of football. It was a tremendous help to have their love and support in everything I did, and I was glad to be able to share some of the fun aspects of the job with them.

I will never forget taking my daughter Dede, who was about 10 at the time, with us on a trip to play Iowa State. She was dressed in a sweat suit, with her pigtails tucked underneath the hood, just in case somebody wanted to give her trouble about being a girl. After the game, we had the news conference with the reporters, and she sat outside waiting for me. I got caught up in all of the activity and got on the team bus and headed for the airport, forgetting all about Dede.

At about the same time we arrived at the airport, a police car with its lights on and siren blaring full blast pulled up right behind the bus. The passenger door opened and Dede scrambled out. "Daddy, you forgot me," she said as she ran up to me. That was something our family remembered for a long time and never let me forget.

We had some special players on those early Missouri teams, including All-American Ed Blaine, who later earned his doctorate degree and is now Director of the Dalton Research Center in Missouri. He followed up his All-America career by later playing for Vince Lombardi with the Green Bay Packers. He is a wonderful person, very intelligent and the kind of role model we were proud to have as part of our team.

Our good fortunes continued in 1962, when we went 8-1-2, losing only to Oklahoma. We beat Nebraska for the fifth year in a row, but this time did allow a touchdown, winning 16-7. Their touchdown came on a bizarre play. We had the ball on the Nebraska 8-yard-line, and during a TV time-out decided to throw a halfback pass. The kid who was supposed to catch the ball fell down, and a lumbering Nebraska linebacker intercepted the ball and went 100 yards the other way for the touchdown.

We earned an invitation to the Bluebonnet Bowl to play Bobby Dodd's great Georgia Tech squad. We won 14-10, and that game showed off some of the terrific talent we had that season. Bill Tobin, a great administrator in the NFL, ran 77 yards for a touchdown in the fourth quarter, helped by some blocks from two players who went on to play well in the NFL, Andy Russell and George Seals. Andy later became the captain and a leader of the Super Bowl-champion Pittsburgh Steelers, and George played well with the Chicago Bears for many years. Jim Johnson was our quarterback and was voted the most valuable player in the game.

I also was invited to be one of the coaches for the annual Hula Bowl game in Honolulu, and I took Jo along, thinking it would be mostly parties and a vacation. Instead, I had to spend time trying to call coaches and get more players to fill out our roster. Hawaii at the time was not nearly as developed as it is today. I think there was only one hotel on Kaianapali Beach, and it was the first real trip Jo and I had taken to a place like that. It was a very nice experience and memory for us.

After we returned to Columbia, I was surprised to get a letter from Father Edmund P. Joyce, the executive vice president of the University of Notre Dame. He wanted me to meet him in St. Louis to discuss Notre Dame football and football in general.

I was pleased, and readily agreed to the meeting. Father Joyce was known around the country as an educator who understood coaches and recognized how much an outstanding athletic program could add to the overall quality of a university.

We agreed to meet at the Chase Hotel in St. Louis, and we spent about five hours together. We talked about everything, but mostly about football. I didn't know at the time, but found out later, Notre Dame officials had been watching me since my days as an assistant coach at Michigan State, which is a big rival of Notre Dame. It was a confidence boost for me that somebody at Notre Dame thought I was a good coach, although I honestly had no intention at that point of entertaining any new job offers.

Notre Dame's football fortunes had fallen slightly in those years, and what Father Joyce wanted to know primarily from me was how I was able to run a good program, and keep it clean, within the framework of a good university. He asked me to come and tour the Notre Dame campus, but I was reluctant to do it. I had a great relationship with the President of the University of Missouri and I honestly thought that if I wanted to pursue the Notre Dame job, he would let me, regardless of the status of my contract.

As my meeting with Father Joyce ended, I asked him what he thought he was going to do. He said he probably would hire Hugh Devore for a year, and then go through an intensive search for a permanent head coach. As that summer went on, I received a number of phone calls and letters from Hugh, encouraging me to take the head coaching job. He said he would happily agree to become my assistant coach, and would be loyal and work hard for me.

I was flattered and embarrassed that this great man would give up the head coaching job at Notre Dame to be my assistant. He honestly thought that would be the best move for the university, and he was so loyal to the school, that was his number-one motivation. As it turned out, Hugh coached the Irish in 1963; then they hired Ara Parseghian from Northwestern, and he was there a long time and did an excellent job.

One of the highlight games during our 1963 season was against Arkansas and Frank Broyles, the man I had replaced as coach. The game was in Little Rock, and marked the first time the schools had played since 1944. Of course, in all of the hype leading up to the game, all of the reporters remembered Frank's comments about how you couldn't win at Missouri, and that "they should go to the Ivy League." We had been lucky enough to be successful, and some reporters used that to try to embarrass Frank as we led up to the game.

The game was a defensive battle, but we scored late and kicked the extra point and won 7-6. Frank was very kind and gracious, and I appreciated the way he handled a very tough situation. He was a great coach and is a great administrator, and more important, is a great friend.

We finally lost to Nebraska that year, 13-12, but my other memory from that year is a very sad one. On Friday, November 22, we left Columbia for our annual game at Kansas, and were in a hotel in Kansas City when we learned President Kennedy had been assassinated. The Presidents, Vice Presidents and Deans of the two universities huddled in a room at the hotel, trying to decide what to do. Like almost all of the university officials around the country, they decided to postpone the game for a week. The only game that wasn't postponed was Oklahoma's game against Nebraska, because Oklahoma coach Bud Wilkinson had worked for President Kennedy, and he convinced the others involved in the decision that President Kennedy would not have wanted the game postponed.

The news of the day, in my mind, was far more important than a football game. We sat in the hotel and watched the events unfolding on television, most of us still in shock. One of the network commentators came on and recited the poem *O Captain, My Captain*. That prompted a big debate in our room about the author of the poem. One English professor said it was Tennyson, but as it turned out, I was the only one in the room who had the right answer, Walt Whitman.

I knew this was a historic moment, albeit a tremendously sad one. As we gathered our players together in the hotel, I tried to share with them my opinions about Kennedy, and about the references to Camelot and Lancelot. I talked about how he was a man in the prime of his life, who had overcome a lot of obstacles to become one of the most powerful men in the world. There were many lessons for all of us to ponder, and I think everyone was in agreement that postponing the game for a week was the best decision that could have been made.

When we did play the game, we won 9-7, closing out another successful season.

Our 1964 season was moderately successful—we won six, lost three and tied one. We did beat Kansas, 34-14, and the tie was against Oklahoma, 14-14. Beating Gale Sayers at KU was always a highlight.

I knew early the next season, 1965, that it was going to be a special year. We had found a talented running back from Corpus Christi, Texas, a few years earlier and he was now ready for his senior season and his spot as one of the best players in the country. I'm talking, of course, about Johnny Roland.

Johnny was highly intelligent and was an excellent student. He was a two-way player, also excelling as a defensive back. Johnny was the first black to became captain in any sport at Missouri, and he was just a ferocious team player.

I always accused Johnny of taking notes. Whenever a player didn't know what to do or had a question, he went to Johnny. Everything on our schedule was timed out to the minute, and Johnny always knew exactly where everybody was supposed to be and when they were supposed to be there. He had to have a photographic memory; that was the only explanation for his knowing everything that he did.

Johnny broke onto the scene as a sophomore, when he scored three touchdowns in his first game, at California. That was just an indication of how good he was going to be, and he maintained that high standard throughout his entire career.

I was a little sad as we prepared to play Kansas in 1965, because I knew it was going to be Johnny's final regular-season game at Missouri and really was going to mark the end of an era. There were two great running backs on the field that day—Roland and Sayers.

Johnny finished his career the same way it had begun—by scoring three touchdowns. We won 44-20, and Johnny finished with more than 160 all-purpose yards. When you saw Johnny run, it just seemed so unreal because it was amazing. He was even more amazing when you realize that he was a unanimous All-America selection that year, as a defensive back.

He went on to the NFL in 1966 with the St. Louis Cardinals, switched exclusively to running back and was named the league's Rookie of the Year. He injured his knee the following year, and that really hampered his career and kept him from ranking as one of the greatest running backs ever.

We had another All-American that year, tackle Francis Peay, and he also went on to a great NFL career, and later went on to win several big games as head coach at Northwestern. It's fun to see players like that go on, but the hardest part about coaching in college is that you know you are not going to have them for very long and that you will have to say goodbye.

We had one more chance to enjoy watching Johnny, Francis and the other seniors play when we accepted a bid to play in the Sugar Bowl against Florida, which had an outstanding quarterback —Steve Spurrier. That was Spurrier's junior year; he would go on to win the Heisman as a senior the following year. We played well and won the game 20-18 and finished the year ranked sixth in the national polls.

I was disappointed about one thing on our bowl trip to New Orleans. I didn't get the chance to ride on a streetcar. Somebody on the bowl committee heard about it, and they invited me and my family back as their guests the following year and had a streetcar at my disposal, with me as the conductor. I had a good time driving that streetcar around New Orleans, and I thoroughly embarrassed all of our kids.

I was worried we would have a letdown in 1966 after losing players like Roland and Peay. We opened the season with games against Minnesota and Illinois, and were lucky enough to win them both.

Against Illinois, we fell behind 14-0 before we began to climb back in the game. We had tied the game at 14, when their great running back, Cy Pinder, took a handoff and started speeding downfield in front of our bench. One of our captains, Jim Whitaker, was a lot smaller than Pinder, but he was a tough kid. Whitaker met him head-on, and the hit was so ferocious that not even one person on our bench cheered. You could tell that Pinder was hurt, and one of the most concerned people on the field was Whitaker, who was a pre-med student. He was out there with the doctors, huddling around Pinder. It turned out he suffered a dislocated kneecap, and while he did come back to play again, he never was as effective a player as he had been before the injury. Jim, who now is a successful surgeon in Kansas City, told me, "Coach, I didn't mean to hurt him." I tried to reassure Jim that nobody thought that. He regained his composure and stayed in the game and with less than a minute to play, intercepted a pass right in front of our bench and ran it all the way in for a touchdown. I stayed with him down the sideline every step of the way—I could do that then.

We had kind of an up-and-down season after that. We lost to UCLA, then posted shutout wins over Kansas State and Oklahoma State before we got shut out by Nebraska and Colorado. We had two games left, at Oklahoma and against Kansas.

While preparing for the Oklahoma game, I was scared and nervous the entire time. I just dreaded going down there. We decided to pass on our first two plays, but had just one problem—both were intercepted. The coaches huddled on the sideline to decide what to do, and it was unanimous to junk the passing game. We didn't throw another pass the rest of the game, running every down, and we used one touchdown, a field goal and a tough defense to come away with a 10-7 victory.

On our way back to Columbia, I was reminded of some of the other great celebrations we had enjoyed at the airport after big victories. This was another special moment. A crowd of 10,000 fans met us at the airport, including my daughter Sarah. As we walked down off the airplane, Sarah ducked under the police rope holding back the crowd and came running up to me.

I was expecting her to say something like, "Daddy you're the greatest coach in the world," but what she said was, "Daddy, Daddy, Mommy didn't think Bill Bates could kick 53 yards." That's how long Bill's winning field goal was against the Sooners, and I don't know if he would have made it either if he had not been kicking downhill and with the wind. It was a gamble that went our way.

We beat Kansas 7-0 the following week to end the year with a 6-3-1 record. Again we were invited to a bowl game but the players voted to turn it down. I actually think the coaching staff was glad about the decision, because we were all emotionally and physically drained and I don't know that we would have done a good job of preparing the team for a bowl game.

That team taught me some important lessons about motivating a team, ones I never forgot for the rest of my career. We could have been really down going into the game at Oklahoma, and it would have been very easy for us to just go through the motions and lament our bad luck.

What I saw and remembered before that game, however, was how you can use your veteran players to motivate the younger players on your team. That way it's not only the coach who is trying to motivate the players; they are working to help each other. A trick I used for some games was when we would be having the team meeting before the game, I would excuse the seniors. I knew they knew everything I was going to say and they were going to motivate themselves. I moved the juniors, sophomores and freshmen down into the front of the room, and I talked to them about motivation and desire. I promised them that if they gave a supreme effort and played to the best of their ability, I would do the same thing for them when they were seniors.

This made those kids go out and try extra hard, because they wanted to be treated the same way when they were seniors.

What I had to remember as a coach was that I could never lie to my team and I never wanted my players to lie to themselves or each other. This leads to a sincere cooperation from everyone involved, and teamwork is one of the most important ingredients in a team's success.

The mid-1960s was a difficult era for everybody in this country, but especially for those who had to work daily with young people. There was growing unrest on college campuses around the country, protests against the war in Vietnam and retaliation and objections to people in charge. There were antiwar riots and violence that resulted in buildings being burned down and people being killed. At Missouri we didn't have as serious problems as they did at a lot of schools, and I was extremely grateful for that.

I honestly believe part of the reason we avoided a lot of those problems was due to the caliber of young men we had on our football team and our students at the university in general. It was the lead story on the news every night, dominating the newspaper stories and television broadcasts, and yet our people refused to get caught up in what was happening. We were the last team in the conference to integrate our football team, but we were the first to integrate the coaching staff when Prentice Gautt joined our family in the middle '60s. We had good people who remained calm and we were able to keep our focus on trying to be the best football team we could be, along with telling our kids to do the best job they could in school.

By 1967, it was hard to believe I had been at the same job for 10 consecutive seasons. I was proud of that stability. I've always believed that loyalty was important, and I also believe stability is the key to success for both a coach and a program. If you look at the most successful programs in college football today, most of the coaches are at the same schools they were at several years ago. There is a reason Joe Paterno has been at Penn State for so long and why that school always has a great program. Tom Osborne was that way at Nebraska, and there are countless other coaches you could name, too.

We had accomplished a lot at Missouri in my 10 seasons, and I was proud of our record. The programs in the Big Eight Conference had changed a lot in those years, especially with integration, and there was no such thing as an easy game anymore. That can be both good and bad, because you never want to be overconfident and experience a letdown, but it's also nice to have games that you believe you can win, even if you don't play your best football. The football season is long and intense, and if you have to really be at

100 percent peak effectiveness every week in order to win, that only adds to the pressure on the coaches and the players.

Some of the pressure comes down to split-second decisions during a game, when you have to make a call to kick the field goal or go for it on fourth down; to pass or run; what kind of defense you should run; etc. You can have all of the film study you want, you can know a team's tendencies, its strengths and weaknesses, but it still comes down to a gut decision, a hunch, as to what you should do and whether it will work or not.

We had such a moment in the second game of our 1967 season, at Northwestern. We had beaten SMU 21-0 in our opener, but Northwestern was playing very well. We were ahead late in the fourth quarter, when we decided to run a play on fourth-and-one instead of punting, even though we were in our own territory. I knew it wasn't the by-the-book call, but I just thought it was the right call for that situation, and my assistant coaches agreed. Luckily, we got the first down and went on to win the game.

Experience is a big factor in making decisions like that, and the more I coached, the more I instantly knew what I wanted to do in each situation. That's not to say the calls I made or the plays we ran always worked, because they didn't. Sometimes it might not have worked at the moment, but planted a seed that would pay dividends later in the year.

One play I always tried to run at least once early in a season was a fake field goal. Sometimes I thought it was the right call and would work, helping us get a touchdown and seven points instead of three, and sometimes I just wanted to run it for the benefit of the other teams on our schedule. Everybody was scouting all of those games and had the game films available, and seeing us run a fake field goal would give them something else to practice and think about when we played that team. You always wanted to make certain the other team didn't really know what you were thinking, and never to be so predictable that they knew exactly what was coming in each situation.

One play I remember came years later, in 1977, when I was coaching at Notre Dame. Just before the first half ended, it was third down, and we were almost in range for our field goal kicker,

Dave Reeve. Instead of trying to get the first down or even a touchdown, we ran a play that looked like we were setting up a field goal attempt for fourth down. A murmur went through the crowd, which sensed what we were doing, disappointed that we were going to try for the field goal.

The Southern Cal players and coaches heard the fans and they also figured that was what we were doing. I was the only one who knew differently, that the play we actually were going to run on fourth down was a fake field goal. Ted Burgmeier, the holder for the field goal attempt, picked up the ball and ran it for a first down. On the next set of downs, Joe Montana passed to Ken MacAfee for a touchdown. Nobody remembered the play on third down, but it was the key play in pulling off the fake and later letting us get that touchdown.

Another factor that is sometimes lost in preparation before a game and action during it, is motivation. I had that in mind as we got set to play Nebraska in 1967.

We had enjoyed great success against the Cornhuskers during my first five years at Missouri, winning all five games, four by shutouts. Then in 1966, we were drubbed in the game at Lincoln, maybe the worst loss one of my teams ever had, and I thought about that game a lot as we got closer to the rematch in 1967.

We were playing well and we had a 4-2 record as we got set for Nebraska. Thinking about the loss the previous year, I had one of my assistants, Keith Weber, find a recording of the Nebraska fight song.

The song begins, "Stand up and cheer for Nebraska, good old Nebraska U." The 1966 game had been on national television, and after every touchdown and the following commercial break, the Nebraska band would strike up that song. The band was sitting directly behind our bench, and it seemed we had that song blasting away at us the entire game. I know I didn't want to hear that song again, and I don't think our players did either. So we decided that during the week leading up to the game, we would play that song nonstop in our locker room from 1:00 in the afternoon until 7:00 at night. I put away all of the other records and forms of entertainment, so that was the only thing our players heard that entire week. We couldn't have been more sick of that song.

On the Friday night before the game, we practiced on a practice field because the stadium field was covered. At the end of practice, we met in the dressing room and could hear the song blaring. I yelled to Keith, "Go get that record." Keith went inside, got the record and brought it back to me.

Acting as serious as I could, I threw the record on the cement floor, planning to break it into a thousand or more pieces, as I shouted, "I don't want to hear this song ever again!" Something backfired. The record bounced off the floor, back up into the air, and didn't break. I picked it up, threw it down again, and darned if the thing didn't bounce up in the air again.

What we had was a vinyl record, which was unbreakable. I look back at the incident now and realize that if I had done this as a young coach, I would have panicked. Instead, blessed with a little more experience, I decided to break it over my knee. Then that didn't work either.

Here I was surrounded by all of these strong young men, and I couldn't break the darned record. It's laughable now, but our staff and assistants tried their best not to make me look like a fool and die of utter embarrassment. Finally, in complete frustration, I just threw the record as far as I could throw it, like a Frisbee. If I had had a blowtorch, I could have melted it, but that was the only way you were going to get rid of it.

Believe it or not, we won the game. We also won the Nebraska games the next two years, in 1968 and 1969. All of those games were special moments in my career.

After the 1967 win, we were celebrating with a party at our house. The coaching staff was there, media members, family, friends—basically anybody I ran into after the game—and the party was going great when the doorbell rang. I answered it and saw John Weaver, the President of the university. I had told him during the week how much I admired a hat he was wearing, and he told me, "If you win Saturday, it's yours." He had come over to the house to give me the hat.

I already had the game ball from the game, awarded to me by the players, and those two items were among my most prized possessions for years until they finally were raffled off for charity. I couldn't look at either the hat or the ball without breaking into a chuckle about what a time I had trying to break that record.

We finished the year 7-3, but the players voted not to go to a bowl game. This was the beginning of a stretch of really good seasons for us. We improved to eight wins in 1968 and won nine games in 1969.

There were some people who were concerned at Missouri that I might be looking to change jobs, and as an enhancement to try to keep me from leaving, I was given the additional duties of athletic director in 1967.

Don Faurot remained a great friend of mine and of the university and basically did whatever he could to help me and everybody else who worked there. I was very thankful to have him there to give me advice and counsel whenever I needed it.

I was happy to get the additional responsibilities, but at that time I honestly had no intentions of leaving. All of that happened very suddenly, and years later I often wondered why I ever did decide to leave.

One of my tasks as athletic director in 1967 was to hire a new basketball coach. We had won only three games—total—in the previous three years and none came in conference games. We were about as low as a team could get, playing in old Brewer Field House, and it was an almost impossible situation.

I was surprised, however, by how many applications we received for the job. The faculty committee on athletics reviewed them and pulled out two that they thought were from the best candidates for the job. One was from Norm Stewart, a Missouri graduate and former basketball player who was the coach at Northern Iowa. The other was Bill Fitch, who was coaching at Minnesota.

I think either would have been a good choice, but since it was my decision and recommendation, I picked Stewart. He was younger, and I thought he might bring a little more eagerness and vision for the future.

Never in my dreams did I believe when we hired Norm that 32 years later he still would be the basketball coach at Missouri. He had a tremendous career and retired after the 1998-99 season to start enjoying his life. We became great friends, and one of my most treasured possessions is the ball he gave me from his 600th career win at Missouri.

My last really big job in the late '60s was to help lead a drive for a new spacious fieldhouse. Gov. Warren Hearnes was a close personal friend, as was the president of the governing board, Bill Billings and MU president John Weaver. With the help of numerous people, Hearnes Center was built with financial aid from the state (a rarity in Missouri). It still stands as a truly remarkable building and has served many thousands of Missouri's finest young people.

I've noticed over the years that some universities have problems between their head football and basketball coaches. Whether it's an ego thing, or a popularity thing, or financial, those coaches seem to battle with each other and never get along, always trying to outdo the other guy. I was proud Norm and I never had any problems like that. He was always very supportive of the football team, and we tried to get him as much support and assistance as possible. He didn't need as much in later years after he was able to turn our basketball fortunes around and make Missouri a contending team almost every year.

Having the basketball situation in better hands allowed me to think more about my other job as football coach, and I was excited in 1968 because I thought we had a good team with a good chance to win the conference title and get back to the Orange Bowl.

We lost the opener to Kentucky, 12-6, but then began to play well. We beat Illinois 44-0 in Champaign, and went into Lincoln and beat Nebraska 16-14. Our season came down to the final game, against Kansas. The Jayhawks had a great team that year with players such as John Riggins and Bobby Douglass, and beat us 21-19, winning the conference championship and the trip to Miami to play Penn State in the Orange Bowl. We accepted a bid to the Gator Bowl to play Bear Bryant's Alabama Crimson Tide. This turned out to be a super break for us and maybe Missouri's biggest win.

Bear Bryant was the king of coaches. He always treated me with the highest dignity. I recently came across a letter he had written to me, inviting me to come down and spend some time with him. I was able to do that soon after I retired from coaching, and that time together will always be a special memory. He was kind of doing the Gator Bowl a favor by bringing his team to Jacksonville for the game, which was nationally televised.

Of course, there weren't as many bowl games in 1968 as there are today, so most college teams were grateful to get an invitation to play in any of them. I still believe going to bowl games, appearances on national television and the campus itself are three of the biggest factors in being able to bring in high-quality recruits for any program.

Alabama was a heavy favorite for the game, but that didn't bother me. I knew it was an important game for Missouri, for some of the reasons I mentioned above, and I was confident that our kids would go down there and play well. We decided to train in Florida before the game, and the NCAA rule was that you had to select a site within 100 miles of the game. We picked Daytona Beach and had a great week of practice. The weather was ideal, the kids were focused and we had one of those days when everything clicked. We won the game 35-10, and the game was not as close as even that score indicates.

It might have been the biggest defeat ever for a Bear Bryant team, but after the game he was very complimentary toward me and our team. He was very kind to my family, and we developed a very nice friendship which continued for years.

After a nationally televised game such as the Gator Bowl, I frequently received a lot of letters, and one that came in the mail after this game was from Frank Leahy, the former head coach at Notre Dame.

This letter said, "Of great interest to me was your call in the first quarter with 2:52 left, your possession, fourth down and half a yard, with the ball on Alabama's 30-yard line." That's how specific his attention was, and showed what a precise man he was about details. I had called a short-yardage play-action pass on the play he mentioned, and it went for a good gain and a first down. It's funny how coaches will notice things like that and realize it could have been one of the turning points of the game, even at that early juncture in the game.

We didn't have much time to celebrate the win over Alabama, because I was going to Honolulu to serve as a coach for the Hula Bowl. Two of our players, Roger Wehrli and Jim Anderson, also had been selected for the game, and I ordered room-service breakfast in our room for them and their wives, Jo and myself and four of our children before our 6:30 a.m. flight.

Nobody cared that we hadn't had much sleep and had to change planes both in New Orleans and San Francisco. By the time we got on the plane in San Francisco for the final leg of our trip, my mind was focusing on the game and I realized that our team, the West, might be in a little trouble. We had 14 players on the plane, and the East squad had a full complement of players and coaches. Our head coach, John McKay of Southern Cal, would not be coming out to Hawaii for four more days, until after his team played in the Rose Bowl. Two of his players also had made the team, so even with the best of conditions, we weren't going to have much time to practice—really only one day for many of the players.

I was still thinking about our game plan when we got to Hawaii, and I picked up a newspaper and saw that Bobby Warmack, the quarterback from Oklahoma who was to be our quarterback in the bowl game, had been injured in the Sooners' bowl game and would be unable to play. I already was worried about our team, and now we didn't have a quarterback four days before the game was to be played.

I called Henry Iba, the Athletic Director and legendary basketball coach at Oklahoma State, because I knew his assistant's son was a good quarterback at Oklahoma State. I realized after I had already placed the call that it was 4 a.m. in Kansas City, where he was.

I knew I had woken Iba up, but I still was dumb enough to ask, "Hank, did I wake you up?" I know from my own experience that even if the answer to that question is an obvious yes, everybody always says no. That's exactly what Iba said when I told him I needed to talk to him about their quarterback.

"No, Danny," he replied in his familiar raspy voice. "I was waiting for your call."

He agreed to help, and our new quarterback, Ronnie Johnson, arrived on Friday, in time for our one day of practice. We had added another player on Wednesday, when at halftime of the Rose Bowl game, I called the press box and asked USC's sports information director to ask Frank Sagge to come out with McKay and the other

USC players already invited—a list that included running back O.J. Simpson.

Until all of the players arrived, we worked out with the players we had. I got my son Tiger to play defensive back so we would have even numbers. He was 14 at the time.

As luck would have it, the one day we had with a full squad for practice was scheduled to be Friday, the day before the game, and the island was hit with a torrential rainstorm. We had to practice inside a gym, and to make matters worse, I found out McKay was ill and would not be able to coach. I suddenly found myself as the head coach.

O.J. Simpson was the one who delivered that news to me, and he said he knew I was short of players and coaches, and he would do anything he could to help. He actually did a lot more than I asked of him. It turned out another young college coach, Mike White, was vacationing in Hawaii and volunteered to help. He went on to a great career in college at California and Illinois, became head coach of the Oakland Raiders, and was an assistant coach with the 2000 Super Bowl champion St. Louis Rams.

The biggest problem during the game was the field in the old stadium. It was six inches lower in the middle than it was at the sidelines, and you can only imagine how much mud was on that field following the heavy rainfall. I kept wondering what had happened to this beautiful Hawaiian vacation we were supposed to be enjoying. I remember going to the beach with my video camera, trying to get pictures of Wehrli and Anderson surfing, but this young lady kept walking in front of the camera. When I showed the film later, it was difficult to focus on the surfers.

Considering every obstacle we had faced, we played extremely well but lost a close game. What stood out more to me than the score, however, was the people that my family and I came into contact with during that week that we otherwise might never have had a chance to meet. That is the beauty of bowl games and all-star get-togethers like that.

One player who fell into that category was Gene Washington, who was a great receiver at Stanford and went on to star for the San Francisco 49ers.

Even though we were losing two great players and team leaders in Wehrli and Anderson to graduation, I thought we could build on our successful 1968 season to be even better in 1969. One of the reasons I was excited about the year was our scheduled game at Ann Arbor against Michigan.

Michigan had a good team as well, and they ended up winning the Big Ten and representing the conference in the Rose Bowl. We led the game at halftime, but I withheld any type of celebration because I knew there was a lot of football left. We made some good adjustments and won the game 40-17. John "Nip" Weisenfels, an attorney today, led our defensive unit. Joe Moore shouldered the burden for the offense. Today Joe is a high school teacher. As we left the field, I happened to think back to the last time we had come in and won at Ann Arbor and had so many problems after the game trying to get into our locker room with the locked door. This time the door was unlocked, and we went right in to begin celebrating a fantastic win.

We had a lot of other big victories during the year as well. We defeated Nebraska 17-7 and rolled past Oklahoma 44-10. The Sooners coach was Chuck Fairbanks, and because of a delay in introducing the starting lineups on national television before our game, we had a few extra minutes to chat.

Chuck's wife, Puddy, had been our babysitter when we lived in East Jordan. He had played at our rival Charlevoix, and he had played on my freshman team at Michigan State. He had a great player in running back Steve Owens, who won the Heisman that year, and the Sooners jumped out to a 10-0 lead. We then were able to shut him down, however, and get our offense going and roll to the big win.

We finished the year by scoring 109 points in our last two games, a 40-13 win over Iowa State and a 69-21 romp over Kansas. We did get the Orange Bowl bid that year, and headed off to Miami to play Joe Paterno and Penn State. We actually received invitations from the Cotton, Sugar and Gator bowls, in addition to the Orange Bowl, but that was the one the players voted to accept.

Notre Dame was playing Texas the day before our game, and we knew that if the Irish could upset Texas, the number-one-ranked team in the country, our game would decide the national championship. Unfortunately for us, however, Texas won, so the championship was decided before we ever took the field.

One of my favorite memories from that game occurred on the morning of the game, when Joe Paterno and I both took off our socks and shoes, rolled up our pant legs and had a nice, quiet, private walk along the beach. We joked about the looks we got from alumni from both schools as we walked. We shared a lot of private thoughts. I have the utmost respect and admiration for him.

As we prepared for the game, I saw that Penn State was obviously well coached and well prepared. They had two running backs who stood out to me—Franco Harris and Lydell Mitchell. You didn't have to be a great judge of talent to realize that both could play, and they went on to stellar NFL careers. They also had a couple of other players who would become household names—linebacker Jack Ham and defensive tackle Mike Reid.

It was a defensive game and we lost 10-3, hurt most by seven interceptions. I blamed myself for the loss because I only did an average job of coaching and I didn't design enough help for our quarterback, Terry McMillan, who had enjoyed a great career at Missouri, including being named the MVP of our bowl win over Alabama the previous year.

One of the factors that hurt Terry in the game was that he was a third-string quarterback coming back home. He was from the Miami area, and I think those distractions affected his preparation for the game. He went down early in the game, and I should have brought in Mike Farmer and then brought Terry back later in the game, but I didn't do that. I was disappointed by the loss, but I couldn't let it dampen our spirits too much for what had really been an exciting season. We ended up with a 9-2 record and a national sixth-place ranking in the final polls.

Looking back on it, that team might just have been the best team Missouri ever had. It was the last Mizzou squad to go to the Orange Bowl, and I know it was one of the finest teams I ever coached.

One of the toughest aspects about coaching is that a lot of your thoughts and observations come through hindsight. Coaching is such a spontaneous profession, with so many decisions having to be made on the spur of the moment, that you never have enough time to sit back and reflect and enjoy things as they happen. That's really the way I feel about that 1969 team. I knew at the time the team was good, and I enjoyed the year tremendously, but in retrospect, I wish I would have had more time to enjoy it because we really did have a lot of special people on the team that year who went on to lead successful lives.

Some of those players were returning in 1970, including running back Joe Moore and wide receiver Mel Gray. Joe was one of the greatest running backs I ever coached, ranking just behind Johnny Roland. He was going into his senior year and I was expecting great things from him. Unfortunately, in just our fifth game of the season, at Nebraska, he separated his shoulder. As he walked off the field, the doctor calmly told me, "Coach, he's out for the year," and he was correct. Losing him was a big blow to our team, and I felt even sorrier for Joe personally because he had been looking forward to a big finale to his college career. He was a number-one pick in the NFL draft by the Chicago Bears.

Mel Gray did turn in some outstanding performances, and I wondered sometimes how he did it. I don't think he ever weighed more than 165 pounds, even during his great NFL career with the Cardinals.

The week after we lost Moore during the Nebraska game, Notre Dame was coming to town. The game was originally scheduled to be played in St. Louis, but the Columbia stadium had a bigger seating capacity, so both schools agreed to move it to Columbia. Ara Parseghian never had a bad team at Notre Dame, but I've always thought this was one of his best.

Their quarterback was Joe Theismann, and he turned in the play of the game early in the second half, which broke our backs and led them to the win. We were ahead 7-3, and Notre Dame faced a third-down-and-long situation. Al Onofrio, the defensive coordinator, came up to me and said, "I'd like to blitz on this play." I said, "Bring everybody."

We did, and our two linebackers each had a clear shot at Theismann. Instead, he eluded them and threw the ball behind his back to a running back, Ed Gulyas. The play went for a first down, and Notre Dame later scored on the drive and pulled away in the remaining portion of the game.

Despite the loss, I was proud of our players. They had played hard, and they had played a very competitive game against one of the best teams in the country. Notre Dame only lost one game that year, to Southern Cal at the end of the year, and then beat Texas in the Cotton Bowl.

The hardest part of the year for me was that we finished with a 5-6 record. It would turn out to be the only one of my 22 seasons as a college football coach that my team finished with a losing record. Despite the disappointing year, I was still enjoying the job and the university. Everybody had treated me, Jo and our family extremely well. I had a 10-year contract, renewed annually; two courtesy cars; a great insurance policy with a cash value that had reached $500,000. I had the rank of full professor with academic tenure, which meant I could not be fired.

Next to Bear Bryant, I had the most lucrative television show for a college football coach. It was in prime time on Sunday night in St. Louis with Bob Broeg, the Hall of Fame sportswriter, sponsored by Coca-Cola. I also had a lucrative contract for a radio show with Harry Caray.

I had never met Harry Caray before I went to Missouri, although I never told him that. We did two shows a week during the season for 12 years and became very close friends. My friends had predicted that I wouldn't last a week with Harry because of the differences in our personalities, but it worked out well for everyone. Harry had a reputation for asking extremely tough questions, particularly about close games, but he honestly never asked me a question that was even remotely difficult to answer. At least in our relationship, he was perfect. He had a good sense of how to approach a coach during the emotional moments after a game, whether you won or lost, and he always treated me well.

The shows were broadcast on KMOX in St. Louis, one of the most powerful radio stations in the country. The stable of announcers who have worked there over the years is amazing: Caray, Jack Buck, Joe Garagiola, Bob Costas, Gary Bender, the late Dan Kelly, Dan Dierdorf, Broeg, Mike Kelly, Bob Burnes and now Jack's son,

Joe Buck. Another announcer there, Mike Shannon, joined the station after his baseball career, but I remember him as a great high school quarterback. He came to Mizzou, and I think would have been a great football player, but after one year he decided to play baseball and joined the Cardinals' organization.

Both the television and radio shows were tougher that year than they had ever been, primarily because of our losing record. I think the disappointing season actually reenergized me a little to know I was going to have to do a better job of recruiting and a better job of coaching for us to again become a winning team. I also knew that a big part of the reason for our 5-6 season was injuries, and that was just a fact of life that a coach has to deal with and really can't predict or avoid.

I had a lot of friends in the coaching business who had left the college ranks to go into the pros, and some of them told me the best job in this business was being a head coach and general manager in the NFL. I was very happy at the college level, however, and never really spent any time thinking about job possibilities in the pros until late in 1970, when I received a call from Dominic Olejniczak, the president of the Green Bay Packers, inviting me to dinner.

Olejniczak was a Green Bay businessman who was most proud of the fact that he had hired Vince Lombardi as coach in 1959 and had brought Tony Canadeo, one of the great all-time Packers, back into the organization. The Packers had hired Phil Bengtson after Lombardi retired. He was Vince's choice. I think Olejniczak was starting to get some pressure to replace Bengtson. He wanted to just talk about the position with me and find out where I was in my life and if I might have any interest in coaching in the NFL.

It honestly wasn't something I had thought about or spent much time analyzing. I thanked Olejniczak for thinking of me, enjoyed the Christmas holiday and then headed off to the national coaches convention, which was in Houston that year.

At the convention, Olejniczak called again—to tell me I was their first choice to become the new head coach and general manager of the Packers. I didn't have an immediate response, but told him I would have to think it over and get back to him.

I was flattered by the offer, but I also knew it was going to be an extremely tough decision. I took a long walk with Doug Weaver, my former assistant coach, also a lawyer, head coach and athletic director. We talked over all aspects of the job, and he encouraged me to look at all of the positive reasons for taking the job.

Jo and I had a long talk about the job, and she encouraged me to do whatever I thought was best. We were both very happy at Missouri, our children were happy, and we were enjoying a great life. During our time in Missouri, Jo's mother lived with us for 13 years after Jo's father passed away, and she was a great addition to our household. Even though we had many special times with friends and family in Missouri, we also realized, however, that offers and possibilities like this didn't come along every day, and so we had to consider it very seriously. I had talked with Art Rooney Sr. previously, but it had never gone this far.

Dominic asked me to meet him in Kansas City, and I did. I had tried to keep the meeting a secret, but one reporter in Kansas City, Dick Wade, found out about it and wrote that I was leaving Missouri to become the coach of the Packers. The news shocked a lot of people, and I was just disappointed that it had leaked out in that manner and I hadn't had time to properly tell everybody that I would have liked to have told personally of my decision.

We had a good meeting, but I still had not officially accepted the job. He went back to Green Bay and I went back to Columbia. The Packers had interviewed two other coaches, Joe Paterno and Frank Kush, but Ole—as we came to know him—told me he wanted me to get the job. I still wasn't certain what I was going to do.

When he called the next time, I knew I had to give him an answer because the media was applying a lot of pressure on him. I said the answer was yes, I would take the job. To illustrate how uncertain I was, the night before I left, I had Tommy Reamon in my rec room at home on a recruiting visit. As I drove away, my neighbor, Greg Hill—who went on to a great career with the Tigers as a placekicker—held his scholarship application at my car window so I could sign it. I have to admit I was torn by the decision and didn't know if I was making the correct decision or not. I still have a tremendously warm feeling for the University of Missouri.

I think either Joe or Frank also would have been a good choice and done a good job. The first two checks I signed with the Packers were covering the expenses for their interviews.

One thing I never asked Ole was why, considering the pro backgrounds of Lombardi and Bengtson, they had decided to concentrate on college coaches in their job search. It didn't really matter what their reasons were. All I knew was that I was suddenly facing the greatest challenge of my life. My attorney, Paul Klavercamp, jumped through the ceiling when he found out that I had accepted the job without a signed contract, which was just another example of my trusting nature.

Chapter Six

THE GREEN BAY PACKERS

The Green Bay Packers had been the dominant franchise in football in the 1960s, but without even asking any questions in my first discussion about going to work for them, I knew that if they were looking to hire a new head coach and general manager, the picture must not be too rosy.

It turned out I was correct, and in a big way.

I was stunned to find out, shortly after reporting for work in Green Bay, that almost half of our roster was unsigned. That meant that just to field a team, we had to negotiate and re-sign those players, plus prepare for the NFL draft, select those players and then try to get them signed before training camp.

All of that had to be done while at the same time figuring out ways to improve a club that had finished last in both total offense and total defense in our division, the NFC Central, in 1970. We weren't even a close last; we were last by a large margin. We had some problems with age—some of the players who had been great on those championship teams in the 1960s were now getting older and couldn't play as well as they had a few years earlier. It never is an easy decision about what to do with a player who is in that position, and I hadn't counted on having to make so many of those moves so quickly after joining the team.

One of the first telephone calls I made the day it was announced that I was taking the job was to Bart Starr, the Packers' quarterback. I told him how much I was counting on him, and he pledged to make my transition to Green Bay and the pros as smooth as possible. It definitely didn't help matters when he was injured and unable to play.

We also lost another class guy and terrific player right away when Forrest Gregg decided to retire. He and Bart were the kinds of players who would somehow find a way to win games for you all by themselves. Forrest went into coaching and later took a team to the Super Bowl. We developed a good friendship and he was very kind in publicly giving me credit for convincing him to stay in coaching at San Diego a few years later. He said he had depended on Coach Lombardi for advice, but in Lombardi's absence was turning to me and asking for my judgment. I will always appreciate his kind comments.

We had some quality players, people like Gale Gillingham, a guard who could pull and lead a play as well as anybody in the league, and Carroll Dale, a wide receiver who gave everything he had for every second in every practice and every game. The Packers' first-round pick in the 1970 draft had been a tight end, Rich McGeorge, and he also was a quality player.

As we studied the team and began to prepare for the 1971 draft, I knew we needed help in a lot of areas. We reached a deal with Denver to send quarterback Don Horn to the Broncos for defensive tackle Alden Roche and their first-round pick. We used that pick to select John Brockington, the big fullback from Ohio State. I should have used my knowledge of college players even more.

One advantage I might have had over some people in my position was evident during draft preparations. My years at the collegiate level had provided me with a fabulous collection of friends and colleagues, and if I needed to verify information or find out something about a college player, I usually just had to make a couple of telephone calls and I had all of the information I needed.

That was part of the reason I was convinced Brockington could become a star in the NFL, and he did. He became the league's offensive Rookie of the Year, and in each of his first three seasons at

Green Bay, he rushed for more than 1,000 yards. We continued to have good success in the draft each year.

I knew the Packers were expecting a lot from me, and they were paying me very well to do the job for them. They more than doubled my base salary, and added lucrative incentive bonuses—such as a $15,000 payment if we beat the Minnesota Vikings in the playoffs. I also had contracts for a radio show and a television show. When school was over in Columbia and Jo and the kids were able to move, we bought a beautiful house on 10 acres out in the country. It had a tennis court, a gift from Russ Overmier, a great Packer fan, a barn for the kids' horses and a lake. It froze in the winter, and I spent countless hours playing hockey with Tiger. Those are special memories that I will always cherish. Some of our greatest memories are from the time we spent in Green Bay.

No matter how hard I worked, however, it became evident pretty quickly to me that what I was doing was more than a one-person job. I couldn't do all of the administrative front-office work and still put in the time I thought was necessary to function as the coach of the Packers, preparing game plans and getting the players ready to play. There physically were not enough hours in the day for one person to do all of the work that needed to be done.

What I wanted to do was find a young, bright, hardworking person I could hire and work into the front-office job. I called Bob Broeg, my journalist friend in St. Louis, and Bing Devine, working for the baseball Cardinals (no relation), and they both suggested a man working in the Cardinals' office named Bob Harlan. He had no experience in football, but he met every other qualification and came with high recommendations from both Bob and Bing. We brought him to Green Bay and I, too, was impressed with Bob and we offered him the front-office position.

That was my first experience with making the natives restless. Of course, I knew about the Packers' tradition and the fans' expectations, but I never expected the media or the fans to get so worked up about my decision to bring in a person like Bob to help out in the front office. Here was this new guy Devine, and for one of his first important decisions, he hires a kid who had been working for a baseball team. It was almost like I had committed an unbelievable blunder. The move was even unpopular with some members of the team's Board of Directors, who cited my lack of experience in the NFL, as well as his lack of experience, period.

Because of all of that second-guessing, it has been fun to watch Bob move up over the years and become one of the most respected and successful executives in the league. He is now the President and CEO of the Packers, and he is justifiably referred to as "the savior of the Packer organization."

I must point out that one person who stood behind me in the decision to hire Bob was Ole, who also supported my choice to bring in Lee Remmel as the Public Relations Director. Lee had been the beat writer for the *Green Bay Press-Gazette* and had no NFL experience, but I thought he could do a good job. I'm proud to say he also is still with the organization and is one of the most respected PR officials in the league.

While some of those off-the-field decisions left me hurt mentally, it was on the field where I experienced physical pain.

We opened the 1971 season at home against the New York Giants and quickly fell behind. In the second half, we started to mount a comeback and were within a field goal of winning the game. The Giants had possession, and attempted a pass which one of our defensive backs, Doug Hart, intercepted. He was returning the ball right in front of our bench, and bodies were flying everywhere. I was attempting to be a traffic cop, but after I realized I was in the way, I turned and tried to move, but my foot got stuck in the tarp near the bench. It had rained throughout the day, so the field was slippery.

Bodies slammed into me—and broke my leg in five places. I probably was in shock, but I knew immediately it was broken. Within seconds, our team orthopedic surgeon, Dr. Jim Nellen, was leaning over me and I remember telling him, "It's broken between my ankle and knee, in several places, but it's not a compound fracture." The doctors quickly had me brought into the training room.

While lying on a training table, I listened as we missed the field goal that would have won the game. We lost 42-40, but I still was proud of the effort our players had put in. The broken leg was placed in a really big cast, which I had to wear for 10 weeks, but I was back at our offices the next morning to review the films of the game. I never missed a practice or a game, thanks in large part to the help of one of our former Missouri quarterbacks, Gary Lane, who was on my Packers' staff. He devised a wheelchair contraption that I was able to use to help get me to Milwaukee the following Sunday for our game against the Broncos, my first victory as an NFL coach.

Lane had been a great quarterback at Mizzou but didn't make it in the NFL. He was a big pre-Montana-type scrambler, who today would be a number-one quarterback in the league because of his abilities. It was a different league back then, however, and he turned to coaching. He is now a referee in the NFL.

As had been the case at the collegiate level, I was blessed with an excellent coaching staff with the Packers. Those guys have to make so many of the decisions and have to work so closely with the players that they are one of the biggest keys to a team's success, without earning nearly enough credit and recognition for the job they do. Having an excellent staff allows the head coach more time to handle the media, conduct business in the front office and all of the other matters that just seem to take up a great deal of a head coach's time every week.

Some of my assistants who had previously coached for me included Hank Kuhlmann, Bill Tobin, Perry Moss, Johnny Polonchek, Rollie Dotsch, and Johnny Roland. All of them have had great careers, and I am proud of all of them.

Those guys had to take on even more responsibility after my broken leg limited some of the things I was able to do, and they had a great deal to do with our success that season. Our next game was against Paul Brown's Cincinnati Bengals, and we were ahead 20-17 late in the game. The Bengals had the ball and were close to field goal range. On fourth down, needing only a couple of yards, he sent out the field goal unit, then took a time-out.

I don't know why, but they changed their plans during the time-out and sent the regular offense back on the field. Quarterback Kenny Anderson tried a sweep, but he was met head-on by safety Willie Wood, one of the all-time Packer greats, and tackled for a loss. We took over possession and won the game.

When I met Coach Brown at midfield, he was very kind and told me, "Danny, every 100 years, listen to your players in these situations."

One of Brown's players, Ken Dyer, had been injured in the game. He hurt his neck attempting to make a tackle and had to be admitted to a Green Bay hospital. I checked in on him every day until he was released, and Brown thought that was nice of me, but I considered it part of my job. I recently ran into Dyer's son at a sports banquet in Phoenix, and when I was explaining how his dad was hurt, I had tears in my eyes.

We had a key game late in the year at Minnesota, and even though we were big underdogs, we played them to a scoreless tie with only a few minutes left in the game. We knew a field goal would win the game. On the sidelines, we were talking about running the clock down and kicking the field goal but we didn't have time to convey that message to the players on the field without risking a five-yard penalty for delay of game.

Instead of the play we should have called, we threw a play-action pass, which got caught up in the wind and was intercepted. It was returned within field goal range for the Vikings, and Coach Bud Grant had his team run down the clock and did kick the field goal that gave them a 3-0 victory. It was a very frustrating loss.

One of the reasons we had not been able to generate any offense in the game was the play of the Vikings' defensive tackle, Alan Page, who later was named the Most Valuable Player in the league that year, the first and only time a defensive lineman had won that award. He definitely deserved it, because he influenced offenses tremendously and forced you to try to design offensive blocking schemes solely aimed at trying to stop him on the line of scrimmage.

The Vikings' entire defensive line, including Carl Eller, Jim Marshall and Gary Larsen, was tremendous. The key to the entire defense, however, was Page. He could handle the middle of the line all by himself, and that made every player around him better. He could rush the passer, go after runners in the backfield and was still fast enough to catch guys going around the end on sweeps. He truly earned his award as the player of the year.

We had good performances from a lot of players, especially John Brockington, and I was pleased with the experience our rookie quarterback, Scott Hunter, gained during the year. A late 31-10 victory over the Bears helped us go into the off-season feeling good about our chances to improve in 1972.

We picked up two terrific players in the draft, selecting Willie Buchanon, a defensive back from San Diego State, in the first round. He went on to become the defensive Rookie of the Year. We chose a placekicker from tiny Hillsdale College in the second round, Chester Marcol, and he became an All-Pro his rookie year. You can't ask for better selections than that.

Looking back at the draft is always a perfect science, because you will see players who lasted until the late round and know that they became an All-Pro. Yes, those things do happen, but there usually is a reason players are picked high in the draft or picked in the later rounds. You can't count on getting lucky on late-round picks, but you had better be able to count on your early picks becoming pretty good players if you want to stick around long as a coach.

As a coach or a player, you sometimes say "what if" about draft picks. You also can sometimes point to one play in one game and wonder "what if." It doesn't seem right that one play can make or break a season, especially early in the year, and sometimes you don't even realize how big that one play will turn out to be until later in the year. In 1972, we won our opener 26-10 in Cleveland, then came home to play John Madden's great Oakland Raiders. We were leading, and had the ball on their two-yard line, when we ran an option play. The Raiders bit on Scott Hunter's fake, and as he pitched the ball to MacArthur Lane, there was nobody near him.

Lane might have had the best hands of any running back in the league; he was not a fumbler. But instead of catching the toss and trotting into the end zone, he saw the ball bounce off his hands and into the end zone. Jack Tatum of the Raiders picked up the ball and ran it 108 yards the other way for a touchdown that cost us the game.

It later dawned on all of us, and other people in the league, that the play should have been ruled a muff, because you are not allowed to fumble the ball forward like that. NFL Commissioner Pete Rozelle called Ole and me to apologize, but there was nothing else he or anybody else could do. The game went into the record books as a loss.

If we had won that game, it would have given us a big mental boost heading into our game against the defending Super Bowl–champion Cowboys, in Milwaukee. Riding the bus from Green Bay to Milwaukee on Saturday, we listened to the Missouri-Notre Dame game on the radio. We had alumni from each school on our team, including Mike McCoy of Notre Dame and Jon Staggers from Missouri, and they made a little wager on the game, which got their teammates involved and choosing up sides.

Missouri was something like a 40-point underdog, so McCoy gave Staggers the 40 points. He didn't even need the help, as the Tigers won 30-26 in a tremendous upset. The entire team was ribbing McCoy pretty good, and I think that helped put everybody in a good and relaxed mood as we prepared to play the Cowboys.

Dallas had most of its players returning from the Super Bowl team, including quarterback Roger Staubach and running back Calvin Hill, but we played a great game and won handily. We now were 2-1, but without that one misplay and blown call, we could have been 3-0.

We continued to play well. With three games to go in the regular season, we were 7-4 and in a three-way tie with Detroit and Minnesota for the lead in the Central Division. One of our victories had been a 23-10 win over Houston, due in large part to a touchdown we scored off a fake punt. I talked earlier about the element of surprise when trying to run a fake field goal, and the same held true with the fake punt. It came at a moment when nobody in the stadium had any idea we would run a fake, and the play worked perfectly. It also was good because it raised the possibility for all of the teams we had yet to play, forcing them to consider that we might run the play again.

Our next opponent was Detroit on a cold, windy day in Green Bay. The Lions won the toss and elected to defend the north goal with the wind at their backs. The decision backfired when we drove the ball on three long drives against the wind and each time kicked a short field goal. We had a 9-0 lead at the end of the first quarter and the Lions had not made a first down. We went on to win 33-7.

The same day, Minnesota went to San Francisco and beat the 49ers, which meant we had to win the next week at Minnesota to clinch the division title and a spot in the playoffs.

It had not taken me very long to get caught up in the Green Bay-Minnesota rivalry. Having grown up in northern Minnesota, I was well aware of the histories of both teams and knew how important it was for the fans of both teams who wanted desperately to win that game. It was even more important this year, since the division championship was riding on the outcome.

They had not yet built the Metrodome in Minneapolis, and you can imagine how cold it was playing outdoors there on December 10, but you would be wrong. It was colder than that, with the temperature and wind chill far below zero. My cousin Rich, his wife Pat, Jo and other family members sat in the stands that day and froze. I think the wind chill was actually measured at minus-37 degrees, not exactly the kind of weather when you want to be playing a football game. But we gave my family and all our fans a lot to cheer about.

It was one of the most emotional days of my life, starting with the moment Jo and I walked into the stadium and saw a message flashing on the scoreboard, "Welcome home, Jo and Dan Devine." Nobody forgot I was a Minnesota kid, and the people there always treated us great whether we came in to play a college game or with the Packers. In three college games against outstanding Gopher teams and in four games against the Vikings, we gave up a total of three touchdowns. Minneapolis treated us very well.

I thought we were ready for the game, despite having to spend one day of practice working out inside the dining room of a restaurant because of all the snow on the ground. The Vikings had to battle the same conditions, but for some reason, I think we had the emotional edge. We won the game 23-7, and even had a long touchdown run by MacArthur Lane called back because of a holding penalty. We had some joyous moments inside our locker room after the win, and Rich and Pat and the other family members came by to say hello. The Packers had won their first division title in four years, and everybody was in the mood to celebrate.

That included our fans in Green Bay. When we flew back into town and arrived at the airport, none of us were prepared for the mass of fans who had gathered for an impromptu pep rally. Mike McCoy had been through some great moments at Notre Dame, but he kept saying over and over, "This beats Notre Dame, this beats Notre Dame." I don't think any of us had ever experienced a crowd quite like it and probably never will again.

Our win against the New Orleans Saints the following week was almost anticlimactic. We began our playoff preparations knowing the odds of beating George Allen's Washington Redskins were tremendous. We gave a great effort, but the Redskins just had a better team and won the game 16-3. They won the NFC title and made it to the Super Bowl, but then ran into the Miami Dolphins, who completed a phenomenal undefeated year by beating Washington in the Super Bowl.

The year was a good one not only for the team, but for me personally. In fact, the 1972 Packer team was the only Green Bay squad from 1968 to 1994 (a 27-year span), that captured a conference championship. I was named the NFC Coach of the Year by the Football Writers of America, and to be included with a group of people that included George Halas, who was like a hero to me, was a tremendous thrill. Don Shula, a good friend, was AFC Coach of the Year.

We had managed to overcome some injuries in 1972 to still enjoy a terrific season, losing people like Gillingham and McGeorge, but we weren't so fortunate in 1973. We shut out Joe Namath and the Jets to open the year, but then suffered through a disappointing year. I could have coached better, and we could have played better, and our final record of 5-7-2 was a big letdown from the playoff high of the previous year.

Willie Buchanon, who had become the best defensive back in the league, broke his leg in a game in Los Angeles against the Rams. We also lost tackle Bill Hayhoe with a broken leg. We lost one game to Minnesota 11-3 when they didn't score a touchdown, beating us with three field goals and a safety. We won our final game, shutting out the Bears 21-0, and that always gives people a little better feeling going into the off-season.

Jo and I were planning on taking three of the kids on a family vacation to Hawaii, in conjunction with the NFL's spring meetings in 1974. There was, of course, snow on the ground, with more coming down when we had to leave to take a flight to Chicago and catch our connecting flight to Honolulu. Dede and Tiger got up early to shovel our driveway, and we took off for the airport in the middle of a snowstorm. Just as we made a turn in the road, we came to a screeching halt. The road had disappeared, covered in a snow drift.

Tiger walked back to the house to get the snowmobile and called the sheriff. The main highway had been plowed, and the sheriff said he would have two cars waiting there for us. We had one snowmobile suit, and Tiger took turns driving us out to the highway, one by one. Our neighbor saw what was going on, and he came along with his horse-drawn hay spreader, which was on runners, and he carried our luggage out to the waiting sheriff's cars. Even with all of that help, we missed our plane to Chicago.

The sheriff called ahead, and we made arrangements to charter a plane. Two limos were waiting when we landed in Chicago to take us to the plane that was boarding for the flight to Honolulu. When we plopped down in our seats, I realized we had made the flight with three minutes to spare. If they had given out an award for the most forms of transportation used in one day, I know we would have won. I guess going to Hawaii was the prize.

The trip was wonderful. We saw all of the sights, and visited the palace of the last monarch in Hawaiian history, Queen Liliuokalani. Our daughter Jill had been studying about Hawaii in school, and when she saw all of the exhibits, she began to cry because of the way the kingdom and the people there had been treated.

Some people don't like going to league meetings, but maybe because we usually were able to take some of the kids and combine them with a pleasure trip, I was able to relax and have a good time. I was fortunate to become friends with many of the NFL team owners, and I will never forget the way I was treated so kindly by people like George Halas and Art Rooney. People like Wellington Mara, Joe Robbie and Max Winter also were very nice to me and made those trips enjoyable as well as professionally beneficial. One league meeting was held in Phoenix and, as a bonus, Sarah, Lisa and Jill attended with us.

After the meetings, we took one of the commuter planes to Maui and returned to Kaianapali Beach, where we had stayed during the Hula Bowl years earlier. The area had grown tremendously. We had taken a bike ride on our previous visit and not seen a car, but this time we tried it and had to cut the ride short because of all the traffic. It was very relaxing to walk on the beach and watch the whales. The kids tried to collect as many coconuts as they could find.

We were looking for an area to go swimming one day in Kaui, and after driving for about 30 minutes, we came upon a little sign on a cardboard box perched on a small stake: Poipu Beach.

There were no dressing rooms, and we didn't see any shops waiting to rent canoes. All we could see were perfect conditions for body surfing. For the next eight hours, we just absorbed the incredible beauty of this perfect beach. We swam, body surfed and sunned ourselves. No one even wanted to take a lunch break. It was a perfect family day. Today, that beach has four huge hotels and a championship golf course.

We took a cruise to the Caribbean during one off-season, and Jo and I took five of the kids with us. The children learned how to snorkel, and also how to shop. The children thought they were getting super bargains when we were in Haiti, and we ended up with 36 items that had to be checked through customs when we got back to Miami. One of the inspectors said they couldn't check all of the stuff, so they just waved us right through. Of course, my bag of dress clothes was the only thing that we couldn't find in Miami, and I was going directly to Milwaukee to give a speech. This was in February. Tiger went with me, and we landed in a blizzard. We had to go on a quick shopping spree so I would have proper clothes for the banquet. We were in beach clothes.

We enjoyed many great trips like that when our children were young, many to some of the most beautiful places in the world. I've always enjoyed the water and the beach. I also love the mountains here in Arizona. I will never forget doing a football clinic at the University of Connecticut, then spending a couple of days body surfing on the beach in Narragansett, Rhode Island, with my wife. There is something special about walking on the beach and playing in the water. It is a great, relaxing feeling, and I often found myself thinking, as we took those long walks on the beach, about if I was truly happy doing what I was doing.

I remembered before taking the job with the Packers how my friends said the greatest job in football was working as a head coach and general manager in the NFL. After three years, however, I had come to the conclusion that it wasn't all it was advertised to be, at least for me. I had been happier coaching in college, and I couldn't see myself continuing to coach in the NFL for an extended period. Before the 1974 season began, I made up my mind that if somebody contacted me about coaching at the college level again, I definitely would consider it.

I made that decision even before the year turned out to be one of the most difficult of my life. The players' union called a strike. Most teams stayed out of the training camps. Green Bay was targeted by the players as one of the key teams, because the town of Green Bay is a big union town. The head of the players' union was Ken Bowman, an attorney who also happened to be a Packer player, having been a very good center for Lombardi, Bengtson and me.

The players set up picket lines, and a lot of hard feelings developed. It wasn't as bad in some places, like Minnesota, where Bud Grant was much more relaxed. Because of my dual title as general manager, I squarely was labeled a member of management, and that made me the enemy.

Having to negotiate contracts with the players, and then having to coach them on the field, was difficult even under the best of circumstances. I've always felt a coach could perform better if he didn't have to concern himself with salaries and incentive bonuses. The coach's job should strictly be directed to trying to put the best players he can on the field and trying to do whatever it takes to get his team the victory. I'd like to think I never coached any differently because I also was the general manager, but I can't honestly say I did that.

That issue came to a boiling point during the strike in 1974. The Packers' Board of Directors ordered me to play the preseason with rookies. Some other teams took the same stance, hoping the strike would be broken before the regular season began. We had to take buses to cross the picket lines, and every time we did it, I became more and more uncomfortable.

Growing up, my hometown of Proctor, which means so much to me, was close to 100 percent unionized. A devastating strike had

Captain Dan Devine (front row, center, No. 62), University of Minnesota–Duluth, 1947.

A studious Dan Devine in his senior year of college.

Dan and Jo Devine and their twins picnic amid the military housing at Michigan State.

The Chicago Tribune *called Duffy Daugherty's 1954 Michigan State coaching staff the greatest ever. Included on that staff were (front row, left to right) Burt Smith, Sonny Grandelius, Daugherty, and Dan Devine; (back row, left to right) Bill Yeoman, Bob Devaney, and Don Mason.*

Coach Devine is carried off the field following ASU's 20-0 victory over Arizona in 1956.

Coach Devine with ASU's 1956 co-captains Charlie Mackey and Dave Graybill.

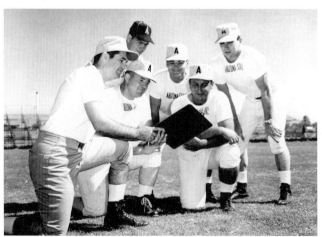

Coach Devine (left) and his talented Arizona State coaching staff of (kneeling, left to right) Gordon Serr and Al Onofrio, and (standing, left to right) George Stevenson, Frank Kush, and Tom Fletcher.

ASU's undefeated (10-0-0), nationally ranked 1957 squad.

Sideline action at ASU–Frank Kush (left) and Dan Devine.

One of Missouri's all-time greats, Johnny Roland, played for Dan Devine.

Devine's first Tiger captains in 1958, Charlie Rash (left) and Don Chadwick.

Devine traveled to Europe in 1960 for a coaching clinic.

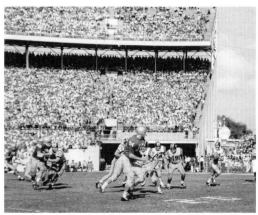

Quarterback Fred Brossart rolls out against Georgia in the 1960 Orange Bowl.

Devine and 1968 Missouri captain Carl Garber.

Missouri players Gus Otto (back row, left) and Bill Tobin (back row, right) help Coach Devine recruit Steve Kenemore in 1965.

The 1969 Missouri team was one of Devine's best.

Coach Devine at Green Bay.

Coach Devine at Missouri.

The 23rd head coach at Notre Dame.

The Devine family, circa 1970.

Jo and Dan Devine being welcomed to Green Bay in 1971.

Jo Devine settles in at Green Bay in 1971.

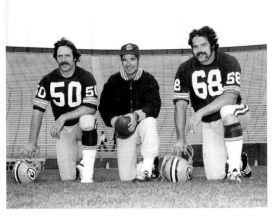

Devine and 1972 Packer captains Jim Carter (left) and Gale Gillingham.

Receiving the NFC's 1972 Coach of the Year Award.

Dan Devine and comedian Jerry Lewis.

Coach Devine weathers the elements with Packer quarterback John Hadl, the NFL's Most Valuable Player in 1973.

Another chum of Devine's is baseball great Stan "The Man" Musial.

Good friends (left to right) Bob Broeg, Dan Devine, and Jack Buck.

Devine settles into his new office at Notre Dame, with reminders of his past triumphs.

At the Mayo Clinic in 1974, absorbing the news of wife Jo's MS diagnosis.

Jim Stock (left) and Ed Bauer (right), Coach Devine's first Fighting Irish captains.

Putting in late hours to earn the national championship.

The 1977 Notre Dame tri-captains (left to right) Willie Fry, Terry Eurick, and Ross Browner.

Devine with his greatest Irish player, Joe Montana.

A beaming Dan Devine after his squad "showered" him following a 1976 victory over Alabama.

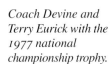
Working on the Fighting Irish depth chart.

Coach Devine and the 1977 Notre Dame-Southern California scoreboard.

Coach Devine and Terry Eurick with the 1977 national championship trophy.

Father Joyce and Coach Devine enjoying one of their many banquet appearances.

Devine chats with coaching legend George Allen.

Receiving the John F. Kennedy Award in 1978.

Leading the 1978 defending national champions into the new season.

Devine and 1978 tri-captains (left to right) Jerome Heavens, Bob Golic, and Joe Montana.

Dave Waymer, Dave Huffman, and Kris Haines admiring the final score of the Cotton Bowl in 1979.

Vagas Ferguson receives his coach's thanks in 1979.

Devine presents a game ball to Scott Zettek after Notre Dame's 1980 victory over Miami.

Harry Oliver's game-winning kick versus Michigan in 1980.

With former Irish captain and friend, Rocky Bleier.

Coach Devine with an all-time great Irish running back, Allen Pinkett.

Kids galore at Notre Dame's 1978 photo day.

Coach Devine and a friend at an orphanage in Mexico City.

Visiting a youngster at the Shriners' Hospital.

Steelers coach Chuck Noll with the
Irish head coach.

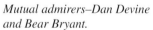
Sharing a laugh with Gerry Faust.

With Barry
Switzer at the
1982 Hall of
Fame dinner.

Mutual admirers–Dan Devine
and Bear Bryant.

With Bob Golic (center) at the
20-year reunion of the '77
Irish champs.

Coach and Mrs. Devine are honored at
halftime of the 1985 Notre Dame-Michigan
State game, prior to his induction into the
National Football Foundation Hall of Fame.

The 1977 Fighting Irish reunion.

Rudy Ruettiger and the coach who played him.

This 1998 Notre Dame ticket honored five of the greatest Fighting Irish coaches.

With broadcasting great Walter Cronkite.

With good friends Harry Caray (left) and President Ronald Reagan (center).

(Left to right) Bill Shover, Bill Bidwell, Wellington Mara, and Devine were instrumental in bringing the Super Bowl to Tempe, Arizona.

Three of ASU's greatest coaches: (left to right) Bruce Snyder, Devine, and Frank Kush.

The Devine grandchildren gathered in the mid-1990s for this photograph.

University of Missouri Provost Brady Deaton and University of Missouri chancellor Richard Wallace surround Dan Devine as he receives an honorary degree at the 1999 Honors

An exterior view of the Devine Pavilion.

once gripped the town and affected everyone living there. I had always been a supporter of unions, but here I was stuck squarely in the middle of this dispute which I had absolutely no control over and it really created a bad taste in my mouth. It was the first time I had heard the word "scab" since I left Proctor.

We went through the picket lines in an old bus, with the windows up. There was no air conditioning, even though it was summer, and we could hear the veterans yelling at us. The police were there, and made certain the bus was allowed through the lines, but I was always afraid that we would hit somebody.

Our training camp was at St. Norbert College, and we had no way to keep the rookies away from the striking veterans as they moved around the campus in their free time. The veterans were trying to pressure the rookies, and it was hard for those players to know what to do. They knew this training camp was their opportunity to show they could play in the NFL and make the team, but nobody expected the strike to last forever, and going against the striking veterans would make those rookies' lives hell when the veterans did come back. I don't think I got more than three hours of sleep a night during that time.

Ken Bowman is still a good friend of mine today, but the differences between our sides had to put a strain on that relationship. I ran into him one time on the campus and he said to me, "Coach, don't take things so seriously." I didn't smile or chuckle. I did take it too seriously. I still had three daughters in high school and there were other problems developing that I didn't want to face. In spite of all the difficulties and distractions, we somehow managed to win our four preseason games.

A year earlier, Jo had begun to develop the first symptoms of multiple sclerosis. She had been an active person all of her life, and an excellent athlete. She used to score in the 80s in golf consistently, but her scores began to go into the 90s, and then she couldn't break 100. We couldn't figure out what was happening until one day, when she went in for an eye exam. During the routine checkup, the doctor recommended that Jo see an eye specialist, and he in turn sent us to the Mayo Clinic in Rochester, Minnesota. Doctors there made the diagnosis of multiple sclerosis.

The news was difficult enough, but the rumors from people who didn't know the true story were worse. There were stories that Jo was having problems with alcoholism. I can see how people who are in high-profile positions, either in politics or the entertainment world or sports, really have their lives affected and in some cases ruined by unfounded rumors like this. We tried to put a stop to those kinds of stories as quickly as possible.

There were other rumors which spread about the tough times we were experiencing in Green Bay. One of our dogs was named Earth, and one morning at 5 a.m. during hunting season, I heard what I knew was a rifle shot. I went outside and found Earth. He had indeed been shot. Rumors circulated that some disgruntled fans or anti-Devine people had shot my dog. I honestly don't believe that was what happened. My guess is that some young folks were out joyriding in the country, probably had been drinking, and Earth probably had taken after them chasing their car and they shot him. Our dogs always were fenced in, but Earth knew how to get out when he wanted to.

He was lying in the middle of the yard when I found him, but luckily we were able to get him to the vet in time and he recovered from his wounds.

We weren't so lucky with another of our dogs. It was only a couple of days later, ironically, when the dog wandered over to a nearby farm and began chasing the farmer's ducks. The farmer, a neighbor who we knew very well, fired a gun at the dog, intending to scare him and get him away from his ducks. Well, the bullet happened to hit the dog and killed him. He had every right to shoot at the dog, and he knew it and I knew it.

Still, he felt terrible about what happened. I saw him walking toward our house, carrying the dead dog in his arms, crying uncontrollably. He kept saying, "I didn't mean to kill him," and I knew that was true. Still, more rumors spread, even though it was a total accident, and that night I was down at his house, playing basketball with his kids.

All those rumors reflected badly on the good people of Green Bay. Most of the people we met were very genuine and nice to us, and it was unfortunate that a few incidents and rumors such as that marred our stay there. Negotiators from both sides finally reached an agreement to end the strike, but a lot of hard feelings remained for a long time.

It just so happened that while we were in the middle of the strike and all of the other problems, I received a phone call from Dr. Joe Kearney, the athletic director of the University of Washington. He told me they were looking for a head coach, and he was calling to offer me the job.

I told him, "The season hasn't even started. How do you know you'll want me when the season's over?" He said, "Well, we'll take a chance on that, but I'm offering you the job." Their coach, Jim Owens, already had told Kearney that he would be retiring at the end of the year. Joe Kearney was one of the all-time great ADs and is still a good friend, and Jim Owens was a superior coach.

I wasn't certain how that made me feel. I liked the confidence he was showing me by offering me the job, basically six months in advance. I have never wanted to take anyone else's job, which is the way I think most coaches feel, and that's one of the reasons I never applied for any job after first going to work at Michigan State.

The one factor I recognized, however, was that if I did decide to leave Green Bay and the NFL after the 1974 season, I knew there would be some other good job possibilities.

During the season, Joe came to Green Bay for some games, ate dinner at our home and even went on the road to watch some of our games. It eventually leaked out to the media in Seattle, as we knew it would, that Joe was trying to hire me to become the coach at Washington. That didn't bother him, and he still continued to try to convince me to take the job.

Jo and I thought about taking a trip to Seattle to visit the campus and the area, but we didn't have to go. The school virtually brought the campus to us through literature and other materials, all showing the beautiful blue skies and yacht-filled lakes. It looked like a beautiful place, and I knew it was a top university.

Even though I had kind of decided in my mind what I wanted to do, I still owed it to the Packers' management and the players, and also to myself, to do the best job of coaching I could during the year. If I was leaving, the one thing I wanted to make certain of was that I left the new coach with a better team and a better situation than the one I inherited. And I did.

One of the moves we decided to make, which I thought would really help us, was trading for a new quarterback, John Hadl. We gave up quite a bit to get John, but not as much as other teams had given up for Jim Plunkett and Roman Gabriel. Hadl had been the NFL's MVP in 1973, so he could really help us *now*. We were getting a huge offensive transfusion. John had All-Pro years ahead of him when we brought him to Green Bay. It was my privilege to coach Earl Morrall, Bart Starr, John Hadl and Joe Montana. They were quite a National Football League MVP foursome. I also coached Gary Lane, three-time Big Eight Player of the Year, who would have been an NFL MVP had he played quarterback 25 years later.

I also traded linebacker Tom MacLeod to Baltimore for Ted Hendricks and a second-round pick. In the next year, 1975, Hendricks earned two first-round picks for Green Bay from Oakland for being traded there. His loyalty to me made him unpopular in Green Bay. These three draft picks were extra bonuses the Packers needed to replace the picks given in the Hadl trade. These extra picks for Hendricks and Robinson meant that we got John very reasonably in the overall picture.

We also got a second-round pick from Washington when the retired Dave Robinson returned to the league. John Hadl's first start was a 20-3 victory over the Chicago Bears. His second start was a 19-7 win against Minnesota. His third start was a 34-0 win over San Diego.

My Missouri teams had played against John when he was at Kansas, and I always was a great fan of his and respected his ability. I couldn't have been more pleased with how John played. He stepped right in and took over.

We had three games to play, and I really thought I had the kind of team that was capable of also winning those games and playing our way into the playoffs. Unfortunately, that didn't happen, and the inner turmoil and politics that were surrounding our franchise partly contributed to our losing our last three games.

One of the disturbing parts of that season to me was the fact that I didn't have 100 percent loyalty from the board. I know that in any situation where you are working with that large of a group of people—close to 70, counting all of the players and coaching staff—that you are going to have cliques and have people who don't get along with each other. I've seen it everywhere I've been. But I had a rapport with 95 percent of my players.

One player who was tremendously loyal to me, and I never will forget it, was Ted Hendricks, the outstanding linebacker. He was an All-Pro on three different teams and played in four Super Bowls. Ted called me a number of times at home during the 1974 season, just to talk. He called one night after he found out one member of the team's Board of Directors was negotiating a new contract with a player without my input. I had already known about it, but Ted thought he was letting me in on a scoop and it was important for him to get it off his chest.

It wasn't as if the entire board was working against me. I think it really was just one member. The player involved was one of the best guys on the team, and probably was worth what he was being offered, but I didn't like it that the negotiations were going on behind my back. It made his first contract in 1971 look like peanuts.

Anytime you are battling situations like that, you have to find a release and a way to forget about your problems or they will drive you nuts. One of the things I did that year was get involved with a lot of the pickup shirts versus skins basketball games between the players. They invited me to play and be a point guard, because I certainly didn't want to get mixed up with all of the big guys underneath the basket. Those games helped develop a good bond among the players, who banded together across all lines—positions, size, race, veterans, rookies. It was a unifying experience and also provided good relaxation. It was ironic that bonding like that was going on at the same time a few people were displaying a lack of loyalty to the team.

I probably should have brought the whole issue to a head a lot sooner than I did, and I guess somebody with a more forceful personality, like Lombardi, probably would have done that. I just kept hoping that Ole, working with the board, would be able to solve the problems, but it turned out he wasn't able to do that.

Team owners and presidents who show great loyalty and respect for coaches when they are going through a tough season definitely have my respect and admiration. It is easy to get caught up in the "lynch mob" mentality and look for a scapegoat in the midst of all your problems, and the most obvious one available usually is the coach. It can't just be one player who is the cause of a bad year, and it is an old cliché that you can't fire all the players.

Loyalty is one of the reasons I had such tremendous respect for Art Rooney, the longtime owner of the Pittsburgh Steelers and one of the great men in football. In the midst of a 1-13 season the Steelers were suffering through under Coach Chuck Noll, some of the players took it upon themselves to pay a visit to Rooney's office. They wanted him to hear their complaints about Noll. Mr. Rooney listened politely, then said two things: "You can poop in your hat, and when you leave the office, I'm going to call Coach Noll and tell him that you're here." Art was truly a special person. I have a distinct memory of him which came a few years later, moments after his team won its first Super Bowl. I happened to be there and he saw me, and in the midst of the big celebration, he pulled me into a private room to talk about Notre Dame football.

The Packers were playing our final game of the year at Atlanta. We had finished our final workout at Green Bay and were preparing to get on the bus to head for the airport when a team official came out to me with a message. I had just received a phone call from a "Father Joyce from Washington, D.C." I knew immediately who was calling and why—Ara Parseghian had retired at Notre Dame.

I went in and called Father Joyce, whom I had spent time with and developed a good friendship with when I was coaching at Missouri and when he was searching for a coach several years earlier. The conversation lasted less than a minute. He was calling to tell me the head coach's job at Notre Dame was open, and he offered me the job.

Now, I had more to think about on our plane flight to Atlanta. Because of the way the University of Washington had been courting me all year, I already had decided to tell Ole after the team returned from Atlanta that I was stepping down. I wasn't still entirely certain that I would take the Washington job, but I knew there would be other opportunities. I still was able to prepare mentally for the Atlanta game. The Atlanta game was by far the top priority.

I told Father Joyce I would be comfortable with whatever terms he came up with, which was another bad decision in the mind of my attorney. I hadn't consulted him when I took the Green Bay job, and I didn't consult him again this time. I knew I was dealing with honorable people, and I trusted Father Joyce that he would give me a fair deal. He did, giving me a base salary of $35,000 a year and a $10,000 bonus for going to a bowl game. This was well before salaries skyrocketed.

When we arrived in Atlanta, I made arrangements to go to dinner the night before the game with Jack Buck, my broadcaster friend. He was broadcasting our game for CBS TV. I had a great friendship with Jack, as well as a great working relationship on KMOX, where we did a weekly show, and when he asked me about my future, I knew I couldn't lie to him. I said, "Jack, I can't tell you this for the record, but I won't be returning to Green Bay as coach after the season."

He asked me where I was going, and I told him I couldn't say, but that it was considered by most people to be the number-one collegiate job in the United States. He guessed it was Notre Dame. I had to make him promise that he wouldn't use the information, and he was true to his word. I couldn't have trusted a lot of people in the media with that information or it would have gone out on the air immediately. Jack always has been a friend I could trust.

We played the Falcons in a driving rainstorm and lost 10-3. We could have had a tying touchdown, except for losing a fumble inside the one-yard line after a long drive. We had lost a game to the Eagles in much the same manner. Of the eight Packer losses in 1974, two were by one point, another was by two points and another was by a touchdown.

I said goodbye individually to the players after the game. I really felt we had a good team with a great nucleus returning for the next season. Willie Buchanon was coming back from his broken leg. John Brockington and MacArthur Lane were among the best running backs in the league. Adding Ted Hendricks gave us three quality linebackers. We also had a very good group of assistant coaches, and I was grooming Vince Tobin, as well, to be a part of that staff. Vince is now the head coach of the Arizona Cardinals.

We flew back to Green Bay. After we arrived, I called Ole and told him I would like to drop by his house for a few minutes to talk. I told him I had decided to resign. He said, "The majority of the Packers' board, as recently as yesterday, have given you full and complete support."

I told him I understood the situation and appreciated his support, but believed this decision was best for myself, my family and the Packers. I really respected Ole.

Then I placed a call to Joe Kearney to let him know of my decision. He was en route to Miami, but I reached his assistant and explained everything to him. I actually was relieved that I didn't have to talk to Joe; it would have been much harder saying no to him after all of the work he had put in during the season to try to convince me to take the job. Joe told me later that as soon as he heard Ara had resigned, he told his wife, "We've just lost Dan Devine to Notre Dame."

It was strange. When I went to bed Saturday night in Atlanta, I was the head coach of the Packers, the future head coach at Notre Dame and at least one person thought I was going to be the head coach at the University of Washington. It was an unsettling time, but I told myself I was doing the right thing.

We scheduled a press conference for the next day in Green Bay to announce my resignation. Then Jo and I flew to South Bend for the news conference to announce that I was taking over as coach at Notre Dame. I told Jo, "I'm emotionally spent. I haven't had a day off since June. The strike was fantastically draining. The season was fantastically draining. Even announcing that I'm taking a new job is very difficult."

I could tell from the minute the news conference began that I was coming into another high-pressure position, but I expected that. Ara and nearly all of his predecessors had enjoyed great success at Notre Dame. The fans and alumni expect their teams to be successful. The school administration expected their players to graduate and then win (in that order). At any place where they have those high expectations, whether it is Green Bay, Notre Dame or anywhere else, you are going to be following in the footsteps of some pretty good people. If you're willing to settle for a mediocre position, maybe they won't have much of a history with big names. If you're going to coach in the NFL or for a prestigious college, however, you can be assured that all of the coaches who came before you were highly qualified.

I was thankful to have had the experience of coaching with the Packers and in the NFL, and I was convinced the situations and lessons I had learned there had made me a better coach. I made so many good friends while there, including Jerry Mortell, who recently retired as the Packers' official timekeeper. He was and still is one of my closest friends. Green Bay was good to us in many respects, especially in giving us good friends who were so kind to us.

Chapter Seven

NOTRE DAME

Even though I was very excited about the challenges and opportunities that were waiting for me at Notre Dame, I also had to admit I was tired, emotionally and physically. The NFL season is rough on the players, but it's also rough on the coaches and their families. You work the entire season without a day off, and you often are putting in 14-hour days or even longer.

Now, just at the point in the year where life can slow down a bit and you can catch your breath, here I was starting on another treadmill. I would have enjoyed a few days or weeks to recharge my batteries before getting started, but I found out that just wasn't possible.

Ara had decided to retire on his own. I was grateful for having him still around to coach the Orange Bowl, which gave me a chance to talk with him about the players, and he was candid and honest.

It also was an advantage for me to be able to watch the Orange Bowl game, to kind of get my own opinions and ideas about the players. You can always watch films of the previous year's games, but you get a much better idea about what is going on when you are watching the game live. You don't know what's going to happen, and you get much more emotionally involved than sitting in a room watching it on tape. Notre Dame won 13-11.

I watched the game on television while recruiting.

A lot of people don't realize when they begin their coaching careers how much more work is involved than merely designing an offense and defense and calling the plays during the game. If that's all there was to it, it would be a simple job and a lot of people could do it. But being a head coach of either a major college or a professional team is a multidimensional task. Two of the toughest parts of the job are the relationships with the media and handling the pressure of everybody wanting a piece of your time.

A coach also has to be an expert on physiology, anatomy, kinesiology and psychology. Those elements don't change from job to job, but the biggest part of the job at Notre Dame that I was not prepared for was the extreme pressure placed on my time.

Even in spring practice, I found out that by the end of practice, and after taking a shower, going to the training table for dinner, conducting meetings and then going back to the office to return all of the phone calls that had accumulated during the day, it often was midnight and I still had a lot of work to do. I found out it was sometimes impossible to return a call to a friend, even those in the media.

I had been away from campus life for only four years, but it didn't take long for me to realize a lot of things had changed in the interim. We were still experiencing the effects of the Vietnam War, and students were becoming increasingly outspoken in their beliefs and attitudes not only against the war but against everything and everybody in society that they thought was wrong.

When I walked into my first team meeting shortly after the holidays, I found one player who was kind of lying on the floor. He had longer hair than I liked and a big hole in his blue jeans. I admit I was tired and worn out from a lack of sleep and worrying about getting my family moved and settled, and I said something I probably shouldn't have said. This guy had just lit my short fuse, however, seeing him lying there like that.

I said something like, "Why don't you sit in one of the chairs and get a decent pair of slacks? Certainly if you're going to represent this great university you should be more cognizant of current trends."

That player flunked out of school that spring. Most of my guys adjusted to me, as I did to the times.

I found out later that their style of dress was more acceptable than I would have liked, so I was forced to mellow a little bit. One player who taught me how to do that was Dave Huffman, a kid who played center for four years for me at Notre Dame and was definitely a free spirit. He was a great young man and a super player. We were able to get along only after we sat down and had a long talk and came to an agreement. He would obey all of the team rules off the field, but he was free to pick his own friends and do his own thing. From the moment he walked through the practice field gate, he was mine until the evening meetings were concluded. We never had anymore problems after that.

No matter whether I was at Arizona State, Missouri or Notre Dame, I always tried to tell my players how important a commitment they were making by agreeing to be part of the football team. It took all of their time and energy, and at the same time they were making a commitment to do their best in their schoolwork, because the academics at those schools also were very demanding. It was important to me that our players excel at both football and academics.

I was fortunate to see many of my former players go on and earn graduate degrees and move into the career fields of medicine, law, engineering, dentistry, economics and other professions. I was extremely proud of all of those kids, because in that era it would have been very easy to let those goals slip away.

In the turmoil of the times, I think all college coaches had to say, "Are you willing to sacrifice these other things on campus to devote yourself to obtaining these other goals?" We wanted to win, but we also wanted to do it legally and wanted our players to enjoy all of the benefits their scholarships provided.

Over the years, I came to resent the widely accepted belief that all coaches cheat or that a young man cannot earn a medical degree while participating in intercollegiate athletics. People can do both, but they have to want to do both. As a coach, I never did break or even shade the rules. On many occasions I have asked people to name a profession, and I can quickly name the number of my former players who have gone on to become successful in that occupation.

I have also learned to appreciate the wisdom of treating my players as people first and players second, giving adequate attention and importance to their talents and problems and futures beyond athletics. Dealing with them as athletic resources alone and discarding them when you think they can be of no further assistance to you is a mistake that some coaches make, and I think those sins come back to haunt them. I have seen over the years that treating players as people first usually helps improve a team's success rate as well.

My conversations with Father Joyce helped educate me on the situation that I was inheriting and the level of talent that we had returning for the 1975 team. I also got briefed on the schedule, which was always something I wanted to know. I was a little surprised when I showed up for our first spring practice and found only half the team was there. I always thought football was the most important part in these kids' lives, but was pleasantly surprised to learn that the missing players were busy studying for exams. We learned to run practices in two shifts to accommodate everybody, and even postponed a scrimmage so the kids could complete their academic requirements. As I said, I wasn't expecting that to be the case, but I agreed with it 100 percent.

The other surprise I quickly received after settling into the job was that the recruiting of new players was, in some ways, more difficult than at either Arizona State or Missouri. I had assumed it would be easy, with just the mention of Notre Dame being enough to attract a lot of the top players from around the country. I also thought the kids who did come wanted to be there and wanted to do their best, but I found out that wasn't always the case.

During one of those early spring practices, it was obvious that one of the younger quarterbacks wasn't playing well and showing good command of the plays. It was the night before a scrimmage. I asked the quarterback why he was struggling, and he admitted to me that he had been shooting pool the night before instead of studying his playbook. His name was Joe Montana. I learned later he was just nervous.

I'm certain I was pretty rough on him, probably too rough, but I wanted him to realize that he had to improve and give himself the best chance he could to become the best football player he could be. He had entered spring drills as the last quarterback on the depth chart, and yet he was the starter in the spring game. I knew I had uncovered a gem and just had to find a way to polish it.

The officials who made up our schedule had not done me any favors. We opened with a late Monday night game on national television at Boston College, then had to come back five days later and play one of our biggest rivals, Purdue, on the road. A week later we had to play Northwestern, giving us three games—almost a third of our season—in a 12-day span.

We beat Boston College 17-3, but the game was more memorable because it set a BC attendance record. We didn't get back to the team hotel until 2 a.m, but fortunately we had arranged to have a buffet waiting for us. The coaching staff ate, then slept for a few hours before getting up to watch films. The players got up at 10 a.m. for a "cowboy breakfast" of steak and eggs, then we flew back to South Bend.

Other than the traffic jam, I will never forget my first game at Notre Dame because of the festivities that surrounded that day.

When we got back to South Bend, we knew we only had a couple of days to prepare in the heat for Purdue, and we just decided to not overwork the players in practice and basically run the same game plan we had against Boston College. Maybe because we were a little more rested because of the light week in practice without pads, we played extremely well and won 17-0.

With the outcome decided, I inserted that young quarterback from the bottom of the depth chart, Joe Montana. He threw one pass, and it was intercepted.

We had a little more time to prepare for Northwestern, but all of those plans were altered when our starting quarterback, Rick Slager, was injured early in the game. Joe was second on the depth chart, so I sent him in to play when Rick got hurt. Joe passed for one touchdown and ran for another and we won the game, improving our record to 3-0.

I really hadn't seen enough of Joe, either in practices or in the games, to determine how good a quarterback he was going to be;

there was no film on him. Because he was on the bottom of the depth chart when we came, he wasn't even getting much work in practice. For some reason I kept finding myself drawn to him, however, and just thought he was the guy I was going to develop as our quarterback. I don't think I've ever seen anyone progress and move up as quickly as he did.

I still on occasion today catch myself looking at Brett Favre and saying, "My gosh, there's a big Joe Montana." Or I will look at Steve Young and say, "There's a left-handed Joe Montana." But I really think there honestly was only one Joe Montana, and all of the Notre Dame fans were about to find out all about him.

Our next game was against Michigan State. We had a decision to make at quarterback, because Rick Slager was healthy and ready to play. Instead, I picked Joe as the starter. Looking back on it, I know he wasn't ready and that I was rushing things. I was just so excited by his potential that I wasn't as patient as I should have been.

Joe didn't play well. He completed two of five passes, for a total of 19 yards, and was intercepted once. We lost, 10-3, in a very disappointing game against Michigan State.

What I didn't take time to realize, while thinking about the loss, was how young our team was. In addition to Joe, who was a sophomore, we had a lot of key people on our roster who were freshmen and they were just finding out what college football was all about. One of our starting linebackers, Bob Golic, was a freshman. Jerome Heavens was a freshman running back who would eventually lead our team in rushing for two of his four years. Jim Browner, as a freshman fullback, was also developing into an outstanding strong safety, and we also were getting good contributions from Dave Huffman and Joe Restic, who as a freshman, set a Notre Dame punting record.

I decided to start Slager at quarterback the following week, at North Carolina, but when we fell behind 14-6, I put Joe into the game. He led us down the field on one possession, converting a two-pointer on a pass, then, with 1:03 remaining, he threw an 80-yard touchdown pass to Ted Burgmeier. The play was more Ted's than Joe's because he made a great catch and spun out of a defender's reach, then sprinted 80 yards past everybody else on his way to the end zone. We went on to win the game 21-14. It was the beginning of Joe's reputation as the "comeback kid" at Notre Dame.

I tried to find out as much about Joe as I could, and looking back over what had happened the previous year, I learned he had completed only one of six passes in his freshman year and had been intercepted once. He had run the ball four times, gaining zero yards. Two other freshmen had more pass attempts—and all three were playing on Notre Dame's junior varsity team. Watching him against North Carolina, it was hard to believe it was the same young man.

The following week at Air Force, Joe started the game but threw two interceptions, and we found ourselves behind 30-10 with about 13 minutes left. Later, we put Joe back into the lineup, and he rallied the team back, running for one touchdown and passing for another, and we eventually won the game 31-30. When you looked at the statistics after the game, you saw that he hadn't really been overwhelming—he completed seven of 18 passes with three interceptions—but somehow we had found a way to win. That was quickly what I was most impressed with regarding Joe—he was one of those special young men who almost always finds a way to win, no matter what it is. Captain Ed Bauer had a fantastic game.

In my mind, Joe was now firmly entrenched as our starter as we prepared for our biggest game of the season to that point, against third-ranked Southern Cal, at home. Again, Joe's stats were not all that impressive, but he had led the team to a lead in the fourth quarter. The Trojans had a great running back in Ricky Bell, and we knew he was going to be getting the ball most of the time on the last drive. We tried everything we could to stop him. Vince Evans was USC's quarterback, and near the end of the game he faked the handoff to Bell and kept the ball himself and scored the winning touchdown. Almost all of our players had tackled Bell, and I couldn't blame them because I would have done exactly the same thing. It was a devastating loss, but I was still proud of the effort all of our young players had put in.

We played Navy the following week with Joe now as our starter, and just when I thought Joe was going to be making even more progress, he broke the index finger on his throwing hand, sidelining him for the rest of the season.

Joe was not the only exceptional young man on that football team, however. There also was a player on the roster named Rudy Ruettiger, and anybody who has seen the movie *Rudy* knows all about him.

He was a walk-on with no scholarship aid. He came to practice every day and worked so hard that on numerous occasions I'd send him in from practice early, a reward for the effort he was putting in.

Rudy became a very close friend to Jo and me. Jo and the rest of my family first met Rudy in the summer of 1975, when he visited our home numerous times, which was in Bremen, Indiana, near South Bend.

After his graduation, during one of my trips back to Notre Dame, we discussed writing the story of his life. At this point, we made a phone call to Angelo Pizzo, the screenwriter of *Hoosiers*. Angelo and I talked for a long time. Finally, Angelo said, "This movie will be a success only if you agree to be the heavy."

I told Angelo I would do anything to help Rudy, including being the heavy. I didn't realize that I would be such a heavy heavy. The story basically detailed Rudy's struggle to achieve success in life.

I didn't think much more about the project until I received this huge script in the mail. I didn't read it, or else I probably would have questioned a couple of errors. As it turned out, the movie has some distortions, which is often the case with the public record. But by the same token, it's a good, healthy movie; it's one you can take your kids to see and not have to worry about. It provides people with a lot of enjoyment.

The senior vice president of Columbia Pictures is Paul Smith, brother of one of my dearest friends, Dr. Pat Smith, whom I hired as the team physician at Missouri.

Paul and Pat took me to a fabulous dinner at the studio. I told Paul, and later, Angelo, that I thought it would have been a better film if they had just told Rudy's true story. Paul also rented a theater in Columbia, Missouri, and sent a crew to show the premiere of the movie to me and my friends. Dr. Smith's wife, Karen, cried through the whole showing. Rudy's done a lot of interviews, and in every one he's truthful and kind about me.

Just recently I received an award, in Las Vegas, for service to college football. Rudy made the presentation, and he did a beautiful job. I've appeared with him on numerous programs, and we remain close friends. He now lives in Las Vegas and is a great inspirational speaker. He also attended a retirement dinner in St. Louis for me.

Probably in part because I was so tired after going straight from the Packers' job into the Notre Dame job, the 1975 season wore on me more than any season I could remember. Football seasons seem so short, you can't believe it when they're over.

As we neared the end of the season, getting ready to play Georgia Tech in the final home game of the year, it dawned on me that it would be the perfect opportunity to reward Rudy for all of his hard work. I told the coaching staff on Monday, "I want to dress Rudy for this game."

Everybody agreed it was a great idea, and Rudy had to pinch himself, I think, to make certain he wasn't dreaming. I think he didn't really expect to play in the game; just being in uniform on the sidelines was a big enough thrill for him.

I wanted him to play, however.

He thought of himself as a defensive player. We had to score to force a kickoff in order for Rudy to get in the game.

He had his moment in the spotlight. He deserved to dress and play; he had worked very hard during his years at Notre Dame.

The final game of the year was in Miami, and as we got off the plane, Ed Bauer, the captain of the team, handed me a written team statement that showed the players' unqualified support of my work at Notre Dame and their complete faith in me. It was beautifully written and it still means a great deal to me. It absolutely wasn't necessary, but it certainly was a good boost to my morale, if nothing else. It was an effort that Ed organized, with the help of Steve Quehl and Captain Jim Stock, and was complete with the signatures of every member of the team.

We won the game easily and finished with an 8-3 record and were invited to play in the Cotton Bowl, but we declined their invitation. However, I did set some ground rules for future bowl invitations.

One thing I have always stressed to my teams is that if they wanted the support of the other athletes on campus, then they had to be willing to support the other teams as well, including women's teams. We had an opportunity to do that during our spring practice in 1976. We allowed the women's field hockey team to play a game on the synthetic-turf practice field, while we moved over and practiced on a wet grass field. We all then went over and cheered on the field hockey team, which included my daughter, Sarah. Taking the football team to the field hockey game turned out to be a morale booster for all concerned. I really didn't have any ulterior motives in mind, other than helping out another Notre Dame team, but it left everybody with a good, warm feeling.

There were very limited women's athletic programs in those days, and even though all six of my girls were very good athletes, they were not able to have access to the kinds of opportunities that young women have today. The Title IX act in 1972 ensured that women got equal opportunities, and it's exciting now to see so many young women getting the chance to succeed in athletics.

Whether it's men or women playing sports, one lesson I learned a long time ago is that sometimes they are going to get hurt. Unfortunately for the Notre Dame football team in 1976, the player who was injured was Joe Montana. He separated his shoulder in a pre-season practice and was lost for the year. It was just the beginning of a difficult season.

We lost one defensive tackle to injury, and had another declared academically ineligible, even though he met the NCAA and Big Ten standards but just missed the Notre Dame requirements (He needed a 2.0 GPA and had a 1.999). I thought those were enough problems to last an entire season, but more were to come.

Despite those early distractions, we actually started out the year well. We lost the opener to Pittsburgh, a team that would go on to win the national championship behind Heisman Trophy winner Tony Dorsett, but then we beat Purdue, Northwestern and Michigan State—my first visit back to East Lansing since leaving in 1955.

We improved to 4-1 with an easy win over Oregon, then went to South Carolina and won a close game, 13-6, in a place where it is very hard for visiting teams to win. Winning was one highlight, but another was seeing President Gerald Ford, who was there to receive an award.

As we came back onto the field after halftime, I passed just a few feet away from him and reached over and gave him a friendly pat on the back. "Great to see you again, Mr. President," I said. A year earlier he had been at Notre Dame making a speech, and sent word that he wanted to visit with me and Digger Phelps, Notre Dame's basketball coach.

All that week, I had practiced what I was going to say when I met him by going up to Jo and the kids and saying, "It's a pleasure to meet you, Mr. President." I really was afraid I was going to blow it and say something stupid. After his speech, the Secret Service agents ushered him into a private room with Digger and me, and we had a great conversation. He did surprise me, however, by telling me it was nice to see me again, as he walked in the door.

He then explained that he had met me on a couple of occasions when I was an assistant coach at Michigan State. The Secret Service kept trying to get him to leave, but he just wanted to stay and talk, and it is a great memory.

We were 6-1 going into a game against Georgia Tech in Atlanta. The night before the game, I couldn't sleep, which happened a lot. I went out for a walk with my friend, Jim Dougherty, an attorney in Miami who had been a big booster of Notre Dame for a long time.

As Jim and I walked, I thought I recognized a young man walking in front of us. I grabbed Jim's arm and said, "Is that Mark McLane up there?" McLane was one of the captains of the team that year, along with Willie Fry. At about the same moment, McLane saw Jim and ducked inside a bar.

I told Jim to go get him and bring him back to the hotel. I ran back to the hotel first, just to be certain he wasn't in his room and had a double walking around the streets of Atlanta. Mark wasn't in his room, a curfew violation. When he came into the hotel, I told him I wasn't certain what I was going to do, but I was inclined to drop him from the team. That's what I ended up doing.

Word quickly spread among the players, and it was the main topic of the pregame meal the following day. I was upset about it, because I didn't know if I had done the right thing, but several of the older players came up to me privately and said they supported my decision. They really believed letting him stay on the team would have weakened the team's discipline, and I believed that was true as well.

I didn't look at it as a great coaching decision, but as a failure on my part. I had not succeeded as a coach in getting the most out of a good football player. I don't know how big a distraction it was to the team, but we lost to a good Georgia Tech squad.

We didn't get any favors in our schedule to have time to re-group. Our next game was at home against nationally ranked Alabama and Coach Bear Bryant. Our kids rebounded well, however, behind quarterback Rick Slager and tight end Ken MacAfee. Slager hit 15 of 23 passes for 235 yards, six of them to MacAfee for 92 yards. After Slager was injured, Rusty Lisch made his Notre Dame debut and picked up two key first downs to let us put the game away, 21-18.

That game also marked the debut of freshman running back Vagas Ferguson, who had been working out with the freshman team. He rushed for 107 yards.

Coach Bryant was a good friend, and he gave me a huge compliment after the game, saying, "If Danny had been coaching Alabama and I had been on the other sideline, Alabama would have won." I don't think that was true, but I appreciated him saying it nonetheless.

We won again the next week, beating Miami 40-27, but then went out to Los Angeles to play Southern California in the final game of the season and lost 17-13. I think we were jinxed in those games, no matter where I was coaching. Anytime I took a team into Southern California to play, we had problems.

Before the season began, we told the players that if we received a bid to a bowl game, we were going to accept it. They didn't really care about the monetary implications for the school, but I explained that the money we would get from a bowl game would help provide more money for scholarships for minority students, and we were not going to be in a position to turn the bid down. They understood the reasons now.

The bid we received was to the Gator Bowl, where we played Joe Paterno's Penn State Nittany Lions. We played a solid game and won 20-9. Afterward, Paterno looked at the list of players we had returning, plus knowing Joe Montana would be back from injury, and predicted we would be the national champions. I suppose I should have thanked him for that comment, but all it really meant for me was more pressure from the media and fans.

It's easy for a coach to look as if he is doing a terrific job when he is surrounded by great players. On our team in 1977 were some great players, led by Joe Montana.

Joe was still having difficulty coming back from his shoulder separation the year before, and the trainer was not pleased with his progress as we got ready to open the season. Our trainer, Gene Paszkiet, and the team doctor didn't think he was ready to start the first game. As a coach, you can't risk playing guys who are not completely healthy, especially in the first game of the season, or you are running the risk they are going to get hurt worse and be out for a lot longer period of time.

With that in mind, we made the decision to go with Rusty Lisch at quarterback against defending national champion Pittsburgh. Lisch played well and we won a tough game, 19-9.

A week later, on September 17, we had an afternoon game against Ol' Miss in Jackson, Mississippi. Our dressing room had no air conditioning and was hot! I vividly recall that during the pregame warm-up, the stadium's public address announcer gave the temperature and the humidity—and the crowd's reaction was fantastic. You don't normally get that kind of crowd reaction over the announcement of the temperature. I should have somehow prepared our team better for the weather conditions.

We lost a tough game 20-13, but Ol' Miss deserved to win. They played better than we did, and when you prepare your team for the season, you've got to prepare for everything. That's why I've always been an advocate of the running game—you are going to need to rely on it more times during the season than you will a passing game. But you need both.

All through my career, the coaches on my staff and my players told me that I was always the same on Monday night, whether we had enjoyed a big victory or a heartbreaking loss on Saturday. This was not an easy thing for me. I might add that there were a number of necessary things in coaching that weren't easy for me.

Losses affected me greatly, but I tried not to take them in the house when I got home. As much as I tried not to show my feelings to the family, I'm sure that they sensed what my emotions were, particularly Jo and Tiger.

When we had our meeting with the squad the day after the loss to Ol' Miss, they knew me well enough to know how I would be. But by Monday, when we hit the practice field, I'm proud to say I was able to accomplish this leveling off and start preparing for the next game. A coach simply can't replay Saturday's game on Tuesday and still get ready for the next game. If you have a Tuesday night TV show, you have to wing it and not get your emotions up again. Perhaps no one took losses harder than I did, and no one got over them sooner than I did. That helped contribute to my winning seasons, realizing that if I lingered too long over one loss, it would affect our preparations for the next week, and then I would be moping about two losses.

In a "normal" week, the players and coaches would all gather on Sunday and I would review the game and talk about what we did well and what we could improve on. We would watch the film of the special teams, then would break up into offensive and defensive meetings. The respective coordinators ran those meetings, but I tried to spend time with each unit. I tried to concentrate on the offense, particularly working with the quarterbacks. Those meetings were, of course, supplemented with one-on-one meetings with a lot of the players during the week, and I've always been proud when my players thought they could come in and talk with me about anything that was on their minds, whether it had anything to do with football or not.

We were 1-1 for the season, but in my mind we were struggling. Watching the game film early on Sunday morning, I noticed that three of our best players had played their worst game. A number of our very good players had played a very average game. I made a gamble.

Instead of having each unit watch only its portion of the game film, I decided to have the entire squad watch all three films. I wasn't trying to embarrass any of the players, but I thought it was an occasion when maybe seeing themselves making mistakes—and knowing all of their teammates saw it as well—would prompt them to concentrate better and work harder in trying to make certain they didn't make the same mistakes again.

When we hit the practice field, I knew we would bounce back and have a great season. This was the biggest deviation from my normal postgame time with the players, and it was all over by Sunday afternoon. If that disappointment lingered, it wasn't a bad motivational technique—to dislike losing so much to not let yourself be a part of defeat. It also showed that we had a class group of athletes. I emphasized that we were too good a football team to be playing poorly like that and that we could still be national contenders. Pat's Pub in South Bend had glasses and bumper stickers printed with "1977 National Champions" the next week, after the loss to Mississippi.

Pat had faith in us. We had a great uphill climb. You have to play games one at a time and good things can happen.

Rusty Lisch was not playing poorly, but I really believed we needed to have Joe Montana playing quarterback if we were going to be as good a team as we could be. Ron Toman, our quarterback coach, Joe, a center and our wide receivers stayed after practice on Monday night for extra work. The center snapped to Joe, and he threw to all the wide receivers. He threw all types of patterns. Joe threw the out pattern like a clothesline, although in the pro reports, they thought that he couldn't throw the out pattern. But he could throw the ball anywhere, any distance that he had to throw. It's like the timing of the backs; anybody knows that a 4.3 back is most desirable. But there are hundreds in college and hundreds in the pros who don't run a 4.3.

I went to our trainer before going to the training table for dinner and told him I thought Joe Montana was ready to play that week against Purdue. Gene gave him his clearance, and I told Joe to be ready to play. I didn't say, "You might play"; I said, "You're going to play."

Against Purdue, with a capacity crowd again, 68,000 people, we found ourselves behind 24-14, and the defense was playing poorly. We had relieved Rusty Lisch with Gary Forystek, who was injured shortly thereafter—an injury that really ended his football career. We brought Rusty back during the third quarter, and then put Joe in early in the fourth quarter so he could have the wind at his back, but we were in poor field position. When Joe entered the game, he threw one touchdown pass, David Mitchell scored on an Emil Sitko-type blast, and we got a field goal and won 31-24.

Joe's performance against Purdue was absolutely amazing for a lot of reasons: Purdue had a nice cushion at home and Purdue had always been a nemesis of the Fighting Irish, but most of all, Joe hadn't played in more than a year and was coming off a separated shoulder and a broken finger. At the press conference after the game, I told them that he would be the starting quarterback the next week.

Coaching is not a popularity contest. I have to give Joe an A+ for leadership, and his maturation was obvious. The team reacted positively to this, and Joe started the remaining 21 games of his career.

We won our next two games, Michigan State and Army, but I still didn't think we were playing like a championship team. After the Army game, we were ranked 11th in the country, and I couldn't disagree with that very much.

Earlier in the season, I had made arrangements to buy an extra set of uniform jerseys—green jerseys with gold numbers. Almost no one knew about it. My captains were told in the middle of the week before the USC game that we were going to wear those jerseys on Saturday. They all did a good job of keeping the secret. The decision to wear the green jerseys for the USC game was an important one, probably deciding whether we would be a contender for the national championship or not.

Before the game, we warmed up in our home blue jerseys while the equipment men were setting out the green jerseys at each player's locker. After we returned to the locker room just before kickoff, we had a very good idea that the team was excited—particularly when we saw Bob Golic looking at his green jersey in a mirror. Joe had a tremendous game, running for two touchdowns and passing for two more, as he was named the offensive MVP of the game by ABC.

Coming out on the field in the bright sunlight was the most thrilling feeling I have ever experienced. The crowd erupted and showed the world what green means to the Irish.

People like Ted Burgmeier became legends that day. USC had gone into the game ranked fifth, so the 49-19 victory brought us back into the picture as a national title hopeful, as we climbed back into the top five in the national polls the following week.

In our next two games, against Navy and Georgia Tech, we scored a total of more than 100 points. Joe threw for more than 260 yards in each of those games. Against Georgia Tech, he passed for 273 yards and had three touchdowns in a 69-14 win.

This was an outstanding offensive performance. As with all lopsided scores, you try to hold the score down, but there's really no way to hold it down once a whole team gets hot like that.

Next up was a road game against Clemson, a very tough place to play. It was a big game, because they were ranked 15th in the country. Both teams played well, but Montana was the difference, rushing for two fourth-quarter touchdowns to give us another comeback win, 21-17.

During the game, Captain Paul Harvey of the South Bend police was working the sideline for us, as he has done for years, when someone came up behind me with a broken beer bottle in his hand. As he got close to me, Captain Harvey hit him hard and down he went. After that, I made the team keep their helmets on for the rest of the game.

I was not only mad at that guy, I was mad at an official in the game, after he assessed me the only 15-yard penalty I ever received in my coaching career. I was upset about an offside call on our tight end, Ken MacAfee. Despite those incidents, we were able to rally and win the game.

The next week we beat a good Air Force team 49-0. The confidence of the players was growing, and as a staff, we really felt good about the progress our team was making. In our final game of the regular season, we beat Miami 48-10 and accepted a bid to the Cotton Bowl to play Texas, which was undefeated, ranked number one in the country and featured the Heisman Trophy winner, running back Earl Campbell.

In our final five games, we had scored 69 points, 49 twice, 48 and 43. We really had a lot of confidence that nobody could stop us on offense, and that was a great feeling. We knew we were playing for the national championship, and I believed this team was ready for that challenge.

Playing in the Cotton Bowl was always a happy time, but going into Dallas and playing the University of Texas was another story. We were treated great—until the Texas team showed up. As a coach, I had been to virtually all the other significant bowl games, but I didn't realize how much this game meant to Dallas and the people of Texas until I saw almost everyone, including the officials, put their hands over their hearts when the band played "The Eyes of Texas Are Upon You," the school's theme song.

I knew that this was a good officiating crew, and they had been prepared well. I do vividly recall the waiters singing a heart-pounding song at a team meal: "It's not where you start, it's where you end." I had a very special feeling about this game after that song.

At the Texas Hall of Fame dinner, our team was late coming to the hall because we were practicing, and most of the team's seats were already taken. The rest of the Notre Dame players were scattered around the room. I could tell at the team's Christmas party later that we were ready to suck it up and take our work seriously. Team Christmas parties have always been quite revealing to me. Bob Golic, now a veteran, predicted that we would win in a rout. I used the Hall of Fame dinner situation as part of my comments in a talk to the team.

When motivating a team, where you say it is as important as what you say. I waited until we got to our dressing room before our next practice and then spoke for an hour. I tried to make individual remarks to each of the players. We had a great practice and were perfectly prepared by our staff. I liked what I saw and I gave them two days off, to let them have fresh legs for the game.

In the week before the game, Jo developed some respiratory problems, a situation that must be avoided for victims of multiple sclerosis. Dr. Les Bodnar, our wonderful friend and the team doctor, treated Jo and told me, privately, that if it didn't clear up, he wouldn't allow her to go to the game.

We had a good motel for our headquarters, and one of the things you get out of a bowl game is the fun of being away from home; children get a lot out of a bowl game. Thanks to a lot of thought and prayer, Jo, almost miraculously, got much better. She was able to go to the game and enjoyed it very much. It's important to have a fun time with the family, and that includes winning. So, Jo's coming to the game was very important for me as well as her.

I already had made the decision that if she was unable to go to the game, it would be the last game I would coach. There would have been no changing my mind. But with Jo in the stands, and with things going well, with the exhilaration of the game, I knew this was where I wanted to be and I was doing exactly what I wanted to do.

Before the game, as we were coming down the tunnel to the field, an official came running up and told me that if we didn't hurry, we'd miss the team introductions. We had already been held up for TV reasons. I told him that no one cared. I knew we were perfectly prepared.

As it turned out, we played nearly a perfect game. We stopped Campbell and rolled to a 38-10 win, even passing up a chance for another score late in the game. When the polls came out, we were a unanimous choice as the national champions, and I was very happy for all our players. They had worked hard and deserved all of the attention.

As time goes by, the 1977 national championship that our Notre Dame team won becomes even more meaningful. Very seldom is a college team able to put itself in a position to possibly win the national championship. To actually snare the title is truly a memorable event. Though I coached many great teams, only four were able to put themselves in a position to win the national championship, and only my 1977 team actually won it. This happens in pro ball also. That wonderful man, Art Rooney, waited so long to win a league championship. He then went on to win several championships in a row. In Phoenix, where I live, there are four major pro franchises. None of them has yet won a league championship. The Diamondbacks have been able to put themselves in a position to win the World Series. Just to be able to get into that position is an achievement.

My national championship ring becomes more significant and dear to me each year. The last reunion this team had was in 1997. It was wonderful to get together with all of these fine people. The championship meant a great deal to everyone who made it possible.

I've had some teams that I wish with all my heart could have had a national championship ring. All the pieces just didn't fit together. In 1960 there were a number of circumstances involved that got in the way of winning. I am just grateful for being able to win all the marbles with that great 1977 team.

When we went to Notre Dame, the first coach I hired was Merv Johnson. He was a great line coach and offensive coordinator. He was joined by Joe Yonto. Joe started out as my defensive line coach and later became my defensive coordinator. Joe was hired by Ara Parseghian. He worked on Ara's staff, my staff, and Gerry's staff and also with Lou Holtz. Brian Boulac started helping Merv Johnson with the offensive line. Brian is still at Notre Dame as the Assistant Athletic Director. Brian and I made many recruiting trips together. My last year coaching at Notre Dame, he was my administrative assistant. Joe and Brian were true "Notre Dame Men." They epitomized the qualities of "God, Country and Notre Dame." They were intelligent, hardworking, ethical and loyal. They had little trouble bringing Johnson into the fold to become a "Notre Dame Man" also. Hank Kuhlman and Johnny Roland came with me from Green Bay. I also offered a job to Bill Tobin. He decided to go with Jim Finks and the Chicago Bears. Francis Peay also joined us. So the whole group had known each other and worked together before. I also retained George Kelly, Paul Shoults and Greg Blache. Greg is still in the NFL. This coaching staff did an excellent job during the transition. We all had to work under some very difficult conditions. I'm proud of each of them.

When the 1976 team beat Penn State at the Gator Bowl, it was our first bowl trip together. Joe O'Brien, part of the support staff, was the point man on the trip. The coaches had fallen into a good rhythm and it was a smooth trip. During the trip, we were going to a church service. The whole team loaded on the bus, and as the doors were about to close, Joe Paterno got on and sat down. He pretended that he mistakenly got on our bus instead of his bus. Of course, the squad liked that. Our Christmas party was always a great success and a highlight of the bowl experience. My players always conducted themselves like gentlemen. The bowl games became an important event and memory in these young men's lives.

The 1977 national champion staff consisted of: Tom Connally, Ross Stevenson, Ron Toman, Rick Slager, Francis Peay, Jim Johnson, Joe Yonto, Hank Kulhman, George Kelly, Merv Johnson, and Brian Boulac.

By 1980, we had added Jim Gruden, the father of Jon Gruden—now Oakland Raiders head coach—to the staff. Bill Meyers and Gene Smith both joined us in 1980. They turned out to be great assets to this young, inexperienced team. Like so many staff members, Meyers had that particular loyalty. We are still the closest of friends. Jim and Bill are still in the NFL. The youngest full-time coach I had was Gene Smith. Gene won two national championship rings at Notre Dame. He worked long and hard and eventually became the athletic director at Iowa State, and, in July of 2000, the A.D. at Arizona State.

Someone once asked me what I thought was the most beautiful place in the world. I thought it over and said I couldn't trim the list any smaller than four: "The Grotto in the Fall, the Grotto in the Winter, the Grotto in the Spring and the Grotto in the Summer." While we were still enjoying our ranking as national champions, one Sunday in late spring in 1978, Jo and I went to the Grotto on campus, just behind the Golden Dome. We said our prayers, lit some candles, meditated, then sat together with our thoughts.

In a short while, four young women, perhaps from nearby St. Mary's, also came to the Grotto (a replica of the Grotto at Lourdes), dressed informally for spring, carrying wildflowers, singing "Ave Maria." They left their gift of flowers near the statue of Our Lady, high up to the right of the Grotto's arch. There are countless moments like this at a place like Notre Dame—so special in our thoughts and memories.

One of the saddest parts of being a college coach is that you know you are only going to have players for four years, five if they had a redshirt season, and then they are going to move on. We lost a lot of talented players off the 1977 team, people like Ken MacAfee, Luther Bradley, Ross Browner, Willie Fry, Terry Eurick and Steve Orsini. I knew I was going to miss all of them.

Watching those players leave, however, is kind of like turning the page after a game on Saturday—if you spend too long moping over what has happened, you're not going to be ready for what's coming next. We lost a lot of great players, but we had a lot of great players coming back, and we had a tough season to prepare for.

I always looked forward to games against the teams where I had previously coached, because invariably old friends came back to say hello and renew acquaintances. Our first game in 1978 was in South Bend against Missouri, and I knew it would be good to see those friends again. I wasn't as excited about seeing the Missouri football team, which was loaded with talent, led by an All-America tight end, Kellen Winslow, who would go on to a Hall of Fame career in the NFL.

The only things I heard around campus all week were reminders of the last time Missouri had come in and upset Notre Dame in 1972, the game I had listened to on the bus while with the Packers. Unsaid in any of those reminders was a simple message—don't let it happen again.

Well, we did a good job of controlling Winslow, but unfortunately, Missouri's defense shut us out and we lost the game 3-0. Joe overthrew our tight end down the middle on the first play and things never quite got going.

The loss didn't devastate me, because I thought we had played well; we just happened to get beat. I was more upset the following week when we blew a lead because of penalties and poor ballhandling and lost to Michigan 28-14.

We were now 0-2 and facing a game against undefeated and nationally ranked Purdue, whose star was a sophomore quarterback, Mark Herrmann. We were able to limit his effectiveness, and the only touchdown of the game came on a 26-yard run by our captain, Jerome Heavens, as we won the game 10-6. I won't say it was a must win for the team, but it was very important.

That victory seemed to give everybody around the team a chance to catch their collective breath and realize we still were a good team and had a long season in front of us. Had we lost that game, I don't know what would have happened the rest of the year.

We went in and beat Michigan State, 29-25, on the road and then came home to play undefeated Pittsburgh, which jumped on us for a 17-7 lead. We didn't panic, however, and Montana and Heavens brought us back to a 26-17 win. The game was significant for another reason—Heavens rushed for 120 yards on 30 carries to break George Gipp's all-time career rushing mark at Notre Dame. He had enjoyed a great career at Notre Dame and definitely deserved the record.

A 38-15 win at the Air Force Academy, followed by a 20-0 shutout over Miami, extended our winning streak to five, as we prepared to meet 7-0 Navy, which had the top-ranked defense in the country and also was ranked number one in scoring defense. The game was going to be played at a neutral site, Cleveland.

I've always thought that the best players seem to be able to raise their games another notch when they come up against tough competition, and that was what I was seeing from this Notre Dame team, and it continued against Navy. Vagas Ferguson rushed for 219 yards, which at the time was the school record for an individual game; Jerome Heavens again gained 100 yards; Montana passed for a touchdown; and Chuck Male kicked two long field goals, as we won 27-7.

A 31-14 win the following week over Johnny Majors' Tennessee Volunteers left us in good position regarding the bowl games. Ironically, our kicking game was a big part of our victory. We had two games to play, at Georgia Tech and then the season finale against Southern Cal.

Scouts from almost all of the key bowls were on hand for the game against Tech, which also had a seven-game winning streak. Vagas Ferguson took a handoff from Montana on the second play of the game and took off on a 68-yard run and we were on our way. The victory set up the showdown with Southern Cal.

It's tough to think back about this game, even though it was a long time ago. Thinking about the way our team battled back in the fourth quarter gives me a great sense of pride, but remembering that the team played well enough to win—and didn't—is still an arrow that is stuck in my heart. We lost because of an error. There was only one other time in my entire coaching career, in high school, college and with the Packers, where I felt a mistake by an official cost us a ball game.

With 12 minutes left in the game, we were losing 24-6. What followed was perhaps the best quarter of football ever played by any quarterback. After a 23-yard pass to Dean Masztak, Montana found Kris Haines for a 57-yard touchdown completion. We went for a two-point conversion and failed, but still had narrowed the lead to 24-12.

Our defense held, but USC punted the ball out of bounds at our 2-yard line. We had six minutes left on the clock, Montana went to work again, completing four passes to Haines and one to Masztak, ran for a first down and then gave the ball to Pete Buchanan, who scored on a 3-yard run. This time we kicked the extra point, and now were down 24-19 with three minutes to play.

The defense once again stopped Southern Cal, and doing what we could to stop the clock, we now had the ball again with 1:35 left. Montana scrambled twice and passed twice, moving us all the way to the USC 12. A 10-yard pass to Masztak moved us to the 2 with 48 seconds to play. On the next play, Montana hit Pete Holohan in the end zone, putting us ahead 25-24.

We decided to go for the two-point conversion instead of kicking the extra point. That would have given us a three-point lead, meaning USC could only tie with a field goal. Unfortunately, Montana's pass to Kris Haines was incomplete.

USC now had one final chance, and with the ball on their 40-yard line, our defensive tackle, Jeff Weston, broke through and hit quarterback Paul McDonald as he was attempting to pass. The ball came loose, and Weston fell on it. Everybody on our sideline was going crazy because it certainly appeared to be a fumble, and our recovery effectively ended the game.

Our defense was coming off the field when the referee jumped in and made a delayed call, saying McDonald had been attempting to pass. He ruled it was an incomplete pass, not a fumble, allowing USC to retain possession. Nobody on our sideline could believe it.

Looking back on it, I realize that I should have called a time-out to try to clear up the confusion and give us a chance to regroup. McDonald made the most of his extra chance, completing a pass to Calvin Sweeney at the 25, setting up a winning field goal. USC won 27-25.

It was the only time in my life I didn't know what to say to the players in the locker room. After just staring blankly at the wall for a long time, I finally said, "I've never been as proud as I am right now. Let's not cheapen this great effort. Let's take a shower and go home."

That evening, I was still upset, and everybody around me knew it. Father Joyce and the Chairman of the Board of Notre Dame came by to try to comfort me, and I appreciated their kind words and support, but this loss was going to take a long time to get over.

Thankfully, we had accepted a bid to return to the Cotton Bowl in Dallas, so this wasn't our final game of the year. We were busy preparing for the game against Houston, the Southwest Conference champion, when we stopped to attend the Notre Dame-Valparaiso basketball game shortly before Christmas. I don't know who was responsible for it, but as a gesture to make everybody with the football team feel better, we were presented with a green plaque inscribed in gold. The message read:

Coach Devine and the Team

Thanks for Never Giving Up

The Notre Dame Student Body

My grandson Arlo has this plaque hanging in his bedroom today, and it still means a great deal to me, and I know it did to the players.

The Cotton Bowl game this time was not for the national championship, but we still wanted to go there and play well, wiping out some of the bad taste that was in our mouth after the USC loss. It was cold in Dallas that New Year's Day, and as we arrived at the stadium, I noticed machines were clearing ice and snow off the field. I walked down to the field to offer my advice, and two things happened—I got my feet and socks completely wet and cold before the game even started, and I got bumped by one of the ice removal machines, which bothered me throughout the entire game.

It was obvious the weather conditions were going to be a big factor in the game. The first six scores were the results of turnovers. Montana didn't play most of the third quarter because of chills that had lowered his body temperature to 96 degrees, two degrees below normal. Dr. Les Bodnar, our team physician, always kept chicken soup in an emergency pack. Les warmed up the soup and fed it to Joe while he was wrapped in blankets. We kept sending runners to see how he was doing, and each time they came back with negative reports. Finally, he felt good enough to return to the field.

We were losing 34-12 with 7:30 left in the game, and even some who had watched Montana produce miracles before thought this game was out of reach. I had confidence we could win and kept reminding the team we could and would.

The comeback began with a blocked punt by Tony Belden and was returned by Steve Cichy for a touchdown. Then Joe hit Vagas Ferguson for the two-point conversion.

Our defense again stopped Houston, and Montana drove us down to the goal line, scoring himself on a 2-yard run. Another two-point pass brought us within six points, 34-28.

Another great defensive stand gave us the ball on the Houston 49 with 2:25 to play. We moved the ball to the 36, when Joe scrambled for a 16-yard gain and a would-be first down at the 20, but he was stripped of the ball and Houston recovered. Even some of my best friends turned off their televisions at that point.

Our attitude didn't waver, however, and we stopped their first three plays to set up a fourth down and 6 at the Houston 24. We made an all-out attempt to block the punt, but our eagerness caused us to jump offside. Now faced with a fourth-and-1 at the 29, Houston Coach Bill Yeoman made the decision to try for the first down. Joe Gramke and Mike Calhoun stopped their great running back, Emmett King, for a 1-yard loss. We had the ball back, with 28 seconds remaining.

Montana scrambled for 11 yards, then completed a 10-yard pass to Haines, who stepped out of bounds at the 8. There were six seconds left on the clock as Houston took its last time-out. I thought we had time to run two plays if the first one didn't get us the touchdown, but we would have to be quick. I told him, "Joe, let's run a 91. If it's not there, get rid of it right away."

The last thing I told him was the most significant. "If your first pass is incomplete, you call whatever is most comfortable for you." He knew I would never second-guess him, and that I had complete faith in him. Ninety-one, the first play I had told him to run, was a quick turn-out by the wideouts with a short pass to the tight end if the strong linebacker blitzed. It's a quick three-step drop for the quarterback. The Houston defense pressured Joe immediately and the play didn't have time to develop, so he quickly grounded the ball. There were two seconds left.

Joe looked to the sidelines and indicated that he wanted a hand signal. It was further proof that Joe had worked himself into the spot where he was the most dependable person on the field, even more so than the coaches. We had not used hand signals all year. In order not to be called for delay of game, we gave him the hand signal to call the same play, 91. He nodded his head and brought the team out of the huddle and up to the line of scrimmage.

With no time left, Montana hit Haines in the right corner of the end zone. Dallas native Joe Unis, a walk-on second-teamer, drilled the extra point through the goalposts, and we had an unbelievable 35-34 comeback win. Or at least we thought.

As both teams were coming off the field, I noticed a penalty flag. I was numb—both because of the cold and our comeback. Our guys hadn't seen the flag and were still celebrating. When we saw we were being called for a 5-yard penalty, center Dave Huffman told me, "You know, Coach, it's just five yards longer than an extra point."

I couldn't believe we were going to have to kick the extra point again. I was worried about Joe's accuracy, but I also was worried he might get it blocked. Standing on the sideline, I could hardly watch. Joe didn't flinch, however, and kicked the ball right through the goalposts, and this time we were ready to celebrate.

The locker room was bedlam. Father Joyce and Father Hesburgh joined in the victory party. The comeback was featured in a movie called *Seven and One-half Minutes to Destiny*, narrated by Harry Caray, and was called not only the greatest comeback in Notre Dame history, but the greatest in the history of college football. I wasn't going to argue.

It was a Cotton Bowl tradition that both coaches attend a press conference at a downtown hotel following dinner. At the news conference, Art Spander, a fine columnist in San Francisco, asked a question about where I thought Joe Montana should go in the draft.

I said, "If I were the owner or CEO of a pro football team or had an expansion club, and the ruling was that I could have for my first pick a choice of all the current players in the NFL and all of the players coming out of college, I would use that number-one pick for Joe Montana."

I was sincere in saying that, not just paying lip service to one of my players. Joe had come a long way from his days as the quarterback at Monongahela High School in Pennsylvania and from the days he was a sixth-stringer for the Irish. He was and is one of the finest players I have ever seen in my life.

The night Joe graduated, he came over to our house with his mom and dad and a few close friends. He spent the evening playing foosball with my grandson Keary, who later graduated from Notre Dame and is now in medical school.

I honestly thought Joe should have been the first pick in the draft that year, and if not the number-one choice, certainly among the very first players chosen. His knowledge of the game was tremendous, and he had the leadership skills and the playing ability to move a team better than anybody I've ever seen.

On the day of the draft in 1979, I received a phone call from John Ralston, the former coach and a good friend, who then was a vice president for the San Francisco 49ers. It was the third round, and I was just stunned that no teams had selected Montana. John wanted my opinion about Montana. I knew there were teams that didn't think he was strong enough to throw the out pattern with any authority, but in my opinion, he could throw any pass he wanted, anytime he wanted.

I told John, "If I could still have Joe Montana as my quarterback, I'd still be the head coach in Green Bay." John took that news back to the 49ers' draft room, where Bill Walsh had the final say, and the 49ers made Montana their pick. It obviously turned out to be a good choice.

Looking back on Joe's final career numbers at Notre Dame, it's still hard to believe he was that good. He started 22 of 27 games, he completed 268 of 515 passes for 4,121 yards, passed for 25 touchdowns and ran for 14 more. I knew he was going to be a great professional, and I couldn't believe so many teams had such doubts about him. Three years later, Art Spander quoted me in a column he wrote in San Francisco about Montana. I was quoted as saying *before the Cotton Bowl,* "He's my boy. He's attentive, dedicated, hardworking. He's had problems, but he's matured. He reads defenses better than any college quarterback, and he has the potential to become a great quarterback." I am really proud of everything that Joe went on to accomplish in his career.

From a personal standpoint, I was sad to see Joe leave because it meant we had to come up with a new quarterback and a new leader, and even though I knew somebody would occupy that position, there was no way anyone could replace Montana.

The 1979 season was not a memorable one in terms of being one of Notre Dame's great years. We had some big wins, including our opener at Michigan, when linebacker Bob Crable blocked a field goal attempt on the final play of the game to preserve a 12-10 victory. Later in the year we played South Carolina, which featured Heisman Trophy winner George Rogers, and Rusty Lisch led a Montana-type comeback to pull out an 18-17 victory that the home crowd loved.

The week before the USC game, and our chance to avenge the disappointing loss of a year earlier, I was at the training table for the evening meal. Jo had driven to Chicago to meet our daughter Jennifer. I didn't know it at the time, but driving back from Chicago she had hit a bad patch on the road and slid off the highway. Another driver spotted the car at the bottom of a hill and called for help. A lady riding in that car had stayed with Jo and kept telling her that help was on the way.

While eating dinner, I noticed a policeman enter the dining room. Jim Gruden, one of my assistants, was sitting with me, and I told him, "Oh gosh, someone has lost someone." The policeman kept walking straight toward me, and I had a sinking feeling in the bottom of my stomach.

He stopped at our table, and told me that Jo had been in a car accident. He said he didn't know any other details, but had a phone number for me to call. I ran to the kitchen and called the number, where I was connected to the ambulance. The paramedics were taking her to the hospital and said she had glass in her eyes and mouth and had suffered broken ribs, not a broken back, as some media outlets later reported. I hung up and raced for my car to meet them at the hospital.

When I arrived, Dr. Bodnar was meticulously removing glass from Jo's face. I heard Jo say, "Les, can I go to the game Saturday?"

I had to smile, knowing how much pain she was in, but that our game with Southern Cal was the most important thing on her mind.

Dr. Bodnar gave Jo his permission to go to the game, and Roger Valdiserri, Notre Dame's longtime sports information director, really gave Jo first-class treatment in the press box. Jo thoroughly enjoyed an exciting game, except for the final score. USC won. It was an outstanding offensive game in which the two teams amassed 1,128 yards of offense, and I'm certain college football fans in general who had no allegiance to either team thought it was a terrific game. Losing coaches, however, never think that way, no matter how great a game it was.

One of the best games that I've ever coached in was played in the National Olympic Stadium in Tokyo, Japan, later that season. It was Miami's home game, and it was their idea to play the game in Tokyo. Father Joyce and I earlier had decided it would be a great experience for the players to see a country like Japan. So, we accepted the opportunity presented to us.

The facilities were very strange. Even though it was an Olympic Stadium, built for the 1964 Olympics, there were no dressing rooms big enough for a football team to change in or to use to get ready for the game. We had to tape up and dress at our hotel, the same hotel where the Miami team was staying. Everything about the trip was a new experience. Very few of the people we came into contact with spoke any English. We prepared on the same field as Miami, which was very much a swamp. The basics of football, however, were still there.

John Scully, our center and a great pianist, entertained anytime we could find a piano. I remember very well one incident where the team, which was very well-behaved and a credit to the U.S.A, saw a piano sitting up on some balcony level and asked permission to move it to the ground floor. They were given permission, and it was quite a sight seeing all these husky football players joining together to lift and transport a large piano from that balcony down to the main floor. Scully put on a fine performance, as usual, and it was well worth the effort.

Miami's coach was Howard Schnellenberger, in the early years of turning around the fortunes of that team. Their quarterback would go on to a great college and pro career, Jim Kelly. Our quarterback,

Rusty Lisch, gave us another fine performance, along with the entire squad. We won the game handily, 40-15, and my only regret was that because the game was played in Tokyo, a lot of our fans didn't get to see the game. To this day, I still run into people who saw the game and they seem to think that we played as well as I thought we did.

That finished the year.

In the months following the end of the season, Jo's MS began to cause deterioration in her eyesight. She had a cataract condition in one eye that caused temporary blindness until it was corrected. Then something happened to the other eye, leaving her virtually sightless. All of this was weighing on my mind, and one day in June 1980, as I was driving to the Notre Dame campus, I said to myself,

"Devine, what are you doing? Here you are going to work and your wife's back home and can't even see."

I had made the drive to the campus from our home in the country nearly every day for five years. I often turned off Highway 31, Michigan Avenue, to Angela Boulevard, which traced the southern edge of the campus, with the golf course on the left and a very nice residential neighborhood on the right. Angela then crosses Notre Dame Avenue after a few blocks. A left turn on Notre Dame Avenue puts you in a direct line with the Administration Building—the famous Golden Dome. Or you can pass by that turn and go on toward Juniper Road and the Joyce Athletic and Convocation Center, where my office was, directly across from the football stadium.

That day in June I decided to make the left turn on Notre Dame Avenue and drove on to the Dome. Father Joyce's office was there and he was in that morning. We had a long, long talk. He spoke of Jo with love in his voice, and he has known me for a very long time. We decided that, under the circumstances, it would be best for everyone if I retired as head coach of the Notre Dame football team. He left it to my discretion as to how and when to make the announcement.

I went home and told Jo, and we agreed that it was the correct decision. We always agreed on all the major decisions in our lives. The next day I had lunch with Father Hesburgh, Notre Dame's president, at the Morris Inn on campus. We got there early for lunch but were the last to leave.

Father Hesburgh also has a fondness for Jo. He knew her better than most college presidents would know the football coach's wife. Father Hesburgh agreed with Father Joyce's assessment, and I knew in my heart it was the correct decision.

As the summer wore on, I began to plan the way this announcement should be delivered. I knew that anyone as emotional as I am could get hung up on this. I really wanted to get it done right.

Jo and I and the family were secretive about this decision, so there were no leaks. I saw Fathers Hesburgh and Joyce socially, and it was clear that I was welcome to stay should I choose to do so, but under the circumstances, I also knew that they think a head coach's maximum tenure today should normally be between six and 10 years. They were well aware of the various pressures and the history of this job wearing down head coaches in the past.

I knew of Knute Rockne's injured leg and his phlebitis and, of course, his early death in a plane crash at the age of 43. Frank Leahy was also only 43 when he resigned. He had serious gastric problems during his time as head coach. I well recall the wonderful letters he would write to me, long letters, after my Missouri teams had played on TV. He was always very specific in these letters. One of the most meaningful awards I ever received was the Frank Leahy Award, presented in Chicago by Dave Condon and Ziggy Czarobski.

Ara Parseghian resigned after a most distinguished career at age 53. A man of his physical stature would normally be active into his 70s. I know that I was wearing down slightly, at age 56, and there was Jo's condition to take into strong consideration. It was becoming increasingly more difficult to get through a season, a bowl game, recruiting and spring practices—the usual cycle for a head coach. As time went by and we continued our winning ways, demands on me to make personal appearances also grew immensely.

I had planned, after extensive soul-searching, to first tell the players what I was going to do. I wanted to make certain the administration had enough time to conduct a proper search for my successor, and it was important for me not to leave them in a bind because of everything they had done for me and Jo and the way everybody at Notre Dame had treated us.

I was obsessed with the fact that my team had to be told first. In my plans, I wanted to set up a schedule to talk to the team on photo day (the first day of fall practice), then go to the office of Moose Krause (the athletic director), and then Roger Valdiserri's office, to make a public announcement.

None of it took place the way I had hoped. Why? Well, to be perfectly honest, I lost my guts. I couldn't face my squad at the scheduled meeting. Instead, I filled the meeting with other specifics. This went on for several days. I knew, however, that I had to get this done before the start of the season and before it somehow leaked. Shortly, rumors that I was thinking of retiring began to spread.

This was the most uncomfortable period of my life. Here I had these freshmen I had recruited and whom I truly loved . . . and I wouldn't be there for them. I wasn't that important for the success of the team and the university, but there was enough negativism in the public's eye about the structure and function of intercollegiate athletics. I did not want my decision and situation to be seen as a part of that problem.

As the start of the season drew nearer, I was having a terrible time with all this. It was causing me sleepless nights, for all the wrong reasons. Soon, I had a phone call on a Monday morning from Howard Cosell of ABC. He told me he had the news that I was going to retire and was going to use it. I pleaded my case and said I'd give it to ABC if I could have enough time to tell my squad. I needed to have enough time to tell my team and I'd do anything to get that time. You had to be in my position to understand.

I wanted Dave Diles of ABC to be able to break the story. I called him and told him what was happening, and he made arrangements to be in South Bend that night. Diles was known as a fair, honest and intelligent sports broadcaster. We had developed a close friendship that has lasted all these years. I have spent many happy hours at his farm in Racine, Ohio.

I called a special squad meeting for after practice and dinner. Just before the squad meeting, I met with my staff in an adjacent room and broke the news to them. I assured them that I would help in any way to see that they could keep their jobs under the new head coach or to help them move on to other positions. I had been blessed over the years with tremendously dedicated, loyal and talented assistants, and to a man, these guys understood exactly what I was doing and why I was doing it.

Immediately, the staff and I went to the squad. It was a fantastic, emotional time for me and I was rubber-kneed. I was brief but honest with the team. The older players understood the situation very clearly. Then I called Dave Diles, now at a local hotel, to let him know that he could go with the story. We broke the news together later that night.

For me, this achieved what was imperative—to tell the team before the news broke through the media. I would have liked for it to have been handled the way I intended, but it didn't work out that way, and the two people who I felt were hurt the most by that were Moose Krause and Roger Valdiserri. They deserved the professional courtesy to know about my decision at the right time, in the right way. This has bothered me terribly ever since, but it can't be undone. I just wasn't able to get it done the way I had hoped it would go. In the summer of 1980, Fathers Hesburgh and Joyce both had told me that they trusted me implicitly to get it done. They never once publicly or privately second-guessed what I did.

I really felt making the announcement was positive for everyone, because now there were no more rumors or questions about what was going to happen. We were able to begin the season in a positive mood, and that was important to the team's success.

I didn't know how good a team it would be. We were extremely young and began the year unranked, which did not surprise me. Our starting quarterback for most of the year was a true freshman, Blair Kiel, just four months out of high school. We had a tough schedule, opening with consecutive games against Purdue, Michigan, Michigan State and Miami. If somebody had told me before the opener that after eight games we would be the number-one ranked team in the country, I probably would have thought they were nuts. Yet that was exactly what happened.

We beat a good Purdue team 31-10, and one player I was tremendously impressed with was John Scully, one of the few senior starters on the squad. He stepped forward as a leader and showed the ability that would allow him to enjoy a 10-year career in the NFL.

The game against Michigan was much closer and the outcome was definitely in doubt entering the fourth quarter. Both teams scored, but they scored with 41 seconds to play. We needed a strong-armed quarterback in the game.

When I had recruited Blair Kiel, who was from Columbus, Indiana, I told him about a special formation we planned to use in the Michigan game. It was a short punt formation, which made it appear we were punting, but we really weren't. I knew Blair had the arm to throw the kinds of passes we would need to complete if we were going to be able to win the game. I hated bringing a youngster into the game like that, but I knew it was the only chance we had.

We were on our own 20-yard line, going into the wind, and I thought we needed to get to the Michigan 30 to have a realistic chance of making a game-winning field goal. Blair did his job, and with two seconds left, completed a pass to Tony Hunter, who stepped out of bounds at the Michigan 34. I had to immediately decide whether to call for a field goal, a 51-yard attempt into the wind, or go for a touchdown. I sent the field goal unit onto the field.

Harry Oliver, an inexperienced kicker, had missed closer attempts earlier in the game, but he was up to the challenge this time. He kicked the ball straight, and it seemed to hang in the air forever before the officials under the goalposts both raised their arms, signaling that the kick was good for a fantastic come-from-behind 29-27 victory. Michigan eventually went on to win the Big Ten Championship with a perfect 8-0 record in conference play.

Some of the fans, including my good friend Bob Welch, couldn't watch because they didn't think we had a chance of making that kick. Bob told me later he stood in the tunnel and didn't come out until he heard the crowd erupt in celebration.

It was almost too much for my heart to handle, too. It was so eerie, because the stadium was so quiet while that ball was in the air, even the wind seemed to stop for a moment. Then the entire place was bedlam. To this day, many people swear that the wind stopped when the ball was in the air.

Harry Oliver was a fine young man, extremely loyal to Notre Dame, and I was very happy for him. We still see each other occasionally, and invariably we end up talking about his field goal and that game. It was the third game against Michigan in my coaching career that was decided on the final play of the game, and my teams were fortunate to win all three.

There probably is more folklore and fiction attached to that game than to any other I ever coached. I can recall, as if it happened yesterday, Harry yelling in my ear above the roar in the locker room, "Coach, I did it for you, because you're the one who gave me a chance." That quote still sits in a small frame in my den at home. I use it as a reminder of all the young men it was my privilege to coach over the years.

Our next game was at Michigan State, and it was a tremendously nostalgic trip for Jo and me, because East Lansing was in many ways the start of my career and our lives in football. I went up with the team on Friday, and Jo and Anne Thompson drove up on Saturday morning. The team ate lunch at Win Schuler's restaurant. He was an old and very dear friend and it was good to see everybody there who had been so kind and helpful to us as a young couple just starting out in life. Every place we went and every person we saw that weekend seemed to bring back a special memory. Crossing the Red Cedar River on the way to the game prompted me to recall Jo taking the twins there to feed the ducks before going to band practice.

I thought about all of the people I had met there who had played such a big role in my life, people like Biggie and Duffy. So was Father Mac, the longtime Michigan State chaplain. He had always taken pride back in the 1950s in announcing that there were more Catholics playing for Michigan State than there were playing at Notre Dame.

We had whipped the Spartans the year before at South Bend, and this time they were determined not to let it happen again. It was a good game, but we came out on top. After we had showered and were prepared to leave for the trip back home, I paused for a couple of minutes to take one more walk back inside Spartan Stadium. It was close to dark, and a cold, light rain was falling. I went and sat down on the Michigan State bench. I sat there and remembered how a lot of the good things in my life had started there. It truly was a special place.

The only negative about the game was that our best running back, sophomore Phil Carter, hurt his knee going for an NCAA rushing record and would not be able to play the next week against Miami, still led by Jim Kelly. Jim Stone, who was well liked by our coaches and his teammates, replaced Carter in the backfield and had a sensational day. As the game was winding down and we were comfortably ahead, we found out he was only two yards away from rushing for 200 yards. Everybody wanted to reward his dedication by seeing him reach that milestone, so we sent him back in the game. He was supposed to run a One Sweep, pick up the yards and we would run out the clock. Instead, he broke loose down the sideline and ran for a touchdown, right in front of Miami coach Howard Schnellenberger.

I know Howard didn't appreciate that, but we later became friends and talked about it, and he realized that we hadn't intended for him to score another touchdown. He knew that, faced with the same situation, he would have done exactly the same thing.

A 30-3 win the following week against Army improved our record to 5-0, and we climbed to fourth in the national polls. Our next game was at Arizona, coached by Larry Smith, and he already had earned a reputation for being able to pull off big upsets. We were riding so high that I knew Larry would have his team pumped up and ready to play their best game of the year. Because of that, I decided to make some of the most unsound play calls I had ever done in my career.

Late in the second quarter, we were leading on the scoreboard but found ourselves backed up near our own goal line. Knowing Larry and his reputation and the Arizona crowd, I knew we had to do something to regain the momentum that we had lost. So, I could envision us punting on fourth-and-12 from inside our own 20, and Arizona setting up at midfield, ready to go in and score the go-ahead touchdown.

Just before the pregame warm-up, I had taken Blair Kiel over to a blackboard and diagrammed a fake punt from the formation that I'd told him we would use against Michigan when I was recruiting him. Blair was our number-one quarterback now and also our punter. He was good at both. I was convinced that Arizona would rush 10 men and try to get the defensive ends in tight enough to block the kick. By doing that, they made themselves susceptible to an end run of some kind.

I told Blair before the game that we would be in constant contact from the sidelines, and that if it looked like we might want to fake, we would discuss it and only he and I would know it was a fake. It was just better that nobody else should know about it and cause them worry.

Before Blair ran onto the field at the start of that possession, I said to him, "Just keep an eye on me, Blair, because we might fake it on fourth down if we have to punt."

I had a whistle on a cord in my pocket. I told him that his signal from me was that I would twirl my whistle. That would mean the fake was on. I then told him, "But, you just go ahead and call the punt. When you step up to punt, watch the right defensive end or the man to your left. If he comes in tight, keep the ball and run to your left. If he doesn't rush, go ahead and punt it."

As I think about that now, to give that much responsibility to a kid just out of high school, playing quarterback at Notre Dame, was a little unfair. He was capable of handling it, though.

Arizona did bring two ends on the rush. Blair stepped forward as if to kick it, but he kept it and ran around the left side—80 yards for a touchdown. When you don't plan things, sometimes they work out quite well. One of our freshmen going downfield on punt coverage heard the crowd noise and knew that something different was happening. He turned around and saw Blair, then went down and blocked Arizona's punt returner, so that Blair had a straight shot down the sideline.

I think most of my squad and coaching staff thought I had gone a little haywire. It really was what we had to do to regain momentum and go on to win the game. Actually, it was also out of respect for Larry Smith's ability to upset good teams that led to my decision. The following week, Larry took his team to top-ranked UCLA and beat them. That confirmed to me that we did the right thing. Later, when I was the Athletic Director at Missouri, I hired Larry Smith as the football coach. We needed someone who was honest, a disciplinarian and who would fit into Missouri's Ivy League atmosphere.

We were now the number-three team in the country, playing undefeated Navy at Giants Stadium in New Jersey. We played a nearly perfect game and won 33-0. My good friend, Wellington Mara, the owner of the Giants, stopped me after the game and asked if he could borrow our team for the weekend. Of course, he was kidding, but he was very impressed by how we played.

The win vaulted us into the top-ranked spot in the polls. A year that had begun with so much confusion had now seen us climb all the way to the top. We couldn't celebrate, however, because we still had a long way to go. Our first test was against Georgia Tech. Our game plan was designed around the pass, and we definitely were a running team. The game ended in a 3-3 tie, but everybody in our program really took it as a defeat. With a young team, things like that happen, but my job was to quickly lift their spirits back up and get the players ready to meet undefeated Alabama.

Our tie against Georgia Tech had dropped us to sixth in the country, with undefeated Georgia number one, but it was widely assumed the winner of our game against the Crimson Tide was going to have a choice of invitations to the Orange, Cotton, Sugar or Fiesta Bowl.

The game was in Birmingham, where Alabama plays several of its home games. I was nervous and excited at the same time. There was nothing more exciting than the buildup to a big game, and this was a big one. The players were ready, and I knew we were going to play much better than we had against Georgia Tech.

We won, 7-0, giving me three wins in three career games against Bear Bryant teams. I'm proud of that record, because I really think he was as good a coach as there has ever been in college football. He always was gracious and complimentary as well, and we were lucky to win some of those games. I thought he represented everything good about college football.

When I entered the locker room after the game, my young team was chanting, "Georgia! Georgia!" because Georgia was number one, and they could see the opportunity of jumping into that spot if we beat Georgia in a bowl game. We voted, right there in the locker room, to go to the Sugar Bowl to play Georgia.

When we got home, the entire student body met the team at the circle near the Dome. Jo rode on the team bus from the airport to the pep rally on campus. The bus ride, as you get close to the campus, is simply great and very slow because the students have now come out to meet the team and go the last few blocks together.

The next morning, many of the newspapers around the country carried a photo of Scott Zettek and others carrying me off the field after the game. In my opinion, this illustrates my coaching style, although I didn't realize it at the time. Early in Scott's career, we had several real disagreements. I know that he thought my discipline was not worth much. But there he was as a senior, carrying his coach over to meet Bear Bryant after that big game, in a season where we had our choice of the Orange, Cotton, or Sugar Bowl.

Today, Scott is very successful and writes to me often. It's ironic, because I was once quoted as saying, "If I had to do it over again, I wouldn't have been as tough on Scott Zettek." In his letters to me, the bottom line has been, "Thanks, Coach, for being tough on me because I was a spoiled brat just out of high school. I needed that to get me through Notre Dame and to give me a running start on life." There are some players who acknowledge that they need some straightening out and there are others who don't.

After receiving the Sugar Bowl invitation to play undefeated Georgia, we returned home to get ready for a really good Air Force team. Air Force was again building a successful program and in future years would have good success against Notre Dame. We knew we would have to do an exceptional job of preparation to win the last two games and go into the Sugar Bowl undefeated.

During the week, Father Joyce called me on the practice field. I had installed a phone on the practice field for emergencies. I took the call, knowing it would be very important; he had never called me on the field before.

Father Joyce, always very kind and considerate, apologized for calling and said he wanted my feelings on announcing immediately that Gerry Faust had been offered the job as the new head coach. I could tell that if I felt the announcement would hurt our preparations, the announcement would not be made. I told him that it wouldn't affect us . . . if it were best for the university, he should go ahead and do it. All my life I have entered into decisions rather quickly and confidently. I was positive I could handle everything. I didn't, however, fully realize just how fragile a team's mental and emotional state can be, and it did affect us more than I thought it would.

In football today, you have to be so mentally sharp, especially at a school like Notre Dame, where students work hard in the classroom every day and battle on the football field all week and on Saturdays. In all other cases, my coaching changes had happened after a season had been completed, but here was Father Joyce on the phone, with his question. Before we hung up, I congratulated Father Joyce on his selection. Gerry Faust was a logical choice, even though he had not coached before at the collegiate level. There were many fine, good men who had played for him in high school on our Notre Dame team. He always supported my teams 100 percent.

The announcement was made on the afternoon of November 24, 1980. I never felt pushed or pressured to make the announcement quickly. In retrospect, however, I see that the announcement should have been held until after the bowl game. Because of Gerry's gregarious personality, his love of Notre Dame, and his anxiousness to get started, it was difficult for me to maintain that straight line of concentration that this young team needed. I let that slim line slip; it's the head coach's job to stabilize all situations that can and do arise.

Just prior to Gerry's announcement, we defeated Air Force in a super game. Now came the regular-season finale at 17th-ranked Southern California. We weren't prepared to play that game, and I take full responsibility for that. We had a lot of rain, which left the practice and game fields in Los Angeles very wet. I was unable to get the sharpness and concentration from the players that is necessary to beat a great team like USC. I had felt bad after the 1978 USC game, but Jo and I were almost sick after this one.

Almost all hope of our team winning the national championship was now gone, but we still had to prepare to play undefeated and number-one ranked Georgia in the Sugar Bowl. The leader of the Georgia team was a great running back, Herschel Walker, and we could easily have just gone through the motions and let them roll all over us. It was a difficult situation for the players, and also for our staff, when some of the assistants already had learned they would not be retained on Gerry Faust's staff. I knew they were upset, but they assured me they would still give 100 percent to help us go out on a winning note. I went into the game unsure about what to expect.

After digging ourselves into a hole in the first half, we fought back to dominate the second half. Georgia's yardage came mostly in the fourth quarter, when we attempted to go for a fourth-and-1 and missed it.

Statistics aren't for winners, because the Irish made 328 net yards total to Georgia's 127 yards. Georgia scored on drives of 1 yard and 22 yards, for 14 of their 17 points.

With five minutes remaining in the third quarter, Blair Kiel moved the team 57 yards, with Phil Carter scoring from a yard out. On our next possession, we drove to Georgia's 27, but on third-and-1 at the Bulldog 20, Scott Woerner stopped Phil Carter for a 1-yard loss. Then we missed a 38-yard field goal attempt.

I've often wondered if I didn't get caught up in the fact this was my last game. There were two plays, one on offense and one on defense, when I didn't do my job in helping out two true freshmen by calling time-outs to explain the situation to them. I was thinking more through emotion at that point and not focusing on the technical aspects of the game. They were two big plays.

Georgia held on for the 17-10 win. As we were walking off the field, Dave Duerson—who eventually become a Notre Dame captain—put his arm around my shoulder and told me, "We've wanted so badly to win this one for you." I'll never forget that gesture. I felt Georgia was a fitting national champion. Coach Vince Dooley was very gracious. Naturally, we would have liked to have gone out on a happier note, but I always felt that our team gave 100 percent, and I was proud of that. The technical mistakes were not a result of poor effort. I was also proud that—except for Knute Rockne's 1-0 record in postseason play—my 3-1 bowl mark stands as the best in Notre Dame history.

The next morning, Jo, my daughter Jill, my grandson Sam and I flew to San Francisco. I went there to coach the Shrine East-West game. There was time to reflect on the many great opportunities we had during my tenure for the various teams I coached. Winging westward, I dozed and woke up to find Jill asleep on one shoulder and Jo asleep on the other. Jill is the baby of the family. Today, she is a successful teacher in Gilbert, Arizona.

The East-West game is always a great experience. Going with the two teams and coaches to the Shriners' Children's Home and Hospital and meeting the children gives this game a special significance. These children, like my wife Jo, are too tough and kind to describe what they go through each day. I've seen many players on these teams suddenly realize how fortunate they are to have a healthy life.

When the game was over, I walked off the field with TV analyst Jim Hill. Jim had been my free safety at Green Bay. I really didn't feel any special emotions at that moment; everything had been left on the field after the Sugar Bowl.

Earlier in the season, I had spoken with Jon Gruden, the son of Jim Gruden, one of my assistant coaches, about coaching as a profession. He was just a youngster and I had the chance to give him some insights into the life of a football coach. Many years later, Jon called me. He had just been named the head coach of the Oakland Raiders. He was calling to thank me for having that little talk with him when he was younger, and that he remembered my enthusiasm for coaching.

As I recall that conversation, what I told him was very simple. I was extremely happy coaching and loved working with the players. On my way up, loyalty and hard work were high priorities. Emotions, preparations and discipline are all important factors in playing winning football. Don't be afraid to show your emotions; but above all, don't ever lie to your team and they'll never lie down. Remember that you have a close, parental type of relationship with upwards of 150 young people. Don't take yourself too seriously. It can't be a game for the players if it's not a game for you. I see too many parents of young athletes who take the fun out of it. It makes you wonder why they are doing it.

I'd like to give any young coaches-to-be some advice. First of all—don't overcoach! Many times, I have seen teams working out too hard in their pregame warm-ups. It's the head coach's job to be certain that the team is not overworked and has plenty of energy for the game to follow. You may have noted that teams prepare for the season and bowl games differently now than when I first started coaching.

For example, in 1959, in preparation for the Orange Bowl, we had an intrasquad scrimmage before leaving for Florida. Twenty years later, for the 1980 Sugar Bowl, we didn't hit scrimmage once before the game.

Players are bigger, stronger and faster than they ever were. The squads are smaller. At this level of play and with their skills, it risks unnecessary injuries to go hard late in the season.

If I were a university president truly interested in preventing injuries, I'd raise the scholarship limit. Because of squad size, immature freshmen often get caught up in heated rivalries, when they should be back on campus playing a freshman schedule and spending time in the library.

For me, as I have said many times, football has been a way of life. You've got to be out there on a hot August or September afternoon when everyone's sweating and you've told them they don't have time for anything but studying and football, nothing else, including normal social relationships. Biggie Munn could push a team until they were ready to rebel, and then he'd slowly back off and have fresh legs for the first game. Football demands a certain type of sacrifice. On occasion, I've heard grumpy players ask themselves, "Why am I doing this? Why can't I have the normal things?"

About then, they look up at you the coach, and you've got Phi Beta Kappas and everybody else, and they've got that look in their faces that they know they are stuck with you, for better or worse. In the end, it's all worth it.

I'd close my conversation with the young potential coach today as I did with Jon Gruden years ago: "Your dad and mom are happy. You look happy. Why don't you give it a try?"

Chapter Eight

AFTER RETIREMENT FROM COACHING

One more coaching assignment awaited me before I could drift slowly into retirement. In fact, I never did drift there fast enough; I'm not really there yet. I had previously made a commitment to coach in the Japan Bowl in Tokyo, so immediately after the East-West Shrine Game, Jo and I were on our way to Tokyo.

Every all-star game is different, and the Japan Bowl has an identity all its own because of the international aspects to the game and the fact the Japanese don't get as much exposure as Americans to college football.

One of the differences, of course, is the facilities. As I found out during Notre Dame's trip there to play Miami, the Japanese just aren't equipped to handle a full-sized college team. We were staying and practicing in Tokyo, but the game was played in Yokohama. We only had one 80-yard field for practice, and both teams were on the field at the same time. That gave our coaches the opportunity to stand and scout them, but at the same time, their coaches were standing and watching us. This worked because it was an all-star game, where nobody really cares who wins and who loses, and because the other head coach was Johnny Majors of Tennessee, a good friend.

Both teams ate together, rode buses together and really hung out together for the whole week. The biggest challenge of the week was trying to make ourselves understood to all of the Japanese people around us who spoke no English, because none of us spoke any Japanese.

Two nights before the game, Jo and I were brought into a big room at the hotel. It was beautifully decorated. We didn't know what was going on, but soon realized it was a "goodbye" party thrown in our honor. It was put on by the coaches of both teams, the Notre Dame players in the game—Jim Stone and Pete Holohan—and Japan Bowl officials. It was a wonderful evening, with all of the delicacies and color of an Oriental party. It surprised and humbled us that people were kind to us so far away from home.

One other memorable moment from that trip came at halftime of the game, when cameras were allowed in the locker room. I was talking with Cris Collinsworth, the great wide receiver from Florida who went on to play for the Bengals and now is a television broadcaster. We were talking about the setup of the defense and I told him, "Cris, when you line up wide to the right, I think the cornerback on the right side is playing you up tight. When you're wide left, then the kid from BYU on the corner plays you loose, right?"

Cris thought it over, and with the cameras aimed directly at him, he said, "Where's BYU?"

All I could think of, with the camera now right in my face, was, "Cris, one million Mormon TV sets just got turned off."

I certainly didn't intend that as a religious joke of any kind. It was just an example of how difficult it was to conduct halftime and pregame meetings at all-star games. We even cut a few seconds off at the end of the game because everyone had to catch a flight from Tokyo to Los Angeles.

One player stood out in the game, for the other side. He played quarterback, he was on the special teams, he probably was playing defense, too. He just seemed to be all over the field. He was the MVP in the game, and I remembered his name because he was someone I wanted to make certain I followed in the future. He didn't turn out to have much of a career in pro football, but now he's moved into a different arena. The guy who attracted my attention was J.C. Watts, the former quarterback at Oklahoma, who now is a U.S. Representative from that state and is a high-ranking member of the Republican Party.

After getting back to the States, Jo and I stayed in an apartment in Newport Beach, California, owned by a prominent Notre Dame alumnus. While there, Jo and I took Joe Montana and his wife to dinner, and we ended up scribbling plays all over the linen tablecloth with felt pens at this very elegant restaurant—with the kind permission of the maitre d'. Joe had yet to reach his star status with the 49ers, and years later I told that maitre d' nobody knew how valuable that tablecloth would have been had anyone thought to save it.

After a good period of relaxation, Jo and I returned to South Bend. There, Jo and I were honored at another retirement dinner thrown by the university. Father Edmund Joyce, the executive vice president of Notre Dame and a long and cherished friend, acted as the master of ceremonies. You know that anything Father Joyce is involved with is going to be done in a first-class manner. His dime was always worth a quarter. Both Father Joyce and Father Hesburgh are wonderful holy men and also extremely talented. Father Jerry Wilson, also from Notre Dame, was also an exceptional person and helped to make the dinner a huge success. One of the speakers was Joe Garagiola, a friend for many years even before his son Steve, a Notre Dame graduate, watched the 1970 Notre Dame-Missouri game.

The only bad part about the dinner and party was the weather, which was awful. The captains from all six of my Notre Dame teams traveled from all over the country to be there, and some really had to fight the weather. Willie Fry flew in from New York, and spent a day at O'Hare Airport in Chicago before he finally was able to rent a car and drive to South Bend. Vagas Ferguson, who disliked flying, even in good weather, came in by private plane.

Other friends from all over the country were there, joining the crowd of more than 1,000 people. Vince Dooley of Georgia represented the football coaches association, and there were conference commissioners, bowl game representatives, former players and friends and many members of the media on hand. Bob Broeg and his wife, Lynne, made the drive on icy roads from St. Louis, and I was glad they were able to be there with us. The evening was over much too soon, but it was a night Jo and I will always remember. It meant so much to us and everybody in our family. It was very difficult to say yet another goodbye to my assistants, staff and the players.

While I was sitting there listening to all my Notre Dame captains when it came their turn to speak, I started thinking about why a player is elected captain of a particular team. Being selected captain always was a special honor for me, and I was the captain of every team I played on in high school and college. In my case, in football, it meant that I could block and tackle. In basketball, it meant I would rather pass the ball to another player than shoot it. In baseball, I could and would hit behind the runner to advance him to another base. The opposing catchers always told me they hated to see me rounding third base headed their way, because they knew a collision was coming. In hockey, I think I was a pretty good penalty-free enforcer.

Not every player is cut out to be a captain; that's why they have an election. It's the same as every player not being cut out to be a starter. You don't have to be the captain or even a starter to make a huge contribution to a team. I've never had a captain who wasn't a great player and also a great leader. I was constantly amazed at the high caliber of young men who were elected to that honor. If I was forced to single out one all-time captain, it probably would be Ed Bauer, who already was captain of the Notre Dame team when I arrived in South Bend.

Ed Bauer was not only a fantastic captain, but he is a great person. He is a very intelligent and understanding man. He is a tough football player, a great credit to Notre Dame and a fine person. In his senior year, we were playing Air Force at the Academy (1975); we were trailing 30-10. One of Joe Montana's first passes was picked off by an Air Force defensive back. The defensive back weaved a path all the way down the field, only to be run down from behind by Ed Bauer near our goal line. This saved the day for us. We turned around and scored. If we had given up a touchdown, it might have been too much to overcome. Ed accepted his captain's responsibilities as he has accepted all the responsibilities in his life, with grace and dedication.

Father Hesburgh also delivered a fine speech at the dinner, which included this statement: "A man wears his honor for his shield, and Dan has a huge shield."

Notre Dame had always treated me kindly and respectfully, and that continued even after I retired. During the transition period, I was given an office, assigned a secretary and was paid for another six months. I spent much of 1981 traveling around the country speaking and also giving clinics and lectures. I thought about coaching again, and did some interviews with some college and pro teams, but my heart wasn't in it. I attended Notre Dame's first game of the year, a good win for Gerry Faust and the players over LSU.

One of the advantages of spending time at Notre Dame is that you become friends with a lot of powerful and influential people, including a gentleman named Bob Welch and his wife, Caroline. He had been a huge supporter of Ara Parseghian. We spent a week at his condominium in Fort Lauderdale, and we used his Lear jet to fly to Ann Arbor for the Michigan-Notre Dame game. Some other good friends, Roger and Pam Stanton, planned a huge tailgate party in the Michigan parking lot, and one discovery I made was that it was a lot easier getting to the game on the team bus, surrounded by a police escort, than it was to fight the other 100,101 fans all vying for parking spots, the bathrooms and access to the stadium.

Notre Dame lost a close game, and then Jo and I headed back to South Bend. We soon were off again on a 15-day trip throughout the Southeast, where I was scheduled to make numerous appearances.

Most of the appearances were at quarterback clubs, but one day that stood out was a trip to Tuscaloosa, Alabama. Bear Bryant was still coaching, and he invited Jo and me out to practice. At that time in the development of her disease, Jo was able to walk with help. Bear had two of his managers meet her at the front gate to the practice facility and escort her to the field. Bear was up on top of what was easily the tallest practice tower I had ever seen. It looked like he had a big Coca-Cola machine up there. When he saw us, he climbed down from the tower.

Bear found a red chair, unfolded it and dusted it off, and set the chair down right at the 50-yard line. He told Jo to sit down, and then he blew his whistle and announced to the team, in his gravel drawl, "This is Mrs. Devine sitting here. I want you all to be very careful when you come over this way."

It was a great gesture, and Jo and I really appreciated it. It reminded me of the time that John Robinson, when he was coaching at USC, once stopped his team bus so he could get out and say hello to Jo. His team had just lost badly to ASU.

Bear Bryant and I had developed a good friendship over the years, and the time I spent with him always was enjoyable. He had a habit that when his team lost to a good team, he would invite the other coach to come in and speak to his team. We spent five days there and got to know each other even better.

We also went to the University of Tennessee on that trip, and the night before the Volunteers' game against Auburn, Johnny Majors and his wife took us to Gatlinburg for a wonderful, private dinner. The next day Jo and I watched the game from the press box. I couldn't help but think about how Pat Dye, then the new coach at Auburn, had played against my Missouri team in 1960, in the Orange Bowl. Time had definitely slipped by.

We returned to South Bend, and Gerry Faust invited me to come speak to the team. It wasn't awkward coming to practice and talking with many of the players I had recruited because it had been a smooth transition. We were all Notre Dame men, sharing time and thoughts together.

Jo and I had time to settle down and decide what we wanted to do with the rest of our lives. There were many opportunities available for us, and one thing I had always remembered was when Jo and I left Arizona in 1957, I promised her we would go back some day. Some friends let me know that the job of Executive Director of the Sun Angel Foundation, the fund-raising arm of the Arizona State Athletic Department, was going to be open. I talked about it with my friend and former assistant Frank Kush, and he assured me it would be something I would enjoy.

I still had many friends in the area and liked ASU's football coach, Darryl Rogers, and had the support of the school's administration. It seemed to be a good fit for me at this point in my life.

In the years since I had left Arizona State, the school had grown tremendously, as had the entire Phoenix area. It now had the sixth-largest student body population in the country on one campus, and it was remarkable to see all of the changes that had taken place. It was fun and exciting to walk into Sun Devil Stadium and know the success of our team in 1957 was in a large way responsible for that stadium being built.

When I started working as the head of the Sun Angel Foundation, I joined the broadcast team for Arizona State football. Tom Dillon was the play-by-play man and did a great job. Currently, Tom does play-by-play for Fox and also does the NFL Cardinals games. Broadcasting was an interesting experience for me. It did cut down on the trips that I was able to make to places like Notre Dame and Missouri during the season.

Lee Hamilton was also on our staff. He now does play-by-play for the Southern California Trojans and the Seattle Seahawks. Greg Schulte was a member of the broadcast staff and now does very well with the Diamondbacks baseball broadcasts. Tim Healey was recently appointed the radio voice of the Sun Devils. He's a great guy, working for a great school. While I enjoyed working on the broadcasts, I decided I would rather be more available to travel during the season, so I decided to give up that job.

Dr. J. Russell Nelson was the President of Arizona State, and he instilled a spirit among the students and faculty that excellence is not only attainable but is a prerequisite for graduation. He inherited an athletic department torn by strife, and he succeeded in working miracles in a short period to restore dignity and stature to the University's athletic endeavors. Thanks to Dr. Nelson and the brilliant leadership of former Athletic Director Kevin White, Arizona State has a program that it can be proud of, all on an ethical basis.

We also established the Sun Angel Endowment Foundation in order to ensure the future development of our men's and women's athletic programs. Donations to the Endowment help fifth-year men and women complete their degrees after using up their athletic eligibility. My daughter Sarah, a Notre Dame graduate, has a generous life insurance policy, with the beneficiary the Sun Angel Endowment Foundation. When the Sun Angel Foundation was beginning years ago, its contributions were only to the Athletic Department. Today, the Foundation supports all aspects of University life and contributes to a variety of projects for which a booster group might not be considered responsible. This philosophy permeates to the athletes and helps them better realize that they are a significant part of the student body.

Since its inception, the Sun Angel Foundation has acted under the direction of the university. Jointly, they accomplished a great deal. For instance, in a combined effort with the Funk family, the Angels became the university's largest source or donor of academic scholarships. When I was working with the Foundation, annual scholarships were provided to seven different colleges. We also supported the College of Engineering with a pledge of more than $1,250,000. The Sun Angels also helped fund the law school library, helped resurface the men's and women's track complex, and funded a feasibility study on property near the campus for building a championship golf course for the use of students, the faculty and the public. I was one of three people who put together this idea of a championship golf course. The other two are very close friends, Solly Sollenberger and Henry Delozier. The president of Arizona Public Service (the company that supplies electricity), Keith Turley, was responsible for a gift of 100 acres and worked with many others to get the job done. Keith has since passed away, as has Solly.

I recently attended a small dinner for 16 people, including two university Presidents. The dinner was to honor Keith Turley. Solly arranged the dinner at the Karsten ASU Golf Course. This golf course has greatly improved that area of the campus and also helped our golf teams become some of the best in the country. The course runs along the usually dry Salt River. A project is under way to restore water to the Salt River and bring commerce and entertainment to the area. This huge project was precipitated by the building of the golf course years ago. It will have a major impact on the valley. Working with the Sun Angel Board was one of the finest experiences of my life. I will always remember the Sun Angel Foundation and what it has done for the state.

Before I went to work for the university, directly for the President, I had been appointed by the Governor and President of the university to be Chairman of the state's first Super Bowl Committee. We didn't have the Cardinals here yet, and no city had ever gotten the Super Bowl without having an NFL franchise. With the help of three ASU employees—Herman Frazier, former Olympic gold medal winner and now the Associate Athletic Director, Dr. Brent Brown and Dr. Paige Mulholland—we created a presentation for the NFL owners' meeting in Washington, D.C. The presentation consisted of a slick brochure and a modern video. The owners really enjoyed the presentation. They left us with the impression that when we got an NFL franchise, we would also get the Super Bowl.

Brent, Herman, Keith Turley, and Bill Shover were instrumental in bringing the Cardinals to Phoenix. They sent me back to St. Louis to visit with the owner, Bill Bidwill. I'm not sure how much good I did, but the Cardinals are here and we were awarded a Super Bowl. Governor Rose Mofford made the state's presentation to the owners. Bill Bidwill, a very popular owner among the NFL owners, contributed much to the presentation also.

I never became very involved with the Fiesta Bowl because I was busy with so many other duties for ASU. The best thing the Fiesta Bowl people have going for them is their involvement with the community and ASU. For a fund-raiser in the early '80s, they raffled off several large items. The first prize was Super Bowl tickets. At the last minute, they couldn't get the Super Bowl tickets. I provided four of mine. In 1999, they paid $11.6 million to each team that played in the Fiesta Bowl.

While I was still an employee of Arizona State University, President Nelson wanted to provide a service to the people of Arizona with regard to substance abuse. I was ready for a move and decided to work on this project. Part of the attraction of it was that it brought me back into an educational environment. I worked for five years in the general field of substance abuse, where I worked as Director, Community Education/Substance Abuse. This was very satisfying because it allowed me national scope and close contact with the President of the United States' cabinet. When I was coaching at Notre Dame, the Governor of Indiana was Dr. Otis Bowen. When I was working for President Reagan and ASU, Dr. Bowen was the Secretary of Health and Human Services.

There were many frustrating moments in my work in the field of substance abuse. The most frustrating was that the people who were governing our country did not realize that alcoholic beverages were a drug used as a mood changer. They also fought the recognition of tobacco as an addictive substance. Today, that recognition has been somewhat achieved, but alcohol consumption and tobacco usage are still terribly large problems, with unbelievably large costs associated with them. Of the millions of dollars we have spent to combat substance abuse, only a tiny fraction has trickled down to where it was needed. That is as true today as when I was deeply involved in the field.

Early in my work at ASU, the university sent me to the Johnson Institute in Minneapolis to study the issues of substance abuse. This was my first opportunity to learn about this acute problem. The work was extremely difficult, but very interesting. This work with substance abuse also allowed me to discover the existence of many super but underpaid people who are totally dedicated to the relief of this cancer from our everyday life.

In my life as a football coach, on any given day you could walk away from a missed field goal or a dropped pass, and the world didn't come to an end. That's not true in the world of illicit drug use. There are no winners there at all. There are no banners, no applauding crowds, no glory . . . only exploitation, addiction and death.

In my football career, for every winner after a game there also was a loser. But in our everyday work—whether in the classroom, the work site or the boardroom—we have to make the most of every opportunity we are afforded. The goal is to make all of us winners in whatever we choose to do. It doesn't get any more real than that.

What I learned in my five years of work in this field is that we can create a drug-free America . . . and that it is within the power of each of us to stop the use and proliferation of illicit drugs.

One of the primary facts that I learned in my work is that drug use is not a victimless crime. The innocent babies of addicted mothers are victims. Children and their families are victims every time drug use crosses the threshold of the home. The average American is a victim whenever we pick up the tab of drug use on the job, or when our lives are endangered by someone driving on drugs or after using alcohol. We are all victims when we have to pay for interdiction abroad, or when drug-financed terrorism disrupts our lives.

For me, the solution is fundamentally based on personal choice, to refuse involvement with drugs personally. This can be extended to one's home, one's neighborhood, one's city, one's home state and then our country. We are all involved at all of these levels, but the most basic decision is made on the personal level, to take personal responsibility for one's own decisions.

In my work with substance abuse for the Reagan administration, I had to leave home in Phoenix every Monday to fly to Washington, D.C., or some other destination for that week's business. I would come back, exhausted, each Friday. This lasted for five years, and then I retired from that.

I had yet another retirement party. Once again, Joe Garagiola was the emcee. At the end of a very long but delightful evening, someone asked if I would like to make any concluding remarks, but Joe popped up (perhaps he's heard too many closing remarks from me) and said, "Dan, there's no need for any closing remarks tonight."

Well, maybe Joe should have let me have my say. The next morning, the newspaper headline said: "Devine Goes Back to Missouri." The governing board of the University of Missouri twice had sent interim chancellor Dr. Gerald Brouder to Phoenix in order to convince me to return. I felt needed, and probably that I was ready for a new challenge, so I agreed to go back to Columbia in August of 1992 as Athletic Director.

I had told Missouri officials that I would take the job for one year. One of the hardest aspects about the job was that Jo was unable to go with me, having to stay at our home in Arizona. I knew I had the support and appreciation of the university, but it was tough to be away from her so much of the time. My last contract, written by the chancellor, Dr. Chuck Keisler, gave me a week off every month, so I could be back in Phoenix with Jo, and paid for the transportation as well as a yearly vacation. But I missed Jo terribly.

One of the points stipulated in my contract with Missouri was that my job, in part, was to restore pride and dignity to the university's athletic program. I thought that was very interesting because that was really what they wanted me to do, but I never thought I'd see it spelled out like that. Another stipulation was to raise $2 million in new revenues without using ticket sales. We raised the money almost overnight. That was the seed that grew into the multimillion-dollar complex that's now in existence at Missouri, and I'm proud that the Devine Pavilion is part of this major complex.

What I'm most proud of is that it's for all Missouri students, not just members of the athletic teams. The Devine Pavilion will be used by tens of thousands of future Missouri men and women. The academic center and the new training facilities are models of providing the very best for the student athletes. The University of Missouri has done this at the same time it is raising entrance requirements.

Other duties during my time at Missouri included finding my successor as Athletic Director. I had groomed Joe Castiglione for the director's position, which he took, although he has now moved on to the University of Oklahoma. He surely is an excellent athletic director. There are many other good people there whom we also hired. I endorsed Mike Alden for Athletic Director. To sum up my second tour at Missouri, I was able to halt the horrible slide of 13 losing seasons and get it started back in the right direction, but they still have a bit farther to go to become a perennial power in the Big 12. They have succeeded in growing in attendance to the point where they had 62,000 to see the football game against a below-par Oklahoma team in 1998.

We were able to reverse the slide, once again establish pride in the university and start the unbelievable building program, and we did it all without even beginning to flirt with the NCAA rules and with the highest academic standards of any university in the Big 12.

I am greatly honored to have recently received an honorary doctorate in education from the University of Missouri. Do you think they'd believe that back in Proctor?

In March of 1999, I was able to attend the Bay Area Hall of Fame inductions. Four great athletes were inducted: Joe Montana, Ronnie Lott, Gordy Soltau and Tommy Smith. I attended with my good friends Coach Ben Parks and Michael Steele. Coach Parks, known to everyone as "Coach," is Joe Montana's personal trainer and he also trains Ronnie Lott. Coach Parks picked me up at the airport and drove me to Joe Montana's home. We enjoyed a great visit with Joe in his workout room. We reminisced about the many great Notre Dame moments.

Joe has a lovely wife and family. I remembered meeting Joe and his charming wife, Jennifer, for dinner after the 49ers Super Bowl XIX win over Miami in 1985. In that game, Joe was named the MVP. We didn't have many opportunities to mingle socially after that, not until we saw Joe, Jennifer and children at the 20th reunion of our 1977 championship team in 1997 at Notre Dame. He was so interested in his children, I could tell he was a good father. He has also returned to the people much that has been given to him.

Joe's dad presented him at the induction banquet that evening in San Francisco (which had John Madden as the emcee). Joe Sr. is very proud of his son, and Joe Jr. is equally proud of his Dad. Joe's Mom, Theresa, was a big part of this evening, too. Joe Sr. always supported his son throughout his career, and on this special evening Joe Jr. showed his appreciation for all of that support.

It has been my honor to have coached excellent players over the years, and they are the reason that I am in the National Football Foundation Hall of Fame, having been selected in the first year of my eligibility. The hall's induction dinner and ceremony in New York is by far the best banquet I attend on a regular basis. Its meaning goes beyond winning and losing. It stands for sportsmanship, integrity, character and contributions to the sport of football.

The night I was inducted in New York, I really felt that I had accomplished something. Paul Hornung gave the acceptance speech for the inductees. He did a great job. I'll remember forever how he said that he was so proud to be inducted in the same class as one of the nation's greatest football coaches (me!). That comment, coming from Paul, in front of all these illustrious people, made this small-town boy wonder to himself what had happened to turn his life into this miracle.

I was in the inaugural class of two halls—the University of Minnesota-Duluth Hall of Fame and the University of Missouri Hall of Fame. I'm also in the State of Missouri Hall of Fame, which includes Stan Musial, Dizzy Dean, Branch Rickey, Joe Garagiola, Curt Flood, Jack Buck, Bob Gibson, Bob Pettit, Paul Christman, Frankie Frisch and many other stars. Buck O'Neil, one of the first black members of the Hall of Fame, cried when I told him that I was proud to be in the same Hall of Fame that he was.

A day does not go by when I do not appreciate the countless blessings of my life and thank God for them. My life was formed in the Depression, separated from my family, and we did not have many of the luxuries of life. Yet I had the good fortune to have nurturing, supportive adults in my life who guided my ambitions and drive into useful pursuits. My professional life has been blessed by innumerable warm, strong friendships and very rewarding work at four of the finest universities in the world and the premier NFL franchise—Green Bay.

My personal life has surrounded me with a loving and large family, all with their own unique qualities. I marvel at the opportunity I have had to work with thousands of young men who have succeeded both on the playing field and in their personal and professional lives. None of this had to happen to me, but it did, and I will always be extremely grateful to all of those people who have made my life so fulfilling and rewarding, especially my devoted wife Jo. I can only say one thing to each one of them—thank you.

Chapter Nine

EPILOGUE

The following views summing up Dan Devine come from five key figures who are in charge of the Devine legacy left at Arizona State, Missouri, Green Bay and Notre Dame and from one of his longtime friends, Hall of Fame sportswriter Bob Broeg. The other views are from three respective Athletic Directors—Kevin White, Mike Alden and Mike Wadsworth—and the CEO of the Packers, Bob Harlan.

Kevin M. White, former Athletic Director, Arizona State University, current Athletic Director, University of Notre Dame:

Dan Devine served as the head football coach at Arizona State College for three seasons (1955-57). However, as historians from that period contend, they were the most important football seasons in school history, forever shaping the profile of the institution.

Devine compiled a win-loss record of 27-3-1 (.887) during that time, easily the highest winning percentage of all time for a Sun Devil football coach. Devine's first team fashioned an 8-2-1 slate in 1955, losing two games by a combined total of eight points. In 1956, Devine's troops improved upon the previous season, compiling a 9-1 record. Then, in 1957—which would be his last in Tempe—Devine's charges posted the first undefeated season in school history, a perfect 10-0. In addition to several easy victories, the Sun Devils crushed in-state rival Arizona 47-7 to cap the most brilliant season to date.

Little did Devine, or anyone for that matter, know that his spectacular 1957 campaign accomplishment would impact the school way beyond wins and losses. For it was at that time that Arizona State College was attempting to become a university. To the south, the University of Arizona, which had a stronghold on the state legislature, would do anything to block the name change. It became a heated debate, one that led to extreme animosity between state politicians, academicians, and citizens in both Phoenix and Tucson.

That undefeated season, in which ASC finished ranked 11th in the final poll (its first time ever in the Top 20), sparked great enthusiasm on campus and, especially, within the community. In fact, it generated so much interest that it is singularly credited with getting enough petition signatures on Proposition 200, eventually landing the vote on the November 1958 ballot.

Following the 1957 unbeaten season, Devine, who received at least half a dozen contract offers from schools across the country, left ASC to become the head football coach at the University of Missouri. With Devine watching from a distance, the vote passed by a 2-1 margin on November 8, allowing ASC to become Arizona State University and ending one of the most spirited debates in state history.

To this day, Tempeans credit the momentum of the petition, the ballot and the successful referendum to the marvelous undefeated football season orchestrated by Coach Dan Devine.

Today, Arizona State University ranks as the fifth-largest university in the nation. It could be argued that no other single college football season had more impact on the future of its institution than the undefeated season of 1957.

In 1982, Dan returned to ASU and served as President of the Sun Angel Foundation, a position that he would hold until 1987.

The three-year period preceding Dan's hiring was a challenging time for Sun Devil athletics. Dan Devine's hiring was a statement to the national athletic community that stability would return to ASU because of the recognizable and respected leadership that Dan represented.

During this time frame, a feasibility study was completed for the ASU Karsten Golf Course. An on-campus facility of this nature had been a longtime dream of Sun Angel supporters. Dan worked extremely hard to put the fund-raising framework in place that would bring this project to fruition.

The last year of Dan's tenure saw the Sun Devil football team win the Pac-10 and Rose Bowl championships. The presence created by Sun Angel President Dan Devine established Arizona State University athletics as a power once again.

With that, Coach Devine is affectionately heralded as a wonderful ambassador for both Arizona State University and college athletics in general. He has indeed left an indelible mark, one that warrants both emulation and celebration.

God bless Dan Devine!

Michael F. Alden, Athletic Director, University of Missouri:

I am a relative newcomer to the University of Missouri scene, having become Director of Athletics in August 1998. But having grown up in Central Missouri while Dan Devine was coaching the Tigers, and having worked with him at Arizona State early in my career, I have a keen understanding of just how important Dan has been in the long and storied history of the oldest public institution of higher learning west of the Mississippi River.

The 40-year love affair between Dan Devine and the University of Missouri goes both ways—supporters have an undying affection for him, and he reserves a special place in his heart for Mizzou. Columbia, Missouri, is the community in which he raised his family, and it continues to be a rallying point for the Devine family, some of whom still live here.

Dan Devine came to Missouri as head football coach in 1958 after Frank Broyles had spent a quick year coaching the Tigers following the 1956 retirement of the legendary Don Faurot. Devine quickly put his stamp on the Missouri football program.

With an offense that opted for a power running game and a rock-ribbed defense, Devine had the Tigers in a bowl game in his second season. In his third—1960—he coached MU to the only number-one ranking in its history and very nearly won a national championship. A tainted loss in the regular-season finale (to arch rival Kansas, which later forfeited the victory for using an ineligible player) was all that kept the Tigers from claiming the national title. Missouri won the Orange Bowl that season—its first bowl victory in eight tries—and would likely have won the national championship, anyway, had today's poll system been in place. In 1960 the final polls were taken before the bowl games, not after. Minnesota got the crown despite having lost the Rose Bowl.

Devine and Tiger supporters enjoyed a glorious decade in the 1960s. During those 10 seasons, Missouri was the only school in the nation never to lose more than three games in any season. He took the Tigers to five bowls from 1960 to 1969 and won three of them. He won a pair of Big Eight Conference championships and coached eight first-team All-Americans. One of them, halfback Johnny Roland, recently was tabbed for induction into the National Football Foundation Hall of Fame. Devine himself was similarly honored in 1985.

Off the field, four of his players won NCAA postgraduate scholarships; three were saluted as National Football Foundation Scholar-Athletes, and six achieved Academic All-American status. As Director of Athletics following Faurot's retirement in 1965, Devine hired Norm Stewart as the Tigers' basketball coach, and he also hired an assistant baseball coach, Gene McArtor, who later would take over for a 21-year run as head coach that resulted in his becoming the winningest coach in school history.

When Missouri initiated its own Intercollegiate Athletics Hall of Fame in 1990, concurrent with the university's celebration of its 100th football season, Devine was among the first 20 inducted into the charter class. Little did anyone know then that Devine was yet to make perhaps his biggest contributions to Mizzou.

After Dan left Columbia for the NFL in 1970, and after he won a national championship at Notre Dame in 1977, the University of Missouri endured a period of nearly two decades that was punctuated by leadership changes: five Chancellors, four Athletic Directors and five football coaches. The result was a downward turn in the athletic fortunes, especially in football, at MU.

In 1992, Interim Chancellor Gerald Brouder was faced with filling the Athletic Director's chair. The decision was an important one, considering that MU hadn't had a winning football season since 1983. Brouder sought to make a move that would steady the Tiger ship by bringing various factions together to help chart the future of intercollegiate athletics.

He called on Dan Devine.

Devine eagerly accepted the challenge, cutting short his work as director of a substance abuse program at Arizona State University and, at considerable personal sacrifice, making the return to Columbia, Missouri.

During an all-too-short two-year period, he set in motion the actions that now have the Tigers on the upswing again. He rejuvenated the university's fund-raising efforts and began a series of facility improvement projects that escalated to even greater heights after he completed his reign in 1994. One of those projects, an indoor practice facility, was completed in 1998 and now bears his name: The Daniel J. Devine Pavilion.

He hired Larry Smith to rebuild the Missouri football program, and four years later, the Tigers were back in the bowl business. He laid much of the groundwork for Missouri's venture into the Big 12 Conference. But perhaps the biggest thing Dan did was that he created a new spirit for Missouri athletics.

Tiger fans everywhere will forever be indebted to Dan Devine.

Bob Harlan, CEO, Green Bay Packers:

Dan Devine's contribution to the Green Bay Packers was, from the outset, the aura and approach of a winner, of one who revels in being in the arena and who is accustomed to a leadership role—and to enjoying the fruits of leadership—positive results.

In the case of his Packers' tenure, Dan's impact may be best illustrated by the reaction of one of his former University of Missouri players, Francis Peay, whom he found on the roster when he arrived in Green Bay to become the Packers' head coach in 1971: "As soon as he walked into our first meeting and began to speak, I began to feel the same kind of excitement I felt when he was our head coach at Missouri. There was no doubt about who was in charge."

When solving a problem or meeting a challenge, Dan Devine brings a dogged tenacity, excellent insights, and an unshakable confidence in the likelihood of a good result, a confidence born of consistent success with the same time-tested formula over his distinguished coaching career.

At his best in one-on-one situations, Dan Devine, in the main, exerted his influence most effectively behind the scenes, motivating both players and coaches to extend themselves, the best evidence being in 1972, when, in his second year as Green Bay's head coach, he led a modestly talented team to a division championship and into the Super Bowl playoffs.

Coach Devine obviously took a big chance in bringing in someone to work for the Packers who had no football experience. I was in public relations with the Cardinals at the time and well remember Lee Remmel's first question to me: "What's a baseball guy know about football?"

Dan thought I could handle the Packers' administrative duties and relieve him of some of his burden. He called Bing Devine at the Cardinals' spring practice, who knew I had attended college at Marquette in Milwaukee and was a Green Bay fan.

While working in St. Louis, I had spent a lot of time with Bob Broeg, the prominent sportswriter and close personal friend of Dan's. He and his associates spoke of Dan as if he were seated next to God. So, I was deeply flattered that he called me at spring practice. I am eternally grateful for the wonderful personal opportunity that Dan Devine has provided for me.

Michael A. Wadsworth, former Director of Athletics, University of Notre Dame:

A select list of head football coaches at the University of Notre Dame won national championships during their respective tenures with the Irish:

Knute Rockne
Frank Leahy
Ara Parseghian
Dan Devine
Lou Holtz

The first four names on that list already have been inducted into the National Football Foundation's College Hall of Fame—and the fifth name assuredly will qualify once he's finished coaching and becomes eligible.

That's only a small part of what Dan Devine accomplished as Irish head coach (1975-80), but it is indicative of the significance of his contributions.

His 1977 national championship team provided its own set of magic moments from that particular season alone. There was the famed green jersey game against USC, in which the Irish warmed up in their traditional blue before switching to green just prior to the kickoff. The emotional impact of that afternoon in Notre Dame Stadium won't soon be forgotten; nor will the 49-19 victory over the fifth-ranked Trojans. Then, looking at a Cotton Bowl matchup against a Texas team that was unbeaten and ranked atop the polls, the fifth-ranked Irish forced six turnovers and effectively held Heisman Trophy winner Earl Campbell in check in winning 38-10. The victory was impressive enough to vault Notre Dame to the top of the final polls.

Dan's tenure produced more than a few other noteworthy moments:

- The '76 Gator Bowl victory over a Joe Paterno-coached Penn State team.
- The '79 Cotton Bowl win over Houston in the aptly named Ice Bowl that Moose Krause termed the greatest comeback in Notre Dame history.
- A resounding 7-0 win in '80 against Alabama at Birmingham's Legion Field in a game that earned the Irish a Sugar Bowl invitation to play top-ranked Georgia.

In all, Dan coached 12 first-team All-Americans, including consensus choices Steve Niehaus, Ross Browner, Ken MacAfee, Bob Golic and John Scully. That list didn't include Vagas Ferguson, who became Notre Dame's all-time leading rusher during the Devine era—and Joe Montana, whose career left him as possibly the most recognizable Irish quarterback ever.

But statistics only begin to tell the Dan Devine story. Like any Hall of Fame-caliber coach, his success was based on his ability to communicate with and motivate the young men with whom he worked each day. It's renewed by the former players who stay in touch long after their days in an Irish uniform are done. And they were exemplified by the words on the plaque presented to Dan by his senior players in 1980 after the final home game:

> *To Coach Devine*
> *What we gave, we have.*
> *What we did not give,*
> *We've lost forever.*
> *Thank you for showing us*
> *how to give*
> *and for all we have now.*

> November 22, 1980
> Our last game together
> for Our Lady
> Senior Players 1980

Bob Broeg, *St. Louis Post-Dispatch:*

For more than 40 years, Dan Devine has enjoyed the close friendship of Bob Broeg, the eminent sportswriter of the St. Louis Post-Dispatch, *a member of the Baseball Hall of Fame and for many years Coach Devine's partner in an in-season television show on Missouri football. There is perhaps no better person in Missouri who can speak with the authority and experience of Bob Broeg regarding Coach Dan Devine.*

Dan Devine's second team at the University of Missouri apparently blew a lead in the final minutes of a rainy September Saturday in 1959 at Michigan's Ann Arbor and, as a reporter who should have known better, I blew my stack.

Too often as an Ol' Mizzou loyalist who tried to write objectively—as I would in the next few minutes—I'd seen the original Boy Scout coach, Don Faurot, lose too many big games late, trying manfully to balance the financial books by playing tougher teams.

Momentarily applauded, those heroic near-miss losses merely went down in history as defeats, and this was another one. Michigan, recovering a Tiger fumble, had kicked a field goal for a 15-14 lead with only two minutes to play. Worse, under the limited substitution rules of the moment, defensive back Bob Haas was the number-two quarterback, frozen in the lineup.

With Faurot sitting behind me in the Michigan press box, next to the famed athletic director, Fritz Crisler, I let fly with profanity that Faurot and certainly not my parents ever taught me.

But, lo, racing the clock, Haas engineered a 78-yard drive and with two seconds remaining, he dived into the end zone. Touchdown! 20-15 Missouri!

In my silent joy now, preparing to write, I heard Faurot lean over to me and say, with his cockeyed grin, "Ye of little faith . . ."

Devine recaptures here part of that rally, including unusual behavior by Coach Faurot, but he didn't mention also needling me about my press-box behavior.

I ribbed Dan—I hadn't started calling him Dan'l as yet—and said, "Gee, Coach, if that bus had been on time, I guess you'd have won the game in the last 20 seconds instead of the last two!"

If you didn't know that black Irishman as well as I did over the years, you didn't know his sharp wit, most of it in a rebound, as, for instance, after that famed Notre Dame rally on New Year's, 1979, the glacier game at Dallas's Cotton Bowl. Joe Montana and mates scored three touchdowns in the final seven minutes for an unbelievable victory over Houston, 35-34.

Sheepishly, I'd missed it. Disgusted and with eyes heavy from New Year's Eve celebration and traditional television viewing of the holiday smorgasbord, I'd taken a fourth-period nap before the Rose Bowl game, only to be awakened with the startling final score by my smiling dear wife, a Devine fan, too.

Before I could get off a wire of congratulations to the conquering coach, I received a telegram from him. The deeply devout Catholic must talk to the devil. The wire read:

"YE OF LITTLE FAITH. . ."

Daniel John Devine was unusual from his boyhood, spent largely with an aunt and uncle rather than his own family, to a manhood in which he seemed more what he wasn't. He looked taller than his height—5'9"—and weight-guessers always underestimate. Off duty, he could pass for a friendly druggist and most of his coaching years he seemed like a sidelines' traffic cop in a Brooks Brothers suit.

Whether watching him on the bench or playing with him, I found him a fierce competitor, sensitive, dark-eyed, fighting an inferiority complex that he explains. Even though his mother was ill and his father, too, it was tough spending so many years away from the small-town Wisconsin family of nine in which he was second.

For collaborator Michael Steele, Devine painted a more productive, grimmer picture of Proctor, Minnesota, than he ever did for me, but he did overlook the good-boy aspect given me once by his paternal aunt, Mary Johnson. Maybe it's because she caught early some of that fire that turned him into one of the great football coaches.

Said Mrs. Johnson when I wrote a book about Missouri football a quarter-century ago, "Oh, he had a temper at times, and he was so intense whether he played games or the baritone horn."

Yeah, and when he could take 55 players on a trip and convince them that they were all alone in a crowd of 55,000! But then and now, Devine would agree that his personal habits reflected themselves in his insistence that his teams dress neatly and practice with a tidiness that carries over into a minimum of game-day errors.

Seriously, he told me back there when he narrowly missed a first chance at a national championship, 1960, "I'll save you the trouble of describing me. I'm what you would call a 'fussbudget.' I've got three pet peeves—failure to pursue, failure to block downfield, and failure at all times to behave like a football team. The little things bother me more than the big ones."

Originally a small player with a big heart, a 135-pound sophomore high school back who would build his body up to 175 pounds as a railroad section hand, Dan wanted so much to get into the Air Corps that he ate carrots like Bugs Bunny. The war ran out on Lt.

Daniel J. Devine even though he was fully trained as a B-29 combat bombardier.

I can't believe, based on more than 40 years following him as a coach, that Devine wanted anything else except to become what he became as one of the best, but he fell in love before he sorted out the future, marrying his dearly beloved Joanne Brookhart, grand-daughter of U.S. Senator Smith Brookhart of Iowa.

Dear Jo, herself an outstanding athlete as a young woman, is Devine's hero and mine, too, as a gutsy multiple-sclerosis victim who has defied everything for too long, but still has the spirit and spunk that enabled her in a weakened MS condition to sit through the most famous of Devine comebacks, the one at the Cotton Bowl when Dallas froze over. The mother of seven is a national champion herself.

By the time Danny sorted it out, seeking his first coaching job, the school superintendent at International Falls, Minnesota, rebuffed him "rudely"—Dan's word, but mine with an amen—when the man thought neither the applicant nor his college, Minnesota-Duluth, had a "big name."

You've read about the Devines' spirit of adventure to East Jordan, Michigan, in a cross-country trek with an old car, baby carriage cradled on the front of the car and twin infant daughters who needed Dad's assistance in the night. As he quipped, some of Devine's fascination with an orderly football organization could have resulted from those wee hours when, as a weary student-athlete, he tried to feed Jennifer and Mary Jo on a three-hour schedule. Let's see now, which one wanted a bottle in the mouth or a diaper change? The answer—a feeding chart on the wall.

As you've seen, Dan learned about organization, after his brief, uplifting session at East Jordan, when he turned a perpetual prep loser into an unbeaten area champion. With the help of that over-sized Irish leprechaun, Duffy Daugherty, Danny was Michigan State's junior varsity coach when he asked big boss Biggie Munn about travel plans. Biggie, facing Notre Dame upcoming, thought sure as heck the coach of the Spartans' jayvees could make his own decision about travel plans to Ohio State.

As Devine told me more than once, "I learned a lesson. If you can't trust your assistant coaches, get new ones." Like a chairman of the board, Devine delegated authority and responsibility.

It was a far cry from the ham-and-raisin dinner Jo scraped up for a scrappy, personable kid named Doug Weaver at the Devines' Michigan State Quonset hut. Recalled Weaver, later a prominent head coach and athletic director, "I felt ashamed, eating there. With my GI scholarship, I should have been taking them to dinner."

By the time Devine head-coached Arizona State, his efforts in football helped elevate the college to a university and helped spawn the new stadium that is one of the nation's largest. There he learned, too, his knack of attracting prominent people's attention. Like Dizzy Dean's.

One night at ASU, Devine asked Ol' Diz to say a few words to the Sun Devils before a game. The greatest of the Cardinals' colorful Gas House Gang was at his finest. "I wasn't the greatest pitcher, but I was amongst 'em," drawled the former great pitcher. "You ain't the greatest team either, but you're amongst 'em. Listen to the Coach, hit 'em hard, and let 'em lay."

They did that often enough to win them national ranking for the first time and the coach national attention, too. In view of Dan's reluctance to visit Missouri, coupled with hot chocolate on his jacket aboard the plane, boisterous greeters at the Kansas City airport and an empty-tank trip to Columbia, it's amazing Faurot and Missouri got him—and most fortunate.

Among the reasons the football field at Columbia is named for Faurot, it was the old coaching home-state loyalist's career, plus his judgment in selecting Frank Broyles and Dan Devine as head football coaches at Missouri, both of whom now are in the College Football Hall of Fame.

First night there, a short stop at Faurot's house, the old coach said he was impressed by the younger coach's ability to communicate. "In that one night, heck," said Faurot, "he got closer to my three girls than I could."

Early, the 33-year-old coach convinced his first Tiger team in 1958 and thereafter to live up to the rules of conduct set by his first Missouri squad—no smoking or drinking in season, no gambling of any kind and curfew by 10:30 week nights, 1 a.m. after Saturday games.

A downer came late in the first season, just as it had to Broyles, a brash, fast-talking southern redhead. Frank's first team, a heady 5-1-1 late in the 1957 season, lost the last three straight: 9-7 to bitter rival Kansas after a 39-14 trimming at home by powerful Oklahoma. Somehow it seemed that Frank had oversold himself—and his Tigers—on their chances against a team that hadn't lost a conference game in 11 years.

Devine, who backed down to a similar 5-4-1 record with a late tie gained by Kansas at Columbia, had just come off a 39-0 clobbering at Oklahoma in the Sooners' Norman snakepit. There, astonishingly, the coach did an incredible thing, one to which he pays modestly little attention. Leaping on a training table in the visitor's dressing room, he snapped for attention and said, quivering:

"You seniors, I promise you that two years from now on this field, these sophomores will win the game and dedicate it to you."

In the 1959 season, in a staggering upset at Nebraska, the downtrodden Cornhuskers handed Oklahoma the Sooners' first conference defeat in 13 years and 73 games. Meanwhile, with a chance to take first place at a time champion Oklahoma was ineligible for a bowl game, Missouri fell at Colorado in an upset, 21-20, on two fourth-quarter touchdown passes by Gale Weidner.

Here, Devine and his staff made a bold defensive decision that reverberated throughout college football for years. The coach defines it here. They junked their soft pass defense in which they dropped their ends into the secondary. Instead, they went to a wide-end, six-man line in which they used only one linebacker. They put in an extra defensive back and turned loose their ends to rush the passer.

The next week in a televised game at Faurot Field, they upset sharpshooting Richie Mayo and Air Force's unbeaten Falcons, 13-0. "Out of that game," said Devine, "was born our defensive philosophy that the best pass defense is a strong pass rush."

That 6-2 defense was a major factor in an unbelievable stretch of 10-plus seasons—from Weidner at Colorado to Lynn Dickey at Kansas State—in which Devine's teams never lost late.

They won late and protected the lead against Kansas at Lawrence, 13-9, to win the Orange Bowl bid. Just before the game, Devine found his 13-year-old twin daughters gravely arguing over the nickname of the Jayhawks. One transplanted Missouri miss insisted that KU was the "Hijackers." "No," said the sister, "they're the Sharecroppers."

For the first time, I noted the semi-defensive, semi-belligerent attitude of Devine the Sunday morning after the bid to the bowl game. Why? "Because we didn't get the proper pep sendoff at Columbia. Nobody believed in this team except the coaches."

Devine projected himself as a faculty man with full involvement. He urged student leaders to soft-pedal traditional "Dixie" and emphasize "Fight, Tiger," an original rouser that had been gathering dust on a shelf. He encouraged the band leader to take the university's "Marching Mizzou" band to Miami at athletic department expense.

Devine's rapport with minorities, most certainly blacks, told him that a continuance of "Dixie" and a national fraternity's running around campus with the stars and bars insignia of the Confederacy just didn't set right with young men whose ancestors often had undergone the unthinkable, i.e., as someone else's property.

Dan didn't wear his concern on his sleeve, but his sensitivity manifested itself. As, for instance, a few years later, 1967, at Kansas City's Muehlebach Hotel, the night before the bus ride over to Lawrence for the Kansas game. I saw him fussing down a corridor of the hotel.

"I don't mind if my sophomores eat with sophomores, juniors with juniors and seniors with seniors, but darn it," he said, as one of my friends who doesn't cuss as I do, "I got into the team's private dining room and the blacks were with the blacks, the whites with the whites. I won't stand for that."

Parenthetically, as an aside, Missouri lost the next day to a pretty good Kansas team, 17-6, ending a regular season on a sour note since the championship-destroying '60 season. Befitting Missouri's selectivity then, administration and players, they didn't push for a bowl game on a 7-3 season.

About race, which I don't like to mention, it came up privately after the '68 Gator Bowl game in which, rising to the heights,

Ol' Mizzou "ran through Alabama like a barber's college," as Bear Bryant put it, 35-10.

Dan'l and the Bear got along great over the years, as Devine has recalled, noting Bryant's gallant efforts on behalf of Mrs. Devine, but at the postgame players' party at Jacksonville, the legendary 'Bama coach pressed the Missouri mentor about his relationship with black players.

"Actually," Dan confided, not intended for publication, "I told him that, truthfully, I probably had less trouble with blacks, though not much with any. You can be sure Alabama football is going to integrate."

When 6-4 Missouri went to the Orange Bowl after the 1959 season, subbing for Big Eight champion Oklahoma, the opponent was Wally Butts' Georgia team, top-ranked in the Southeast at 9-1. The Tigers outplayed the Dawgs, but lost only 13-0, because Fran Tarkenton did so well what he would do for years in pro football. He was as elusive as the Scarlet Pimpernel.

Devine, feeling pretty good with a fair-and-warmer outlook for the '60s, sniffed orange-scented air that night at a Miami country club, host to both teams. At one point, senior defensive back Fred Brossart, en route to a medical career in Oregon, took the coach aside for a word.

Afterward, Dan'l couldn't help repeating the conversation. Softly, he said, "Fred wanted to thank me for what I've done. Truth is, because he was a scholar-athlete, I was tougher on him than most others."

In unguarded moments, the feelings of the coach who worked from a tower and behind a fence of detachment let his feelings hang out. As, for instance, when only son Dan Jr., oddly nicknamed "Tiger" by the family before they ever tried Boone County ham, grew up from being his father's Mizzou waterboy to a scholar-athlete as a high school guard, then a wide receiver in a small Wisconsin college, and, ultimately, given a professional look-see by the Chicago Bears, Dan Jr. became a high school coach back in Columbia.

"I'm so very proud of 'Tige'," said Devine one time, "because I think he really likes me, even though, from a kid on up, he'd seen me in my worst sides with my team, as well as the best."

That team in 1960 precipitated not only the finest decade in Missouri's football and Devine's, too, but a record for consistency that none of the major football powers could equal. In that decade, the Black and Gold's poorest season had only three defeats and one tie.

The first one followed an outrageous challenge when Devine insisted the Tigers—feet together, fellas, helmet in your lap!—would (1) win the Missouri opener for the first time in 13 years, (2) beat Oklahoma at Norman, (3) win the conference championship and (4) win the first bowl game for Ol' Mizzou.

The deep, dark secret didn't come out until late in the season. As Devine explained, "I can tell 'bear' stories to the media, but I can't fool my players and I can't be anything to my players except myself. I can't be Knute Rockne . . . Bud Wilkinson . . . Biggie Munn," or, grinning, because you've heard this one, "not even Dizzy Dean!"

The Tigers drove the foe dizzy with a balanced-line attack, set up before the last Orange Bowl game with Georgia and refined. This "T" was devastating, a streamlined device with old-fashioned single-wing blocking. Not only did both guards pull out to lead the interference, along with the fullback and the near-side halfback, but also the quarterback, compact little Ron Taylor, after pitch-flipping a lateral to the ball-carrying back.

A modernized blocking back who pined to pass more than Devine permitted, Taylor displayed a gutty target-leading escort. Devine simplified it for Taylor. As the cocky kid put it, "He told me to take the first opposing jersey I saw in the hole."

Devine had altered the power sweep when watching Taylor block in spring ball. This five-man blocking wedge was so effective on power plays outside end or off-tackle that they prompted Coach Ben Martin of the Air Force Academy to label the play as "Student body left" or "Student body right."

Fussbudget Devine was hard to please. From the sidelines he'd snap on the phone to the press-level coaching box, "What happened on that play?"

Longtime MU assistant Clay Cooper would counter, "It gained eight yards."

"Oh!"

Not every play worked, but the philosophy and policy was best described by Nebraska Coach Bill Jennings, whose Huskers had upset Penn State, Pitt, Minnesota, Army, Navy, Oregon and Texas, yet did not score a point for four years against Devine's Tigers. Said Jennings, "It was a classic case of staying with your basic plays."

With that first-game victory over Southern Methodist, 26-0, the first opener won since 1947 against St. Louis University, the Tigers were off and roaring, aided by the defense of Al Onofrio, the coach Devine had talked back off the golf course at Arizona State and became his successor.

Missouri beat Penn State on their home field, 21-8, helping Danny LaRose to All-American at end, and they came down to the next-to-last game in the season still unbeaten. Graying Galahad Wilkinson's gladiators weren't the greatest, but they immediately scored the first touchdown Missouri had allowed on the ground all season.

In the stands at Norman, where to correct Oscar Hammerstein II, the "wind comes sweeping UP the plain," were many of those 1958 Missouri seniors who had remembered Devine's reckless prediction two years earlier.

They got their money's worth in a game much more exciting than the final, 41-19, Missouri's first win in the red-clay country since 1936. The game hinged on two plays,

Favored by field position and wind after a shanked third-down punt at the Missouri 45, the Sooners were shackled when Devine's Man Friday, Uncle Al Onofrio, switched to a nose-tackle, five-man front, and penetrated his linebackers. They stopped Oklahoma cold, forcing a third-down fumble.

When teams changed directions for the fourth quarter, Norris Stevenson, earlier a long-distance scoring weapon, circled left end off the steeply crowned, burned Bermuda grass of Owen Field. He turned the corner and raced 60 yards for the back-breaking chore.

I still like my lead for Sunday's *St. Louis Post-Dispatch:*

"The meek inherited the earth today. Mild-mannered Norris Stevenson, son of a St. Louis minister, ran 77 yards and 60 yards for touchdowns as unbeaten Missouri beat Oklahoma in Norman for the first time in 24 years. . ."

Missouri football, only 26,000 strong for the first game, went
bonkers as both the Associated Press and UPI ranked the Tigers
number 1 with only a week to go. The tiny airport made difficult
the return of the gallant heroes. Even Columbia radio station KFRU
and business phones crowed through the week:

"We're number 1."

Old foe Kansas didn't think so. Jack Mitchell, probably a better recruiter than coach at Arkansas and KU, had a highly talented
team led by three prospective pro backs—John Hadl, Curtis
McClinton and the one who was ineligible, Bert Coan—and a tradition of upsets.

The Hijackers . . . er, Sharecroppers . . . no, check signals, the
Jayhawks gave Ol' Mizzou an early opportunity with fumbles, but
Mitchell had strung out the attack with a nine-man front, and a
rusty Tiger passing attack wasn't accurate enough. Kansas's victory
before a record Columbia crowd of 43,000—they had begun the
season with 26,000 at the SMU game—cost the national championship.

It taught Devine a lesson, too. "I let the occasion carry us all
away," he said. "I gave the players too much media attention that
week, but I worked them too hard. If I ever get another chance, my
team will have fresher legs. . ."

Before the bowl season, Kansas had been deprived of two victories because of defying a conference rule in using the ineligible
Coan—so Missouri, actually 9-1, was awarded a technical unbeaten
season. Still, the conference championship was number three among
Devine's four-tiered challenge.

The first bowl victory was number four.

Oh-four-six, the old State U. seemed hexed when in the early
going at Navy's goal line, quarterback Taylor was stopped at the
Middies' 2. He lateralled back to a trailing Tiger, only to have an
alert defensive end, Greg Mather, intercept and return 98 yards for
a touchdown. Immediately after that, coach Wayne Hardin's future
admirals recovered a fumbled onside kick.

For Navy, then, the future looked as bright as it did for a
handsome young man who shed his jacket, sat in shirtsleeves in
their section of the Orange Bowl stands, munched on a hot dog,

drank a Coke and puffed on a cigar. Life was so good then for President-elect John F. Kennedy—it was tough to watch him and the game, too—and it appeared good for the Midshipmen, too.

But from the time defensive back Norm Beal intercepted a pass at the Missouri 10 and used Devine's blessed downfield blocking to go 90 yards for a touchdown, the hex was hooked, 21-14, even though Navy's Heisman Trophy back Joe Bellino made a brilliant diving catch of a pass over his shoulder for a touchdown. Poor Joe was a victim of Devine teams' ability to deflate shooting stars. The sawed-off Heisman gained just minus-four yards rushing, and his mates a total of minus-eight.

So, the Devine decade began with a flourish for Dan'l and his den of Tigers. In the turbulent 1960s, man had one of his finest hours, figuratively and literally, with a flight to the moon, but in retrogression to what seemed medieval—also assassination.

An unpopular war was fought. Race riots scourged city ghettos and rural campuses—hey, it's okay to plagiarize myself—and sensitive, soft-spoken Devine can take considerable credit for two things.

At a time when pro football arrived popularly at both ends of the state, St. Louis and then Kansas City, Missouri not only held its own, but twice enlarged the stadium. And as a responsible faculty member, the football coach found his campus heroes able to help keep understandably troubled students happy.

They didn't always win, but, as Dizzy Dean would say, they were amongst the best, winning 77, losing only 22, and tying 6 as the country's most consistent major team. They won on poise and tenacious defense, as manifest immediately in 1961.

With firepower gone—and Devine had reasonably few first-rate quarterbacks in his 13-year stay at Faurot Field—they dipped from the most Missouri points in any season, 295, to 129, the fewest since Faurot's 1955 team went 1-9, but they came within a coaching decision—and an official's—of having a unique 7-0-3 season.

Against Oklahoma in a 7-0 dogfight at home, the Tigers lost when a rough goal-line call on fourth down denied them a touchdown. And in a season of an actual 14-14 tie with California, they lost a 7-6 conference game at Colorado, where Devine opted for that Russian-roulette innovation, the two-point play, with more than six minutes remaining in the game.

"I learned a lesson that day," said Devine. "With so much time remaining, I should have tied the game first."

Highlights came early and late. In late September, by coincidence, the Tigers were scheduled at Minnesota, the team that had nosed them out of the national championship only because bowl ratings were completed before the Gophers lost in the Rose Bowl. And Minnesota's mentor, Murray Warmath, nosed out Devine for Coach-of-the-Year honors.

The late September game was a classic for competition and climate. The game began in sunshine, clouded to a drizzle, froze into sleet and then convulsed with a freak snowstorm. The only score of a punting duel featured by Darrell Krugman's coffin-corner kicking came when Carl Crawford made a leaping catch of a half-back option pass from Mike Hunter, the baseball second baseman whose occasional on-the-run targets were the best lesson of a limited offense.

Devine never would forget the 6-0 game, in part because of the get-even aspect, but mainly because his gutty 5-10, 185-pound center, Jimmy Vermillion, outplayed the Gophers' great pro-bound Bobby Bell.

The Kansas game was equally inspirational. By then, the Jayhawks were heavily favored, not only because they had amends to make for the 1960 forfeit and the same firepower, they also could win the conference championship and the Orange Bowl invitation. Worse—for Mizzou!—five regulars were hurt.

But the magnificent cripples came up with a 14-7 upset over the Jayhawks. So Devine's Hitless Wonders offensively became Wonderful Hitters defensively and, physically battered, the players turned down a Bluebonnet Bowl invitation. Kansas took it instead and romped over Rice at Houston, 33-7.

"I think times have changed," Devine would recall, "but I never tried to influence the players. Twice more they passed bowl games in the 1960s. . ."

They thought better of a bowl bid after a 1962 season that began at Berkeley's scenic Strawberry Canyon, where sophomore Johnny Roland made his varsity debut with three touchdowns in a

21-10 triumph over the Golden Bears. Roland would be remembered as probably the best all-around back in the Tigers' history. The game might well have been remembered for something else.

Trying to block an extra point, Tiger end Don Wainwright dived to his left and ran smack into the driving knee of Missouri's husky other end, George Seals. The injured player, shocked into unconsciousness by the impact, swallowed his tongue and well could have suffocated if Tiger trainer Fred Wappel hadn't had a tongue depressor on his hip pocket.

After the game, I'd had a date to meet Devine and Cal's famous coach, Pete Newell, his former Michigan State associate, at Oakland's original Trader Vic's. Understandably, the coach was late.

"I've been at the hospital," he said. "They told me, curiously, that even though Don is in a coma and will remain so for weeks that the swelling in the brain will subside and that he'll be OK. I've talked to his mother and she'll be here tomorrow, but I won't leave until she gets here."

So the two empty seats on the plane back to Kansas City included one that belonged to the head coach.

A few years later I had lunch with Don Wainwright and his mother. The young man had just finished his thesis for a master's degree. The topic, a water-filled safety helmet for football and, oh yes, considerable praise for the coach who cared.

Over the years, I've encountered many players whose affection for the old coach increased after they had played for him, but perhaps that's normal. Still, there's a reason. As more than one Tiger who got his sheepskin told it, "Just about the only time you could be sure of a private audience in the head coach's office was if you cut a class. Then he'd give you a cutting what-for!"

That 1962 team lost only once, in the next-to-last game, 13-0, at Oklahoma in the raw rain. The defeat was the most decisive for Missouri for three years. And when Kansas rallied for a 3-3 tie late at Columbia, though the Tigers again halted the great Gale Sayers, the Missouri players wanted one more chance.

They were the underdogs to Bobby Dodd's Georgia Yellowjackets, representing an outstanding defensive coach best known for a loosey-goosey bowl-coaching regimen that paid off in postseason victories. Not this time. The Tigers' 14-10 upset was climaxed when captain Andy Russell, a good ball carrier, but a better linebacker, intercepted his second pass.

Although the Tigers tried two passes, both intercepted, their season's total in an 8-1-2 year, 2,549 yards rushing to just 293 passing, didn't keep end Conrad Hitchler from making the Football Writers' All-America team.

Years later, I can recall Hitchler's summing up the coach. This, mind you, was an ex-Marine, who had earned a high school diploma in the service.

"I'll bet," said Hitchler, "he never said more than 10 words to me in four years. If he said 'Hello' or 'Good morning,' he made your day. But then after I'd finished playing, we rode together to St. Louis and he talked my arm off for nearly two hours, about me and my future. It was great."

"I sensed it had all been the psychology of coaching, and I asked whether this was the case—that he chewed on some, patted others and some, like me, he left alone. He just smiled."

Like he did after the Bluebonnet Bowl game when from Houston's fabled old Shamrock Hotel, he hustled to the airport to coach in the East-West game with his thrilled teen-aged daughters, Jen and Mary Jo, as his companions.

Yeah, Devine could lose control now and then, noticeably in the 1963 early-season game against Arkansas at Little Rock's War Memorial Stadium, where an overflow crowd watched the one and only competition between Devine and the coach who had left Missouri for the Razorbacks, Frank Broyles.

Both coaches were up and down like jumping jacks, especially Devine. At one point, when sideline officials were tardy in acknowledging the referee's first-down signal, Dan'l jumped out from behind the visitor's bench and rushed out to help them. Years later I wasn't at Clemson's Death Valley when Notre Dame fought to stay alive in the lair of the country Tigers, but wasn't that about the same? He got his only 15-yard penalty.

In the Arkansas game, six of the state police were there to escort Devine back to the bench. In a tense game, Missouri won, 7-6. Happily, afterward, MU alumni and friends at Kansas City presented Devine with a new clipboard, gold tinted, to replace the one he had fried to the ground in disgust at Little Rock.

Privately, Don Faurot, the old coach and then athletic director, called Devine in to congratulate—and lecture—him. Dan told it long after.

"Don told me, 'Son, you've got to settle down. You'll never last.' He was right, of course."

Devine had a good reason for a chip-on-his-shoulder attitude when he lost his player, Johnny Roland, for the entire season. As a silly prank, another player had swapped three tires from another car's to Roland's. Trouble was, Johnny didn't have the grade point at the time to qualify for an automobile.

Huffed Dan'l, "I wouldn't blame him if he didn't come back. What does he, a Texas kid, owe Missouri? Nothing. He's too smart to switch different-colored tires to his own from a car parked in the same block, but he's too proud to turn pigeon. He could transfer or go to Canada for pro ball. . ."

But Roland went to Kansas City for a job and returned to Columbia in 1964. Missouri just had lost to Nebraska, beginning its tremendous turn-around under Bob Devaney, and finished lower than second. The team could be good if—.

If the defensive secondary was good enough. Quickly, when California's Craig Morton threw three touchdown passes in an opening upset at Berkeley, Devine made his pitch to Roland, aware he was—as he'd continue to prove inside the red zone with a great nose for the goal line—a great offensive back. But for the good of the cause, would he move to defensive back in the three-deep secondary?

He would, salvaging what would become a 6-3-1 season, the decade's poorest, with a ferocity of tackling receivers and defenders even more memorable than his close-in clout when called on to carry the ball.

If mutual respect and loyalty reflect reciprocal gratitude, Johnny Roland could coach wherever Dan Devine coached—Green Bay and Notre Dame—and so could Hank Kuhlmann, who turned down a pro baseball contract at an earlier time when Devine lost possible Heisman prospect Mike Shannon to baseball and also Charley James.

Curiously, that run of Tiger talent by the St. Louis Cardinals' Bing Devine, a pale-faced Protestant unrelated to the dark-complected Roman Catholic, created briefly a breach, but I was happy to intercede. They became good friends and, as Dan relates in his autobiography, they combined in what amounted to a pivotal move in the career of Bob Harlan, now president of Green Bay's Pack.

Devine's 1965 Sugar Bowl team, upset early and beaten otherwise only by Nebraska, new conqueror of the conference, hit the jackpot in the last bonus conflict between the merger in which the venerable NFL absorbed some of the American Football League. Biggest winner was a lanky, powerful offensive tackle, Francis Peay, a transfer student.

"For trying to make him a defensive tackle, I was a prunehead," said Devine, aware that Peay developed such proficiency for making and holding a long block as an offensive tackle that he became the number-one draft choice of the New York Giants.

Peay, pronounced "pay," made the Jints pay, en route to a career as a responsible sociology major who, in one diversion, head-coached Northwestern to a victory over alma mater Mizzou. He complimented Devine this way:

"I learned from him to put something back in the pot," said Peay. "He's an introverted man, but he's also extremely sentimental, sympathetic and sensitive to the rights of others. . ."

Yes, that sensitivity, helpful to the black players, most certainly, manifested itself in other ways. For instance, after the Sugar Bowl game in which Missouri, off to a rousing 20-point lead, held on to beat Florida, led by the Heisman Trophy quarterback who later coached the Gators as handsomely as he played. Steve Spurrier, of course.

When I mentioned at breakfast after the Tiger triumph, 20-18, that maybe Missouri had been a little "lucky" because Florida had tried and missed three two-point conversions, Devine bristled. "If," he said, "they hadn't been making six points rather than seven or eight, you don't think I would have risked that [fumbled] pitchout near our goal line?"

No, because basically Devine was conservative usually when a high risk could cost his team. With really only two topflight quarterbacks in 13 seasons at Missouri, Gary Lane and Terry McMillan, he passed seldom. Actually, he won one bowl game, over Georgia Tech in the Bluebonnet by completing both passes to the opposition, and he went 0-for-2 in the '68 Gator Bowl game with 'Bama that deserves mention.

Actually, though he had key concerns about the kicking game and special-team play, his biggest challenge to his squads was occasionally risking a fourth-and-one effort in his own territory. Basically, Daniel John Devine, a little guy by most standards, loved smash-mouth football, hit-'em hard and let-'em lay, as Dizzy Dean put it.

Although he had a classic rivalry with Nebraska's remarkable savior, Bob Devaney, his lowest ebb was 1966 when he was shut out by the Huskers at Lincoln, 35-0, then was blanked again the next week by Colorado at home, 26-0. The first subpar season seemed imminent, but then they came back and beat OU and Kansas, then the Tigers' top rivals.

Probably best put by a Tiger "pet" on campus, John Kadlec, former star guard, longtime coaching assistant and later fund-raiser and broadcaster. Kad smiled, "Coach let us have the team—the rest of the staff—until Thursday and then he took over."

Smiling slyly, said Kadlec, "Then he'd play with their minds until game time."

So that '66 team went down into the snakepit against Oklahoma and played it so tough that they won on Bill Bates's record 52-yard field goal, mentioned amusingly in Devine's family reaction. At Norman, poor Coach Jim Mackenzie, a former Mizzou assistant, walked through his house, a mute in postgame shock.

A year later, Missouri did it to Nebraska at Columbia, where Jon Staggers survived a shock in a diving grab of an end-zone pass for the winning touchdown, 10-7. I wondered in early '68, having seen the team wobble in early games, and first-place Big Eight powerful Colorado, led by the Anderson brothers, Bob and Dick.

A couple of nights beforehand, Devine broke away to be honored in St. Louis by the prestigious Knights of the Cauliflower Ear, given bejeweled Tiger cufflinks, so large and flashy that they seemed obscene. There, aware of what he intended to say as part of his thanks, I tried to talk him out of it. Hey, Dan'l, Kansas City could be listening on powerful 50,000-watt KMOX radio.

He shook his head and said it, anyway—"St. Louis is my favorite town."

He must have sold the Tigers on themselves, too. They powered a 400-yard-plus rushing game, punishing Colorado, 27-14, but they weren't good enough to avoid late-season losses to Oklahoma and new champion Kansas.

The choice was the Gator Bowl, where the 7-3 Tigers were a definite underdog to Alabama. Bear Bryant's dimpled-darling Tide was the fawned-on favorite of the regional press at Jacksonville and at Daytona Beach, where Missouri trained in the relative pre-Christmas privacy of the white sands.

Reluctantly, Devine sent home a nonconformist center who had challenged the coach once too often. Aware that the kid's father was a high school coach, Dan was more concerned about the parent, aware he had a team with a psychological edge if it didn't peak too soon or lose its poise.

The day's backdrop helped with rain virtually until game time, when Bear Bryant walked onto the field in his traditional checked houndstooth hat. Someone chortled in the press box, "See, the Bear can walk on water."

Well, as Bryant put it with biting sarcasm after a 35-10 drubbing, Missouri "ran up and down the field just as though they were playing a barber's college." Not only did the Tigers grind out 402 yards, all on the ground, but they stretched 'Bama's quarterback, Scott Hunter, on the seat of his white pants 12 times for 45 yards lost rushing. But, c'mon, that was minus in sack time.

The most points allowed by a Bryant-coached team had a national impact, all right. The Tigers catapulted from 16th to ninth in the season's final poll and, despite the loss through graduation of All-America defensive back Roger Wehrli, probably the best player not in either the pro or college Hall of Fame, they had a sanguine future.

The 1969 team, perhaps Missouri's best ever, not only manhandled the Nebraska team it tied for the conference title, but Devine's players won two significant games.

At Michigan, in a game more deceptive than the final 40-17 score, they not only handed Bo Schembechler his first defeat as coach of the Maize and Blue, but also the only home game he lost his first 10 seasons at Ann Arbor. Michigan went to the Rose Bowl, Missouri to the Orange Bowl.

The other key contest, after a frustrating slop stop at Colorado, where circus sand tried to sop up a gooey gridiron, the Tigers were upset, 31-24. The same day, Kansas State beat Oklahoma for the first time since 1934, 59-21, taking the league lead.

If this properly weren't a salute to the coach, a play-by-play still could be as tense as it was when Big Eight commissioner Wayne Duke, headed to the Big Ten, called it "the most exciting ever." Missouri won, 41-38, and earned the bowl bid. Kansas State collapsed.

By now, thanks to the aerial accuracy of Terry McMillan, a junior-college kid from the Miami area, and the racehorse speed of wide receiver Mel Gray, the passing had caught up with the running game and kick returns. The Tigers, ready to explode, leveled Oklahoma, 44-10, and buried blistering rival Kansas, 69-21.

The most points ever yielded by Kansas and Missouri's most ever in the series came with some prompting for Devine, who could grieve over the years in scoring so many points against boyhood idol Sammy Baugh's Hardin-Simmons team at ASU in 1955. With gumshoe perseverance, Dan'l had learned that the dirty-dig *Sports Illustrated* sentence in a preseason piece—"Devine doesn't win the big ones"—had originated with KU coach Pepper Rodgers.

Rodgers, a blithe spirit who bounced to UCLA and then to alma mater Georgia Tech, made capital of the crushing defeat and amusingly, even if apocryphal: "I gave Dan the peace sign," quipped Pepper, "and he gave half of it back to me."

The '69 season took a fairy-tale twist when Terry McMillan, who couldn't even make second string in high school, came back home to the Orange Bowl with a college team of virtually national championship caliber. Here, Devine was sensitive as well as sensible, expressing concern when it was announced that Ol' Mizzou would get a shot at Joe Paterno's Penn State 29-game winning streak.

Dan'l confided, "I worry about the pressure on Terry. He's a good, conscientious kid, generous with his time and talent to the

Campus Crusade for Christ and other worthy causes, but I'm afraid his family and friends will expect too much of him before the game, and I know he's going to have too much pressure in the game."

Devine tried all right, but he would have looked like a switch-hitting scalawag, to doting and proud Miamians, if he had hindered McMillan's pregame activities as much as he would have liked. Heck, at one night social gatherings, Terry fell asleep, and that was before he met Joe Pa's brilliant blue-and-white defense.

Harried, hurried, hit hard and finally hurt more than he would let on even to the coaches, McMillan had a tough night as Penn State got 10 first-period points. Then, playing conservatively and wisely and well, the Nittany Lions failed to score again despite nine Tiger turnovers, seven of them interceptions. Final, 10-3, Penn State.

Devine's esteemed colleague and Mizzou successor, Uncle Al Onofrio, put it extremely well: "From the team that had perfect balance between grind-it-out running and passing against Michigan, we had become a team that scored too early with the big play in the last few weeks."

At lunch the next day, I sat with Devine and Stan Musial at the baseball star's Bal Harbour hotel, the Ivanhoe. "You're still Dan the Man," Stan cracked.

Devine, saluting Penn State's defense as "10,000 times better" than he had seen all season, acknowledged that he would have gone for two points if the Tigers had scored when they got down to the 14-yard line in the final minute. "The more I think of it, though, the more I believe that if we had played conservatively, passing less and setting up field goals, we could have won. If we hadn't had so many interceptions, we had field position good enough for four or five field goals . . ."

Characteristically closing his eyes in a moment of deep feeling, the old coach added softly, "I like Jon Staggers' quote—'If everybody was perfect, it would be beautiful'—but I've got this to say: as we proved against Georgia Tech in the Bluebonnet Bowl, Alabama in the Gator Bowl, and in other games, I've never had a team of mine lose by throwing too little!"

With his great All-America candidate Joe Moore hurt early in the 1970 season—Moore and fullback James Harrison were two top draft choices of the Chicago Bears—the magic of the '60s was lost with the new decade. So was that 11-year streak of never losing late, much less losing in the second half.

With his first losing season assured, Devine had one trick still left up his sleeve. With Kansas about to make it four straight defeats for Missouri, the coach impulsively took Mel Gray out of the dog-house. Double-teamed, Mel had found passers unable to get the ball to him and, overeager, he'd botched plays.

Hurt, the Gray ghost even had run back punts with less than usual enthusiasm, so he had been relieved of the task, but now, Devine's voice was pitched high in the emotion and commotion on the sidelines, the coach barked out, "Mel . . . Mel Gray, get in there!"

Gray ran back the kickoff for 97 yards and a touchdown, the backbreaker in a 28-17 win in a 5-6 season, but one which gave Devine an 8-3-2 record in the bread-and-butter games against the Jayhawks. Honorable successor Onofrio, a winner of giant-killing upsets, lost six out of seven to KU when favored to win five and, sorrowfully, lost his job.

About Devine, he phoned me from a Kansas City hideaway motel to Miami, where I was covering the Super Bowl. He explained that he had been offered the job to coach and general-manage his pro favorites, the Green Bay Packers. I don't know what I expected him to say, but I didn't say it too convincingly. He said he'd pray on it in his room . . .

I knew he was gone. Years earlier, when I urged him to quit one year too soon rather than coach one year too late, he had talked about the rigor of recruiting. Most successfully now, he wouldn't have to wipe many mothers' kitchen dishes when out selling him-self.

As an extroverted introvert, a private person who had to force himself to observe some of the amenities with those other than his athletes or close friends, the coach and GM of a pro team, heeled with triple his salary, would have more time to think football than fuss over fuzzy-cheeked lads or fat-walleted alumni.

For me, I'd miss many things, including those years when I did Sunday night football television with him in St. Louis, a 10:15 show with a tremendous audience. We had sweet-tooth cakes and hot tea sessions when breaking down the plays we'd show—with an ulcer I was temporarily a teetotaler and Dan'l only a light Scotch sipper—and our sessions with the goodies had one lingering memory.

When I began the *Post-Dispatch's* Scholar-Athlete program in 1967, an expensive salute to 150 high schools supported by the Pulitzers' willingness to help reward high school achievements, my biggest booster from the git-go was Dan Devine. That first night afterward, we celebrated in the Jefferson Hotel coffee shop with malted milks and jelly doughnuts.

Devine's rosary pointed north—into the coaching legend of Green Bay and then from the frying pan into the fire with the cathedral of college football, Notre Dame. I honestly wonder if, back to back, any coach ever hazarded such a challenge, most certainly with painful physical purgatory.

At his first official game with the Pack in 1971, leading the cheers in a rally too late against the New York Giants, Devine was trapped by a sideline pile-on and suffered a broken leg, an injury that brought him back on crutches. At Notre Dame, learning about the icy slicks of South Bend, he skidded into a tree before his second season, 1976, and suffered a spinal injury that aged him with a persistent whiplash disaster.

At Green Bay, Devine might have been a figurative pain in the neck, certainly to his squad when he once asked the pros to sit through a game film of a well-disciplined college game, Missouri's. But he had his own disappointments from the outset when a player he most admired, Bart Starr, as a quarterback coach on the field, had a sore arm and little left.

So perhaps with the same cockiness of college coaching with journeymen quarterbacking, he turned to Scott Hunter, a lesser light in Bear Bryant's stable of A-1 passers. Uh-huh, the same Hunter dumped so often by the Tigers in that Gator Bowl game.

Early, Hunter evidenced inexperience when he tried to force a touchdown pass from the red zone when a field goal by Chester Marcol would have produced a 3-0 victory over rival Minnesota. Instead, an interception's long runback gave the Vikings the chance for the same game-clinching placekick.

Still, with John Brockington a wheelhorse ballcarrier and Marcol's kicking overcoming missed opportunities, Hunter was the quarterback when the Packers won the NFC's Central Division in

1972, Green Bay's one and only from Vince Lombardi's famed Ice Bowl win over Dallas in 1967 until 1983 (16 seasons). That bobcatted 1974 strike season was an exception until Mike Holmgren brought back the Pack in '94.

Devine might have fooled just about everybody in that 10-4 season, but not a wily master of dee-fense, finger-locking George Allen. Grasping no real challenge passing, Allen stacked up a five-man front, blunted Brockington and walked off with a 16-3 conference title for the Washington Redskins.

So Devine wasn't Lombardi, but Dan'l had a more productive season and record than coaches who followed him at Lambeau Field, i.e., Starr, Forrest Gregg and Lindy Infante. And he wasn't Knute Rockne, either, when he responded favorably to the invitation of Notre Dame's venerable Father Edmund Joyce, unofficially the director of football for the Irish.

Once before, Father Joyce had called on Devine, back there at the end of Joe Kuharich's dismal five-year stretch through 1962. After their meeting, Devine sent me a scribbled memo from the Golden Dome with an off-the-record comment, "I wanted you to know I was at least once considered by Notre Dame."

The choice then was Ara Parseghian, whose eight years of a good job at Northwestern included the only Big Ten victory in 11 years over Devine-coached Missouri teams. Parseghian's 11-year record at Notre Dame of 95-17-4 was brilliant, highlighted by three national championships and three bowl victories.

Ill health had produced the end of Ara, and—again!—a tough act to follow, but as one who, ill as a kid of 13, cried when boyhood favorite Rockne was killed in 1931, I didn't think the Irish ever appreciated Devine quite enough. The faculty Fathers did, Hesburgh and Joyce, and faculty such as Dean Emil T. Hofmann, for years the favorite academic figure on campus, yes, but not Athletic Director Moose Krause or a few others in the Athletic Department. Maybe they figured him to play golf as Parseghian had and would continue to do, but Daniel John Devine is not a handshaker or back-slapper.

The puzzlement is why Devine's name automatically wasn't linked with those other Notre Dame coaches who also won national championships—Rockne, Leahy, Parseghian and, ultimately,

Lou Holtz. Maybe I'm too sensitive myself because they don't list one of their own, either, Elmer Layden. Poor Elmer, a Four Horseman, hero of Rockne's 1925 Rose Bowl victory over Stanford and a commissioner of the National Football League, had a better won-and-lost percentage than Devine and Holtz, but, alas, he didn't win a national championship. Devine's 1977 championship Notre Dame team, led by incredible Joe Montana as a come-from-behind quarterback, did it all, dramatically.

Devine, schooled in the intensity of the rivalry of Michigan from years as an assistant at Michigan State, beat Bo Schembechler two out of three at Notre Dame and the one mentioned at Missouri. Dan'l's three bowl victories out of four for Notre Dame gave him seven out of 10 overall.

So he really had the College Hall of Fame made before his last season, 1980, when a preseason announcement made him, in effect, a lame duck or a one-legged Irishman. Incredibly, with successor Gerry Faust announced as the new coach before the season ended, the Irish were unbeaten until a regular-season wind-up at Southern California. A couple of gift scores—one of them an unfunny Alphonse-and-Gaston misplay that let a crucial early kickoff lay like a golden egg gift for Georgia in the Sugar Bowl—ended in a 17-10 loss, Devine's 16th in 80 games.

For Devine's retirement dinner, Georgia's great coach, Vince Dooley, who looked so much like Dan'l's dear friend and associate, Al Onofrio, was the featured speaker. I got in a few words, too, remarkable for two things—for once, I wasn't long and, in addition, I didn't Show-Me Missouri football as I've done in this reminiscence. Fact is, I was most impressed by Father Hesburgh's Shakespearean salute to the coach, a tribute that escapes me now.

Voluntarily retired or not, Dan Devine owed more direct support to dear wife Jo, who did need more physical if not moral attention. Back in the soothing Valley of the Sun, the lady could rekindle many things, first when the old coach headed Arizona State's drug-abuse program, then when he admirably heeded a request from Ol' Mizzou to come back briefly as an athletic director who would mend fences and abused alumni's interest and contributions. As always, like the days when he persuaded his teams to play better than they knew how, he delivered. Grateful for contributions past and present, they've built an athletic pavilion named for Daniel J. Devine.

For the kid they've called Danny and Dan—and I call Dan'l—Devine and dear Jo have come a long way from that time years ago when she sighed, thinking of another baby, "Just two months now . . ."

"Yeah," said my coaching hero, "just a couple of months to the start of the football season!"

COACH DAN DEVINE'S YEAR-BY-YEAR SUMMARY

At Arizona State University

Year	W	L	T
1955	8	2	1
1956	9	1	0
1957	10	0	0
3 years	**27**	**3**	**1**

At University of Missouri

Year	W	L	T
1958	5	4	1
1959	6	5	0
1960	11	0	0
1961	7	2	1
1962	8	1	2
1963	7	3	0
1964	6	3	1
1965	8	2	1
1966	6	3	1
1967	7	3	0

1968	8	3	0
1969	9	2	0
1970	5	6	0
13 years	93	37	7

At Green Bay

Year	W	L	T
1971	4	8	2
1972	10	4	0
1973	5	7	2
1974	6	8	0
4 years	25	27	4

At University of Notre Dame

Year	W	L	T
1975	8	3	0
1976	9	3	0
1977	11	1	0
1978	9	3	0
1979	7	4	0
1980	9	2	1
6 years	53	16	1

Bowl Game Statistics

1959 Orange: Georgia 14, Missouri 0
1960 Orange: Missouri 21, Navy 14
1962 Bluebonnet: Missouri 14, Georgia Tech 10
1965 Sugar: Missouri 20, Florida 18
1968 Gator: Missouri 35, Alabama 10
1969 Orange: Penn State 10, Missouri 3
1976 Gator: Notre Dame 20, Penn State 9
1978 Cotton: Notre Dame 38, Texas 10
1979 Cotton: Notre Dame 35, Houston 34
1981 Sugar: Georgia 17, Notre Dame 10

Dan Devine's Assistant Coaches

Arizona State University
Carey, Bob
Coleman, Cecil
Fletcher, Tom
Kush, Frank
Onofrio, Al
Serr, Gordie

University of Missouri
Cooper, Clay
Cowdrey, Charles
Dotsch, Rollie
Fletcher, Tom
Frala, Bob
Gautt, Prentice
Johnson, Merv

Kadlec, John
Kuhlmann, Hank
Mackey, Charles
Onofrio, Al
Rapp, Vic
Rash, Charles
Smith, Harry
Tobin, Vince
Weaver, Doug
Weber, Keith

Green Bay Packers
Cochran, John "Red"
Doll, Don
Dotsch, Rollie
Gustafson, Burt
Hanner, Dave
Kinard, Billy
Kuhlmann, Hank
Moss, Perry
Polonchek, John
Roland, Johnny
Schnelker, Bob
Starr, Bart

University of Notre Dame
Blache, Greg
Boulac, Brian
Chlebek, Ed
Gruden, Jim
Johnson, Jim
Johnson, Merv
Kelly, George
Kuhlmann, Hank
Meyers, Bill
Peay, Francis
Roland, Johnny
Shoults, Paul
Smith, Gene
Stevenson, Ross
Toman, Ron

Dan Devine's Lettermen
(1955-1980)

Over a span of 25 years, Dan Devine has influenced many players at both the collegiate and professional levels. The following is a complete list of Coach Devine's letter winners at Arizona State University, the University of Missouri, and the University of Notre Dame, and a list of the men who played for him with the Green Bay Packers.

Arizona State
1955-1957

Allen, John, 1956
Anderson, Ben, 1955, 1956, 1957
Arredondo, Dan, 1955, 1956
Beard, Danny, 1955
Bell, Frank, 1955, 1956
Belland, Joe, 1955, 1956, 1957
Benedict, Allen, 1956, 1957
Bonderud, Fred, 1955
Bourgeois, O'Jay, 1957
Burch, Fred, 1956
Burton, Leon, 1955, 1956, 1957
Camut, Joe, 1956, 1957
Carr, Al, 1955, 1956, 1957
Carunchio, Dennis, 1957
Coffinger, Mike, 1955, 1956
Della Libera, Gino, 1955, 1956, 1957
Dilley, Chuck, 1956
Drake, Joe, 1957
Erhardt, Ron, 1955, 1956, 1957
Fletcher, Dick, 1955
Fonner, Dave, 1955, 1956, 1957
Ford, Tom, 1955, 1956, 1957
Futch, Tom, 1955
Gedman, Wayne, 1955, 1956
Gieger, Jack, 1956, 1957
Grassl, Karl, 1955, 1956
Grassl, Tom, 1955, 1956, 1957
Graybill, Dave, 1955, 1956
Greathouse, George, 1957

Gumpf, John, 1955, 1956, 1957
Hangartner, John, 1955, 1956, 1957
Harper, John, 1955
Hickman, John, 1955
Hicks, Hadley, 1956
Jankans, Bart, 1955, 1956, 1957
Jankans, John, 1955
Jensen, Cliff, 1955
Jones, Charley, 1956, 1957
Jones, Ken, 1957
Julian, John, 1955
Kerr, Ken, 1956, 1957
Kiefer, Karl, 1957
Koisdowski, Dick, 1955, 1956, 1957
Lambeth, Jim, 1957
Livingston, Terry, 1957
Lundie, Jim, 1955
Mackey, Charlie, 1955, 1956
Mansperger, Dick, 1956, 1957
Meitzler, Al, 1957
Mitcham, Gene, 1955, 1956
Mitchell, Ed, 1955, 1956, 1957
Mulgado, Bobby, 1955, 1956, 1957
Napolitano, Dan, 1955, 1956, 1957
Napolitano, Dick, 1955, 1956
Noel, Bob, 1955
Olenick, Jim, 1955
Osborne, Clarence, 1955, 1956, 1957
Pagnetti, Al, 1955, 1956
Paplowski, James, 1956
Patella, Nick, 1955, 1956
Province, Fritz, 1955, 1956
Rose, Jim, 1955
Rounds, Lee, 1955
Ryan, Mickey, 1955
Sandell, Alan, 1956, 1957
Sedlar, Bob, 1955
Shively, Tom, 1955
Smith, Sumner, 1956, 1957
Spanko, Bill, 1956, 1957
Stanhoff, Mike, 1955, 1956
Stovall, Jack, 1955, 1956
Stangia, Mike, 1955
Swanner, Jim, 1957
Urban, Fran, 1955, 1956, 1957

Vardian, Carl, 1957
Vucichevich, John, 1957
Widmer, Paul, 1955, 1956, 1957
Worsley, Roger, 1955, 1956, 1957
Wunderly, Ron, 1955
Zuhowski, Bill, 1957

Missouri
1958-1970

Abell, Harry, 1963, 1964
Adams, Samuel, 1967, 1968, 1969
Allison, Buford, 1963, 1964, 1965
Alton, Jack, 1966
Anderson, James, 1966, 1967, 1968
Angel, Ralph Richard, 1968
Austin, David, 1970
Barnett, Gary, 1968
Bastable, John M. 1970
Bates, William, 1965, 1966
Beal, Norman L., 1959, 1960, 1961
Bell, Raymond, 1969, 1970
Benhardt, Elmer, 1966, 1967, 1968
Bennett, Michael, 1968, 1969, 1970
Berg, Marty, 1965, 1966, 1967
Bernsen, Rich, 1964, 1965, 1966
Blain, Edward H., 1959, 1960, 1961
Bogard, Daniel C., 1969, 1970
Boston, Kenneth, 1963, 1964, 1965
Boucher, George, 1958
Boyd, Robert G., 1967,1968,1969
Boyd, Roger, 1966, 1967, 1968
Brewer, Richard P., 1968
Brinkley, Lorenzo, 1969
Brinkman, William F., 1959
Britts, Samuel A., 1969, 1970
Brossart, Fred, 1958, 1959, 1960
Brown, Bobby D., 1963, 1964
Brown, Charles R., 1964, 1965, 1966
Brown, Henry, 1967, 1968, 1969
Brown, John W., 1969, 1970
Buerkle, Joe, 1962, 1963, 1964
Buha, Petar C., 1970

Burns, John W., 1970
Calhoun, Joseph R., 1958, 1959, 1960
Caputo, Louis F., 1970
Carpenter, Thomas, 1959, 1960
Carroll, Michael, 1967, 1968, 1969
Case, Joel W., 1959
Chadwick, Donald M., 1958
Chettle, Alan, 1965
Clark, Joseph, 1967, 1968
Clark, Mark M., 1970
Colclasure, Charles M., 1970
Comfort, George D., 1963, 1964
Cook, Greg L., 1967, 1968
Cooksey , James H., 1964
Cowan, John E., 1969, 1970
Cox, David L., 1967
Cox, Lynn E., 1968
Crawford, Carl D., 1961
Crnko, Timothy, 1967, 1968, 1969
Crumpler, Jerry, 1964
Curtright, Jerry, 1958
Darnaby, Bryant 1965
Davis, John C., 1967, 1968, 1969
Denny, Earl, 1964, 1965, 1966
Douglas, John, 1966, 1967
Doyle, Daniel D., 1965, 1966
Eader, Michael, 1963, 1964, 1965
Ewing, Mike, 1966, 1967
Farmer, Michael K., 1970
Feind, William J., 1958
Fink, Paul M., 1970
Fisher, Robert, 1960
Fountain, George E., 1968, 1969, 1970
Frieders, Gary, 1965
Garber, Carl, 1966, 1967, 1968
Garvis, Paul W., 1959, 1960, 1961
Gebhard, Kurt E., 1970
Geiger, Bruce 1960
Gilchrist, Leonard M., 1961, 1962, 1964
Gill, David L., 1962, 1963
Gillespie, John W., 1970
Glosson, Edwin N., 1969, 1970
Gray, Melvin D., 1968, 1969, 1970
Griffin, William E. Jr., 1967
Grossnickle, Gary, 1964, 1965, 1966

Haas, Robert L., 1958, 1959
Harrison, James H., 1968, 1969, 1970
Hauptman, Joseph M., 1968, 1969
Henley, John, 1969, 1970
Henley, Paul, 1959, 1960, 1961
Hertz, Gene L., 1968
Hertz, Tom, 1960, 1961, 1962
Hessing, Brock, 1958
Hinkley, Ken, 1962
Hitchler, Conrad, 1960, 1961, 1962
Holsinger, Dave, 1963, 1964
Hunter, Michael N., 1961
Hunter, Stanley J., 1970
Jackson, Larron, 1968, 1969, 1970
Jansen, Steve, 1962, 1963, 1964
Jenkins, Paul R., 1964
Johnson, Jim, 1960, 1961, 1962
Jones, Curtis, 1967
Jones, Michael, 1964
Judd, James, 1966, 1968
Juras, James C., 1966, 1967, 1968
Kellet, John T., 1970
Kelley, Dan O., 1969, 1970
Kenemore, Steve, 1967, 1968, 1969
Kephart, Michael, 1969, 1970
Kistner, Richard C., 1965, 1966
Klein, Archie B., 1965, 1966
Kombrink, Gary, 1966, 1967
Krugman, Daryl C., 1961, 1962, 1963
Kubinski, Ralph C., 1962, 1963
Kuhlman, Mark, 1968, 1969
Kuhlmann, Hank, 1958
Lane, Gary, 1963, 1964, 1965
Lang, Larry E., 1967
Langan, Mike, 1960
LaRose, Marvin D., 1958, 1959, 1960
Lavender, William K., 1962
Leimbach, J.C. Jr., 1959
Leistritz, William, 1963
Lischner, Barry, 1966, 1967
Loudon, Donald, 1958
Lowder, Eric D., 1968, 1970
Lundholm, Steve, 1968, 1969, 1970
Lurie, Ron, 1962, 1963
Luther, Robert G., 1970

Lynn, Thomas F., 1963, 1964, 1965
McBride, Ron, 1967, 1968, 1969
McCartney, William, 1959, 1960, 1961
McCoy, Roger, 1958, 1959
McDonough, Daniel F., 1970
McKee, Michael, 1969, 1970
McMillan, Terry, 1968, 1969
McMurry, Charles, 1970
Magac, Michael S., 1958, 1959
Mauser, William, 1969, 1970
Mehrer, Edward W., 1958, 1959, 1960
Meyer, John E., 1967
Miles, James, 1958, 1959, 1960
Mizer, Stephen, 1969, 1970
Moore, Joseph L. 1968, 1969, 1970
Moore, Larry, 1966, 1967, 1968
Moore, Terry M., 1969, 1970
Moyer, Max W., 1959, 1960
Mungai, Lee, 1966, 1967
Murphy, Brian, 1966
Nelson, Don, 1964, 1965, 1966
Oliver, Frederick E., 1961, 1962
Otto, Gus J., 1962, 1963, 1964
Palmer, Jackie L., 1961, 1962
Parker, Robert, 1966
Peay, Francis, 1964, 1965
Pepper, Alan, 1966, 1967
Phelps, Garnett, 1967, 1968
Phelps, Monroe, 1963, 1965
Phillips, Roger M., 1961
Pidcock, Donald D., 1958, 1959
Poppe, Dennis, 1967, 1968, 1969
Powell, Robert, 1965, 1966, 1967
Powell, William D., 1964, 1965, 1966
Rash, Charles R., 1958
Rees, Conway, 1967, 1968
Reese, Carl D., 1963, 1964, 1965
Ritter, Robert C. Jr., 1963, 1964
Rittman, Joe C., 1959
Roland, Johnny E., 1962, 1964, 1965
Roper, Charles L., 1970
Russell, Andrew C., 1960, 1961, 1962
Sangster, William M., 1968
Saussele, Ted F., 1963, 1964
Schmitt, William H., 1967, 1968

Waller, James A., 1964, 1965
Walls, Tyrone, 1968, 1969, 1970
Washington, Russell, 1965, 1966, 1967
Weber, Charles, 1966, 1967, 1968
Weber, James L., 1966
Wegener, William, 1958, 1959
Wehrli, Roger, 1966, 1967, 1968
Weisenfels, John R., 1968, 1969, 1970
Wempe, Mike, 1966, 1967
West, Melvin, 1958, 1959,1960
West, Ray, 1965
Whitaker, Jim, 1965, 1966
Widenhofer, Robert W., 1964
Willsey, Jim, 1965, 1966, 1967
Wilson, Robert W., 1969, 1970
Worstell, Owen, 1958
Wyrostek, Thomas P., 1962, 1963, 1934
Yanko, Roger, 1970
York, Larry, 1966
Zieglar, Robert, 1965, 1967

Green Bay Packers
1971-1974

Acks, Ron, 1974
Aldridge, Lionel, 1971
Anderson, Donny, 1971
Austin, Hise, 1973
Basinger, Mike, 1974
Bradley, Dave, 1971
Branstetter, Kent, 1973
Bratkowski, Zeke, 1971
Brockington, John, 1971-1974
Brown, Aaron, 1973, 1974
Brown, Bob, 1971, 1972, 1973
Buchanon, Willie, 1972,1973,1974
Carr, Fred, 1971, 1972, 1973, 1974
Carter, Jim, 1971, 1972, 1973, 1974
Concannon, Jack, 1974
Conway, Dave, 1971
Cooney, Mark, 1974
Crutcher, Tommy, 1971, 1972
Dale, Carroll, 1971, 1972
Davis, Dave, 1971, 1972

Del Gaizo, Jim, 1973
DeLisle, Jim, 1971
Donohoe, Mike, 1973, 1974
Duncan, Ken, 1971
Ellis, Ken, 1971,1972, 1973, 1974
Fanucci, Mike, 1974
Garrett, Len, 1971, 1972, 1973
Gibson, Paul, 1972
Gillingham, Gale, 1971, 1972, 1973, 1974
Glass, Leland, 1972, 1973
Goodman, Les, 1973, 1974
Gordon, Dick, 1973
Hadl, John, 1974
Hall, Charlie, 1971, 1972, 1973, 1974
Hampton, Dave, 1971
Hart, Doug, 1971
Hayhoe, Bill, 1971,1972, 1973
Hefner, Larry, 1972, 1973, 1974
Hendricks, Ted, 1974
Highsmith, Don, 1973
Hill, Jim, 1972, 1973, 1974
Himes, Dick, 1971, 1972, 1973, 1974
Hudson, Bob, 1972
Hunt, Kevin, 1972
Hunter, Scott, 1971, 1972, 1973
Jenke, Noel, 1973, 1974
Kopay, Dave, 1972
Krause, Larry, 1971, 1973, 1974
Kroll, Bob, 1972, 1973
Lammons, Pete, 1972
Lane, MacArthur, 1972, 1973, 1974
Leigh, Charlie, 1974
Lueck, Bill, 1971, 1972, 1973, 1974
MacLeod, Tom, 1973
Marcol, Chester, 1972, 1973, 1974
Mason, Dave, 1974
Matthews, Al, 1971, 1972, 1973, 1974
McBride, Ron, 1973
McCarren, Larry, 1973, 1974
McCoy, Mike, 1971, 1972, 1973, 1974
McGeorge, Rich, 1971, 1972, 1973, 1974
Michaels, Lou, 1971
Nitschke, Ray, 1971, 1972
Nystrom, Lee, 1974
Oats, Carleton, 1973

Odom, Steve, 1974
Okoniewski, Steve, 1974
Patrick, Frank, 1971, 1972
Payne, Ken, 1974
Peay, Francis, 1971, 1972
Pitts, Elijah, 1971
Pureifory, Dave, 1972, 1973, 1974
Randolph, Al, 1971
Robinson, Dave, 1971, 1972
Roche, Alden, 1971, 1972, 1973, 1974
Schmitt, John, 1974
Schuh, Harry, 1974
Smith, Barry, 1973,1974
Smith, Barty, 1974
Smith, Donnell, 1971
Smith, Perry, 1973, 1974
Snider, Malcolm, 1972, 1973, 1974
Spilis, John, 1971
Staggers, Jon, 1972, 1973, 1974
Staroba, Paul, 1973
Starr, Bart, 1971
Tagge, Jerry, 1972, 1973, 1974
Thomas, Ike, 1972, 1973
Toner, Tom, 1973
Torkelson, Eric, 1974
Van Dyke, Bruce, 1974
Vanoy, Vernon, 1972
Van Valkenburg, Pete, 1974
Wafer, Carl, 1974
Walker, Randy, 1974
Walsh, Ward, 1972
Webster, Tim, 1971
Wicks, Bob, 1974
Widby, Ron, 1972, 1973
Williams, Clarence, 1971, 1972, 1973, 1974
Williams, Perry, 1971, 1972, 1973
Winkler, Randy, 1971
Winther, Wimpy, 1971
Withrow, Cal, 1971, 1972, 1973
Wood, Willie, 1971
Wortman, Keith, 1972, 1973, 1974

Notre Dame
1975-1980

Achterhoff, Jay, 1975
Adell, Bernie, 1979, 1980
Allocco, Frank, 1975
Andler, Ken, 1975
Autry, Jon, 1980
Banks, Mike, 1975, 1976
Barber, Ty, 1978, 1979, 1980
Bauer, Ed, 1975
Becker, Doug, 1975, 1976, 1977
Belden, Tony, 1978, 1979, 1980
Bell, Greg, 1980
Bleyer, Bob, 1980
Bleyer, Frank, 1977
Bock, Tom, 1978, 1979
Boerner, Chris, 1980
Boggs, Pat, 1977
Bone, Rod, 1979, 1980
Boushka, Dick, 1977, 1978, 1979, 1980
Boushka, Mike, 1978, 1979, 1980
Bradley, Luther, 1975, 1976, 1977
Brantley, Tony, 1975
Brown, Chris, 1980
Browner, Jim, 1975, 1976, 1977, 1978
Browner, Ross, 1975, 1976, 1977
Browner, Willard, 1976
Bruni, Todd, 1979, 1980
Bucci, Elvo, 1976
Buchanan, Pete, 1978, 1980
Buehner, Rick, 1977, 1978
Burger, Bob, 1978, 1979, 1980
Burgmeier, Ted, 1975, 1976, 1977
Bush, Bob, 1977
Buth, Doug, 1975
Calhoun, Mike, 1976, 1977, 1978
Carney, Mike, 1975, 1976
Carter, Mansel, 1980
Carter, Phil, 1979, 1980
Case, Jay, 1975,1977, 1978, 1979,
Christensen, Ross, 1975, 1976, 1977
Cichy, Steve, 1978, 1979, 1980
Clasby, Rob, 1979, 1980

Condeni, Dave, 1978, 1979, 1980
Courey, Mike, 1977, 1978, 1979, 1980
Crable, Bob, 1978, 1979, 1980
Crews, Ron, 1975
Crippin, Jeff, 1978, 1979
Cullins, Ron, 1975
Czaja, Mark, 1976, 1977, 1979
DeCicco, Nick, 1977
DeSiato, Tom, 1979, 1980
Detmer, Marty, 1978, 1979, 1980
Dickerson, Ty, 1976, 1977, 1979
Dike, Ken, 1976, 1977
Doherty, Kevin, 1975
Domin, Tom, 1976, 1977
Dover, Steve, 1977, 1978
Driscoll, Leo, 1977
Dubenetzky, John, 1975, 1976
Duerson, Dave, 1979, 1980
Duncan, Bob, 1977
Eastman, Tom, 1975, 1976
Ellis, Randy, 1979, 1980
Eurick, Terry, 1975, 1976, 1977
Fasano, Angelo, 1978, 1979, 1980
Ferguson, Vagas, 1976, 1977, 1978, 1979
Fischer, Mark, 1980
Flynn, Tom, 1976, 1977, 1978
Foley, Tim, 1976, 1977, 1978, 1979
Forystek, Gary, 1975, 1976, 1977
Fry, Willie, 1975, 1976, 1977
Gagnon, Robb, 1980
Galanis, John, 1975
Geers, Mike, 1977
Gibbons, Tom, 1977, 1978, 1979, 1980
Golic, Bob, 1975, 1976, 1977, 1978
Gramke, Joe, 1978, 1979, 1980
Gray, Ian, 1979, 1980
Graziani, Larry, 1976
Griffith, Kevin, 1979
Grindinger, Dennis, 1976, 1977, 1978
Grogan, Pete, 1980
Grooms, Scott, 1980
Haines, Kris, 1975, 1976, 1977, 1978
Hankerd, John, 1977, 1978, 1979, 1980
Harrison, Randy, 1975, 1976, 1977, 1978
Hart, Kevin, 1977, 1978, 1979

Hart, Speedy, 1976, 1977
Hartwig, Steve, 1978, 1979
Hautman, Jim, 1976, 1977, 1978
Heavens, Jerome, 1975, 1976, 1977, 1978
Heimkreiter, Steve, 1975, 1976, 1977, 1978
Holohan, Pete, 1978, 1979, 1980
Horansky, Ted, 1976, 1977, 1978, 1979
Hornback, Eddie, 1979
Huffman, Dave, 1975, 1976, 1977, 1978
Huffman, Tim, 1977, 1978, 1979, 1980
Hufford, Larry, 1978, 1979
Hughes, Ernie, 1975, 1976, 1977
Hunter, Al, 1975, 1976
Hunter, Tony, 1979, 1980
Johnson, Pete, 1975, 1976, 1977, 1978
Johnson, Phil, 1977, 1978
Johnston, Mike, 1980
Kelleher, Dan, 1975, 1976
Kidd, Don, 1979, 1980
Kiel, Blair, 1980
Kissner, Larry, 1980
Klees, Vince, 1975
Knafelc, Greg, 1977, 1978, 1979
Knott, Dan, 1975, 1976, 1977
Koegel, Tim, 1977, 1978, 1979, 1980
Kornman, Russ, 1975
Kramer, Pat, 1978, 1979, 1980
Krimm, John, 1978, 1979, 1980
LeBlanc, Mark, 1980
Leon, John, 1977, 1978, 1979
Leopold, Bobby, 1976, 1977, 1978, 1979
Liebenstein, Mike, 1980
Likovich, John, 1975, 1976
Lisch, Rusty, 1976, 1977, 1979
Lopienski, Tom, 1975
Lueken, Jeff, 1979, 1980
MacAfee, Ken, 1975, 1976, 1977
Male, Chuck, 1978, 1979
Marshall, Tim, 1980
Martinovich, Rob, 1976, 1977, 1978, 1979
Maschmeier, Tom, 1975
Masini, Mike, 1980
Masztak, Dean, 1978, 1979, 1980
Maune, Neil, 1979
McCormick, Keith, 1978, 1979

McDaniels, Steve, 1975, 1976, 1977
McGarry, Rob, 1979, 1980
McLane, Mark, 1975, 1976
McLaughlin, Pat, 1975
McMurry, Andrew, 1975
Meyer, Howard, 1975, 1976, 1977, 1978
Mishler, Ron, 1978, 1979, 1980
Mitchell, Dave, 1977, 1978
Montana, Joe, 1975, 1977, 1978
Moore, Elton, 1975, 1976
Moriarty, Larry, 1980
Morris, Rodney, 1980
Morse, Jim, 1976, 1977
Mosley, John, 1980
Moynihan, Brendan, 1978, 1979
Muno, Kevin, 1977
Murphy, Terry, 1976, 1977
Naylor, Rick, 1980
Niehaus, Steve, 1975
Norman, Mark, 1979
Novakove, Tony, 1975
Oliver, Harry, 1980
Orsini, Steve, 1975, 1976, 1977
Pagley, Lou, 1978
Pallas, Pete, 1977, 1978
Parise, Tom, 1975
Payne, Randy, 1975
Pohlen, Pat, 1975
Pozderac, Phil, 1978, 1979, 1980
Putzstuck, John, 1980
Quehl, Steve, 1975
Quinn, Mark, 1977
Rayam, Hardy, 1976, 1977, 1978, 1979
Reeve, Dave, 1975, 1976, 1977
Restic, Joe, 1975, 1976, 1977, 1978
Rice, John, 1979, 1980
Rodenkirk, Don, 1976
Rudzinski, Joe, 1979, 1980
Ruettiger, Dan "Rudy", 1975
Russell, Marv, 1975
Schmitz, Steve, 1975, 1976, 1977
Scully, John, 1977, 1978, 1979, 1980
Shields, Jack, 1980
Shiner, Mike, 1980
Siewe, Bill, 1979, 1980

Simon, Tim, 1975
Slager, Rick, 1975, 1976
Smith, Gene, 1975, 1976
Spielmaker, Daane, 1980
Stock, Jim, 1975
Stone, Chris, 1979, 1980
Stone, Dan, 1979, 1980
Stone, Jim, 1977, 1978, 1979, 1980
Sweeney, John, 1979, 1980
Thayer, Tom, 1979, 1980
Thomas, John, 1976, 1977, 1978, 1979
Toran, Stacey, 1980
Tripp, Tim, 1978, 1979, 1980
Tull, Bob, 1976, 1977
Unis, Joe, 1977, 1978, 1979
Unis, Tom, 1976
VanDenburgh, Tom, 1977
Vehr, Nick, 1978, 1979, 1980
Vinson, Dave, 1976, 1977
Waymer, Dave, 1976, 1977, 1978, 1979
Weber, Robin, 1976
Weiler, Jim, 1975, 1976
Weston, Jeff, 1975,1976, 1977, 1978
Whittington, Mike, 1977, 1978, 1979
Williamson, Greg, 1980
Woebkenberg, Harry, 1975, 1976
Wozneak, Joe, 1979
Wroblewski, Tom, 1977,1978, 1979
Wujciak, Al, 1975
Zanot, Bob, 1975
Zappala, Tony, 1975, 1976
Zavagnin, Mark, 1979, 1980
Zettek, Scott, 1976, 1977, 1978, 1979, 1980